DECLINE OF IDEOLOGY?

# The Editor

Mostafa Rejai (Ph.D., U.C.L.A.) is Professor of Political Science at Miami University (Ohio), where he has been the recipient of an outstanding teaching award. He is the author of *The Strategy of Political Revolution* (Aldine • Atherton, forthcoming), co-author of *Ideologies and Modern Politics* (1971), and editor of *Democracy: The Contemporary Theories* (1967) and *Mao Tse-tung on Revolution and War* (1969, 1970). His articles have appeared in *Comparative Political Studies, Ethics, International Philosophical Quarterly, International Studies Quarterly, Journal of Asian and African Studies, Orbis,* and other journals.

# DECLINE

## EDITED BY

# OF IDEOLOGY?

*M. Rejai*
MIAMI UNIVERSITY

Aldine · Atherton
*Chicago/New York*

*145*

*R38 ld*

*Decline of Ideology?*
edited by M. Rejai

Copyright © 1971 by Aldine • Atherton, Inc.

First published 1971 by
Aldine • Atherton, Inc.
529 South Wabash Avenue
Chicago, Illinois 60605

Library of Congress Catalog Number 79–116537
ISBN 202–24094–X, cloth; 202–24095–9, paper

Printed in the United States of America

DESIGNED BY LORETTA LI

*72-5565*

# Preface

Since the early 1950s, the "decline of ideology" hypothesis has provoked intense controversy in political science and sociology as well as in the intellectual community at large. The argument has taken both empirical and polemical turns. This book concentrates as much as possible on the empirical literature.[1]

The introductory chapter delineates some of the outstanding issues in theoretical and comparative analysis of political ideologies. Part I, consisting of two chapters, sets forth the hypothesis of ideological decline by two of its major spokesmen. Part II brings together a series of papers subjecting the hypothesis to empirical examination in both Western and non-Western contexts. Part III, comprising five chapters, evaluates the hypothesis in both negative and positive terms.

Each part is introduced by a brief note designed to bring out the major issues and guide the reader through the wealth of material on the decline of ideology. Inasmuch as the three introductory notes together constitute a modest introduction to the literature under consideration, the uninitiated reader may find it helpful to begin by running rapidly through these notes.

For one reason or another, it has not been possible to include a number of very worthwhile papers, especially those by James

B. Christoph, Otto Kirchheimer, Edward Shils, Sidney Tarrow, Herbert Tingsten, Ulf Torgersen, and Robert C. Tucker, among others.[2] The selection of material was guided by some specific criteria. To begin with, since the number of available papers turned out to be quite large, I have decided to exclude material published before 1960. Beyond that, I have attempted to give full play to novelty of material and diversity of locale. Thus, for example, Part II includes a paper on Europe in general, one on a western European country, one on a northern European country, one on the United States, one on Japan, and one on the Soviet Union. No paper on Great Britain is included, for instance, simply because the theme of decline of ideology is not as novel in that country as it is in Finland, Japan, the Netherlands, or the Soviet Union. Some of the excluded material is discussed in the introductory notes to the various parts of the book.

I am very grateful to the authors of the papers included here for their kind permission to reproduce their work. I am particularly indebted to Erik Allardt and Roy Pierce, who prepared especially for this volume—and on very short notice—the papers of Finland and France. I should like to thank David Spitz for a critical reading of an earlier draft of the opening paper. Any shortcomings remain my own responsibility.

NOTES

1. Much of the polemical material has already appeared in Chaim I. Waxman, ed., *The End of Ideology Debate* (New York: Funk and Wagnalls, 1968).
2. Christoph, "Consensus and Cleavage in British Political Ideology," *American Political Science Review*, 59 (September 1965), 629–642; Kirchheimer, "The Waning of Opposition in Parliamentary Regimes," *Social Research*, 24 (Summer 1957), 127–156; Shils, "The End of Ideology?" *Encounter*, V (November 1955) 52–58; Tarrow, "Economic Development and the Transformation of the Italian Party System," *Comparative Politics*, 1 (January 1969), 161–183; Tingsten, "Stability and Vitality in Swedish Democracy," *Political Quarterly*, 26 (1955), 139–151; Torgersen, "The Trend towards Political Consensus: The Case of Norway," *Acta Sociologica*, VI (1962), 159–172; Tucker, "The Deradicalization of Marxist Movements," *American Political Science Review*, 61 (June 1967), 343–358.

# Contents

ix

# Political Ideology: Theoretical and Comparative Perspectives

## M. REJAI

The systematic analysis of political ideology is contingent on the resolution of at least two important sets of problems: an agreement on the meaning of ideology and the development of a framework for the comparative treatment of ideologies. The first task has consumed vast quantities of scholarly energy in recent years, though the issue is by no means settled. The second task—though of great potential value for the resolution of certain outstanding conceptual difficulties—has received only scant attention.

At the outset it is necessary to distinguish between political ideology as concept and political ideology as ideology. The analysis of ideology as a generic concept (in terms of its nature, function, and types) constitutes an intellectual activity of a quite different order from the analysis of ideology as ideology (conser-

1

vatism, liberalism, or socialism, for example). Similarly, it is quite impermissible to confuse someone's (e.g., Marx's) analysis of the ideology concept with *his* own ideology (e.g., Marxism). It is of course true that one's analysis of the concept of ideology may be "ideologically" conditioned—as indeed Marx's was—but these questions are analytically distinct. At any rate, the present paper begins with an analysis of ideology as a concept in social science and moves to a discussion of ideology as ideology.[1]

The foregoing distinction corresponds to one drawn by Giovanni Sartori between ideology in knowledge and ideology in politics.[2] The former is a question of determining the extent to which one's knowledge and scholarship are ideologically influenced or distorted, the extent to which one's knowledge is interest-bound, for example. In this sense, ideology stands in contrast to "truth" and "science."[3] The latter is a problem of determining the extent to which ideology plays a role in politics, its impact and functions, for example. In this sense, the functional value of ideology may be more important than its truth value. It is important to bear in mind that the distinction between ideology in knowledge and ideology in politics is not always as neat and clear-cut as one might wish.

## DIMENSIONS OF THE CONCEPT

Definitions of ideology are legion. Some writers emphasize the sociological components of ideology, others its psychological characteristics, and still others its psychocultural features.[4] We are prepared to concede that, since definition is frequently an arbitrary matter, no one definition is intrinsically better than any other. The acid test is utility in scholarly discourse. The superiority of one definition over another lies in the extent to which it provides a more adequate, a more searching, a more powerful explanation of the phenomenon at hand.

An adequate definition of ideology must meet certain explicit criteria. It must be neutral rather than pejorative. It must be reasonably precise without being unduly restrictive. And it must be, at least potentially, operational. Rather than setting down a definition of ideology ex cathedra, our strategy will be to identify and disentangle its major dimensions. This done, we will perhaps be in a position to pull together the loose ends into a coherent definition.

The concept of ideology embraces five important dimensions: (1) cognitive: knowledge and belief, (2) affective: feelings and emotion, (3) evaluative: norms and values, (4) programmatic: plans and programs, and (5) social-base: participating groups and collectivities.[5] Each dimension will be considered in turn.

## Cognitive Dimension

Ever since the French Ideologues, ideology has been widely defined as a "system of ideas." More realistically, ideology should be viewed as consisting primarily of beliefs and only secondarily of ideas.[6] The basic distinction is that ideas are subject to scientific operation (such as testing and verification), whereas beliefs are not.

Belief systems are interrelated sets of notions and attitudes about man and society that are accepted, at least in part, as a matter of habitual reinforcement and routinization. Beliefs, in short, say nothing about the truthfulness or falsity of a notion or an attitude; they imply only a psychological state of acceptance. For our purposes, these beliefs involve characteristically political questions—for example, those of adjustment of conflicting interests, of authority and legitimacy. To this topic we shall return presently.

(Since we have said that ideology consists primarily of beliefs, and since we have distinguished belief explicitly from idea and implicitly from cognition, it is an open question that the title of this subsection "cognitive dimension" is well chosen at all. The want of a better term, however, has left us without an alternative.)

The elements or units of a belief system—and indeed belief systems as wholes—vary along some important dimensions. These include:

1. Constraint and coherence. Although within each individual certain belief elements tend to "go together," the degree of their interdependence is by no means uniform. As a rule, the more "extreme" a belief system, the less logical and coherent it will tend to be. As Rokeach has suggested, it is a characteristic of belief systems that "the parts may be interrelated without necessarily being logically interrelated."[7]

2. Centrality. Within each belief system, a belief element or a small number of belief elements usually plays a key role in unifying the entire system and holding it together (the element of equality in socialist ideology would be an example). Thus, as Converse points out, a change in the central belief element(s) will require adjustment in a wide range of other belief elements. In some belief systems, moreover, the relative centrality of a belief element may change over time (as in the interplay between liberty and equality in recent socialist thought).[8]

3. Richness or articulation. Belief systems can be fairly rich and articulate or fairly poor and inarticulate. The richer a belief system, the more explicit and comprehensive it will tend to be.[9]

4. Openness-closedness. A closed belief system, according to Rokeach, either completely blocks out new evidence and information or so filters and distorts them as to leave no impact on the belief elements as they existed prior to the new evidence or information. In an open system, by contrast, "new information is assimilated *as is* and, in the hard process of reconciling it with other beliefs, . . . 'genuine' . . . changes in the whole belief-disbelief system [take place]."[10] As such, the essential distinction between an open system and a closed system lies in "the extent to which the person can receive, evaluate, and act on relevant information received from the outside on its own intrinsic merits, unencumbered by irrelevant factors in the situation arising from within the person or from the outside." The more open a belief system, the greater the individual's ability to receive, evaluate, and act on information in terms of "inner requiredness."[11]

Since we have already called into question the cognitive truth value of ideology, it would be taking only a small step further to suggest that ideology involves elements of distortion or myth.

This, in fact, is one of the few points on which most writers on ideology agree. Marx and Engels view ideology as false consciousness, writing that "in all ideology men and their circumstances appear upside down as in a *camera obscura*."[12] Karl Mannheim defines ("particular") ideology as "more or less conscious disguises of the real nature of a situation."[13]

Among the more contemporary scholars, Robert M. MacIver is noteworthy for his broad concern with the character of myth and its function in society. He writes in a passage deserving quotation in full:

> By myths we mean the value-impregnated beliefs and notions that men hold, that they live by or live for. Every society is held together by a myth-system, a complex of dominating thought-forms that determines and sustains all its activities. All social relations, the very texture of human society, are myth-born and myth-sustained. . . . Every civilization, every period, every nation, has its characteristic myth-complex. In it lies the secret of social unities and social continuities, and its changes compose the inner history of every society. Wherever he goes, whatever he encounters, man spins about him his web of myth, as the caterpillar spins its cocoon. Every individual spins his own variant within the greater web of the whole group. The myth mediates between man and nature. From the shelter of his myth he perceives and experiences the world. Inside his myth he is at home in his world.[14]

Other scholars have been concerned with the much more specific question of the nature and role of myth in ideology. Thus Gustav Bergmann suggests that an ideological statement is "a value judgment disguised as, or mistaken for, a statement of fact."[15] Lasswell and Kaplan refer to ideology as "the political myth functioning to preserve the social structure."[16] Talcott Parsons identifies the "essential criteria of an ideology" as "deviations from [social] scientific objectivity," which he attributes either to the selectivity with which ideologies approach reality or to the deliberate distortion of that reality.[17] Many other examples could be cited.[18]

The myth in ideology is socially and historically conditioned. It communicates a fairly complex message in simplified form, which is indeed a hallmark of all ideology. Successful communication of ideology and its myth(s) will not take place except through simplification. Simplification is accomplished most notably through the use of symbols. Whether linguistic (words or speech) or nonlinguistic (flags, insignia, documents, monuments, holidays, ceremonies, anthems), symbols capture in an economical fashion large expanses of meanings and communicate these meanings in an instantaneous fashion. "The symbol," Friedrich and Brzezinski have written, "gives concrete form and focus to an abstraction, while the abstraction serves to illumine for the faithful the 'meaning' of the symbol."[19] Moreover, symbols bring "things" together and relate them in a coherent fashion; they promote understanding by making things readily intelligible; and they provoke an emotive response.[20] Finally, as Lasswell and Kaplan have maintained, symbols may have latent as well as manifest functions. Thus, for example, "the significance of a demand for universal education may lie in its relation to a latent demand for a share of power."[21]

## Affective Dimension

What we have been saying about myth and symbol brings into focus another dimension of ideology, its emotive content. This dimension is rather self-explanatory and does not require extended elaboration.

To stress the affective component of ideology is not, of course, to deny all rationality in belief systems. Nor is it to suggest that ideologies will not attempt to hide their affect behind a facade of "objectivity" and "science" (cf. Marx). It is simply to say that there is a rationality-emotionality balance in all belief systems and that the actual balance varies from ideology to ideology. Beliefs may be held with relative emotive weakness or relative emotive intensity, with low or high affect. Regardless of the degree of intensity, a most distinctive feature of all ideology is an appeal to emotion, an eliciting of emotive response. As Bell has written, "what gives ideology its force is its passion. . . . One might say, in fact, the most important, latent, function of ideology is to tap emotion."[22]

## Evaluative Dimension

Belief systems embody normative elements. Ideologies make value judgments in at least two ways: negatively, by denouncing the existing system of social relationships; positively, by putting forth a set of norms according to which social reconstruction is to take place.

The criticism of existing society is undertaken, at least in part, through appeal to high-sounding moral principles. Moral outrage, moral indignation, moral protest—these are indispensable to any ideology. The attack against existing society is presented, rationalized, justified, and thus dignified in terms of appeal to standards of morality.

The positive values of an ideology revolve around such central norms as liberty, equality, fraternity, humanity. The normative propositions, to recall Bergmann's caution, are characteristically presented as factual statements.

All ideologies move toward a "good society," however defined. Some ideologies posit an ultimate value, a final good, a utopia. They are, in Shils' view, "insistent on an actual and continuous contact with sacred symbols and with a fuller manifestation of the sacred in the existent. . . . Ideologies impel their proponents to insist on the realization of the ideal, which is contained in the sacred, through a 'total transformation' of society."[23] (It is interesting to note that the term "utopia" was brought to popular attention in Thomas More's book of the same title [1516], which described an imaginary island. The Greek origin— *ou topos*—meant, in literal translation, "no place." Samuel Butler's choice of *Erehwon* for his utopian novel was not happenstance, since "erehwon" is "nowhere" spelled backward.[24])

It was said earlier that ideology revolves around characteristically political beliefs. We may now amend this statement by suggesting that ideology embraces political beliefs as well as political values.

For our present purposes, we may adopt David Easton's definition of politics as "the authoritative allocation of values for a society."[25] Such allocation naturally involves adjustments and compromises among conflicting interests and demands. It also entails questions of rulership, authority, and legitimacy.

In this context, political ideologies are systems of beliefs and values focused primarily on such questions as: By what criteria are conflicting values and interests adjusted? Who (what person, party, or group) has the authority to play a role in such adjustments, and under what conditions? Under what conditions is coercion justified? Under what conditions is the legitimacy (public acceptability) of a regime open to question? Under what conditions should one regime be replaced by another?

## Programmatic Dimension

The values, goals, and objectives of ideology are embodied in a more or less comprehensive program of activities. Ideologies insist on the translation of values into action. Indeed, Clyde Kluckhohn defines values as "conceptions of the desirable" which require action for their realization. They "are ideas formulating action commitments."[26]

Ideologies, then, as many have pointed out, are action-related systems of beliefs, norms, and ideas. Not only do they posit a set of values, they also seek to relate specific patterns of action to the realization of those values. "Ideologies," Shils notes, "insist on the realization of principles in conduct."[27] This demand for consistency between principle and behavior forms the basis for imposition of ideological discipline and control.

The action and program of ideology may be directed toward the maintenance and perpetuation of the status quo, or, more characteristically, toward the transformation of the existing society. The program of ideology will set forth, implicitly or explicitly, a hierarchy of values and objectives. It may even include a statement of priorities specifying immediate, intermediate, and ultimate goals. In the communist ideology, for example, the immediate goal is overthrow of the bourgeois regime; the intermediate goal, economic reconstruction; the ultimate goal, a classless society.

## Social-Base Dimension

Ideologies are necessarily associated with social groups. Ideology, to *be* ideology, must have a mass base. It must be presented to the populace in such a way as to be readily understandable and, in this understanding, to elicit a commitment to action toward the realization of goals and objectives. As Bell has pointed out, ideologies are essentially mobilized belief systems. "A social movement," he writes, "can rouse people when it can do three things: simplify ideas, establish a claim to truth, and, in the union of the two, demand a commitment to action. Thus, not only does ideology transform ideas, it transforms people as well."[28]

The mobilization-transformation function of ideology is impossible without organization. Indeed, as Samuel H. Barnes has pointed out, organization is the link between belief and action.[29] But organization does not evolve spontaneously. Nor is it put together by the masses. Organization is an elite concept and an elite function.

It is necessary to draw a distinction between ideology for the elites and ideology for the masses. Philip E. Converse approaches this problem as essentially one of greater access to education and information among "elite publics." The belief system of an elite public will tend to be rich, comprehensive, articulate, and coherent; that of a mass public, poor, partial, inarticulate, and incoherent.[30] Similarly, Robert E. Lane distinguishes "the articulated, differentiated, well-developed political arguments" put forward by the elite from "the loosely structured, unreflective statements of the common man." He calls the former "forensic" ideologies and the latter "latent" ideologies.[31] An analogous analysis has been made by Sartori.[32]

The elite-mass distinction gives rise to some intriguing questions: To what extent do ideologies serve as covers for personal ambitions and motives of elite publics? To what extent do elite publics use ideologies to mobilize, manipulate, and control the masses?

Although it might be wise not to attempt blanket, categorical answers to these questions, the possibilities of manipulation and control are of course quite real and frequently present in ideology. In fact, Sartori goes so far as to write that "ideologies are the crucial lever at the disposal of elites for obtaining mass mobilization and for maximizing the possibilities of mass manipulation. That is . . . the single major reason that ideology is so important to us."[33] The form and degree of manipulation and mobilization will of course vary from ideology to ideology. Both would be more intense in extremist ideologies and less intense in moderate ones.

## Summary

In this section we have identified five principal dimensions of ideological belief systems and we have discussed each in some detail. We would rather avoid a summary definition of ideology, for such a definition would necessarily sacrifice some of the intricacies of the concept. Since this option is not realistically open to us, however, we offer the following conception of ideology as consistent with the analysis so far developed.

By political ideology is understood an emotion-laden, myth-saturated, action-related system of beliefs and values, about man and society, legitimacy and authority, acquired as a matter of routine and habitual reinforcement. The myths and values of ideology are communicated through symbols in a simplified, economical, and efficient manner. Ideological beliefs are more or less coherent, more or less articulate, more or less open to new evidence and information. Ideologies have a high potential for mass mobilization, manipulation, and control; in that sense, they are mobilized belief systems.

## TOWARD A TYPOLOGY OF POLITICAL BELIEF SYSTEMS

The comparative treatment of political ideologies has not commanded the attention that it deserves. (We are here setting aside the conventional classifications of ideologies under such rubrics as nationalism, socialism, liberalism, conservatism, etc., since they do not represent analytical categories and since they have not proved helpful in the systematic comparison of political ideologies.)

Comparative analysis can take one of two forms: one can compare a given phenomenon across several nations or one can do so across a span of time within a given nation or nations. The starting point in both cross-national and cross-temporal analysis is the development of a typology or classification of the phenomena to be compared. Indeed, classification is not only the starting point of comparison, it is also "the first step toward scientific investigation."[34] This step is a particularly important one for our purposes, since the hypothesis of decline of ideology—the principal theme of this book—is a hypothesis in comparative analysis.

Though rare, comparative analyses of political ideologies are not totally nonexistent. Among the best known in the literature are a cross-temporal analysis by Daniel Lerner, Ithiel de Sola Pool, and Harold D. Lasswell, and two attempts toward cross-national analysis by Roy C. Marcridis and Giovanni Sartori.

Lerner and his associates set out to investigate the "comparative history of political ideologies" through content analysis of elite communication in five countries (U.S., Britain, France, Germany, U.S.S.R.) over a period of sixty years, 1890–1950. They define ideology as "the special vocabulary which a governing elite uses to reveal its social goals," and they focus on the political symbols contained therein.[35]

The study was part of the broader Lasswell-initiated inquiry into "the world revolution of our time," which posited that the twentieth century has witnessed a trend toward a world of "garrison-prison states" and away from "a democratic international community." A trend of such magnitude, it was hypothesized, would necessarily manifest itself in elite vocabulary, so that an analysis of elite communication should reveal a trend toward a "parochialization of attention" at the expense of democratic and internationalist norms. Thus, "We might expect to find . . . a decline in the democratic vocabulary of the nineteenth century, which includes the key symbols naming, describing, and advocating the social goal of human dignity. These include the symbols of liberty, equality, fraternity, democracy. We might also expect to find a 'parochialization of attention' among elites, indicated by a decline in the traditional vocabulary of internationalism, which includes the cosmopolitan symbols of humanity, brotherhood, the world. Conversely, we might expect to find an increase in the vocabulary of constrictive self-reference, particularly in relation to the national elites and their own survival."[36]

The method consisted essentially of a content analysis of the "flow of symbols" in the "prestige papers" of the five countries over the designated period. It was assumed that, since in every country one newspaper tends to stand out as the official or semi-official spokesman for the ruling elite (such as the *New York Times,* the *Times* of London, *Izvestia, Le Monde, Frankfurter Zeitung),* a content analysis of representative editorials in these papers would reveal the patterns of elite ideological change in each country.

The analysis of 416 symbols in nearly 20,000 editorials in the prestige papers over a period of sixty years revealed that a "constriction of political symbols" and a "parochialization of attention" had indeed taken place, that symbols of democracy and internationalism were losing ground to those of militarism, totalitarianism, and aggressive behavior, and that the *New York Times* and the *Times* of London were the least dogmatic papers in that they showed the least fluctuation in their ideological posture over time.[37]

Macridis' approach to ideology can be quickly summarized.[38] He employs "ideology" as one of four major components for the comparative analysis of political systems, the other three being "decision-making," "power," and "institutions." He identifies four "significant aspects of ideology" for purposes of comparison: sources, functions (especially those of control and legitimacy), diffusion, and relation to "the organization of political authority." Unfortunately, Macridis makes no attempt to carry his thought further or to develop a typology of belief systems.

Sartori employs two important dimensions of ideologies to construct a typology of belief systems: (1) cognition: whether the belief system is open or closed, and (2) emotive intensity: whether the belief system is held with low or high intensity. He identifies four types of belief systems: adamant (closed cognition, high affect), resilient (closed cognition, low affect), firm (open cognition, high affect), and flexible (open cognition, low affect).[39]

A major difficulty with this typology lies in the realm of application—that is to say, in the identification of actual ideologies to "fit" each of the four categories—and Sartori makes no attempt in this direction. The typology reveals other inherent weaknesses when he tries to apply it to the decline of ideology hypothesis.

Sartori argues that the requirement of the decline hypothesis would not be met by a decline in the emotive intensity of ideology, that is, by a passage from "adamant" to "resilient." "A real decline of ideology is safely indicated" by a trend toward relative openness in the cognitive dimension, i.e., by a passage from "adamant" to "firm."[40]

In making this argument Sartori introduces an unnecessary disjunction between the cognitive and emotive dimensions, for, although analytically distinct, the two are in fact closely interrelated. Thus, for example, if the emotive intensity of a belief system is high, that belief system is almost by definition "closed." Similarly, if a belief system is "closed," it is probably because it is held with high emotive intensity. This difficulty suggests that cognition and affect are inadequate or insufficient criteria for a typology of ideologies.

An adequate typology of belief systems must meet some important criteria. It must be abstract enough to permit analytical manipulation and yet concrete enough to accommodate "real" ideologies in the "real" world. And it must be based on a fairly small number of variables, since any attempt to handle large numbers will render the operation unwieldy.

The selection of the key variables is a crucial aspect of typology construction. And yet it is basically an arbitrary operation governed primarily by the purpose to which the typology is to be put and secondarily by the interests of the investigator. However, it is possible to minimize arbitrariness in typology construction through the explicit statement of certain ground rules—such as the ones proposed in the foregoing paragraph.

An adequate typology of belief systems may be based upon two vital characteristics of the ideology concept: the programmatic and the affective dimensions. The programmatic component would consider the goals of ideology, and it would make a distinction between ultimate and intermediate goals. The affective dimension would consider the intensity with which the goals are held or pursued, and it would make a distinction between high-intensity and low-intensity belief systems.

The programmatic dimension is particularly relevant and valuable, for it tends to subsume some other components of the ideology concept. Thus, for example, any discussion of goals necessarily involves elements of cognition and evaluation. Together, the programmatic and the affective dimensions yield a fourfold typology of belief systems especially useful, among other things, for application to the decline of ideology hypothesis. This typology is presented in Figure 1.

A consummatory belief system subscribes to millenarian goals, and it does so with high emotive intensity. The passionate pursuit of utopian objectives goes hand in hand with a blanket

|  |  | GOAL | |
|  |  | *Ultimate* | *Intermediate* |
| --- | --- | --- | --- |
| | *High* | Consummatory | Expressive |
| AFFECT | | | |
| | *Low* | Transcendent | Instrumental |

FIGURE 1. A Typology of Belief Systems

denunciation of the existing society through appeal to standards of morality. The high affect and the low rationality combine to increase the mass appeal of consummatory belief systems while at the same time maximizing their potential for mass manipulation and control. Patterns of action are articulated toward the realization of principles embodied in the ideology, and there is a demand for total consistency between action and principle. Consummatory ideologies tend to be cognitively closed. Examples include fascism, nazism, and communism.

A transcendent belief system subscribes to millenarian goals but with low emotive intensity. It calls for a complete reconstruction of the existing society but the low emotive content is balanced against strong elements of rationality. The low affect and the (relatively) high rationality undermine the mass appeal of transcendent belief systems. Proposed patterns of action are implicit rather than explicit. Consistency between principle and behavior is deemed inherent in the order of things, in the way in which society evolves. Examples of transcendent ideologies include old-fashioned elitism, Social Darwinism, and utilitarianism.

An expressive belief system subscribes to intermediate goals but with high emotive intensity. The passionate pursuit of limited objectives is accompanied by a denunciation of the existing society as evil, corrupt, and immoral. The high affect, accompanied by a degree of rationality, maximizes the appeal of the ideology to those segments of the population to which it is directed (youth, for example). Proposed patterns of action tend to be imprecise and implicit. Examples of expressive belief systems include all varieties of romanticism, including some statements of the New Left ideology.

An instrumental belief system subscribes to intermediate goals, and it does so with low emotive intensity. The "pragmatic" pursuit of manageable objectives is buttressed by a considerable regard for the existing society. A high degree of rationality drains passion out of politics. Instrumental ideologies are partial, segmental, and reformist. Proposed patterns of action are precise and explicit. Such ideologies tend to be cognitively open. Examples include liberal democracy and democratic socialism.

Some of the objections to this typology may be anticipated. It may be argued that the distinction between the consummatory and transcendent categories is farfetched, since the former also involves "transcendence." Such a criticism has a certain plausibility, but it overlooks the criterion of emotive intensity. A consummatory ideology is both utopian and affective, a transcendent ideology simply utopian.

Another objection may be that the typology does not accommodate the status quo ideologies. This objection may be overcome by distinguishing between the varieties of status quo ideologies. Such a moderate status quo ideology as contemporary American or British conservatism would be included in the instrumental category, for to seek to maintain a given status quo is in itself a goal or objective. On the other hand, such an extremist status quo ideology as that of fascism would be placed in the consummatory category. The same may be said of the ideology of nationalism, which itself takes at least three forms: formative nationalism (as in colonial countries), prestige nationalism (as in contemporary France), and expansive nationalism (as in Nazi Germany). Again, the first variety would fall in the instrumental category, the second in the expressive category, and the third in the consummatory group.

The point, in short, is that there are various expressions of conservatism, nationalism, socialism, etc., and that these expressions must be sorted out before they can be placed in the proposed typology.

## DECLINE OF IDEOLOGY: THE TRAVAIL OF A HYPOTHESIS

"Decline of ideology" is a theme in comparative political analysis that can be applied across nations, across time, or both. Its substance may be contrasted with that of the Lerner-Pool-Lasswell study discussed above, in which, in effect, an intensification of (elite) ideologies over the 1890–1950 period was identified. The decline hypothesis is in fact a complementary proposition applied to a different time span, since it identifies a deintensification of ideologies in the postwar era, that is, the period immediately following the Lerner-Pool-Lasswell study.

The decline of ideology hypothesis refers to either one of two propositions: (1) a relative modulation over the last two decades of the ultimacy with which ideological goals are stated, or (2) a relative attenuation of the emotive intensity with which ideological goals are pursued. The hypothesis has relevance for both international and domestic politics.

Considered at the international level, the decline proposition suggests that extremist ideologies—Marxist movements, for example—have, over the last two decades, modified both their global objectives and the intensity with which these objectives are sought. When applied to domestic politics, the decline hypothesis suggests that the formerly intense competition between political parties over national policies has been moderated, that the ideologies of the left and right have to some extent coalesced into a united assault upon certain common problems, and that there has been a relative attenuation of political cleavage and dissensus.

In terms of the typology proposed in the previous section, a decline of ideology hypothesis would require an alteration in the programmatic or the affective dimension of ideological belief systems. This would suggest any of five propositions: (1) replacement of a consummatory belief system by a transcendent one; (2) replacement of a consummatory belief system by an expressive one; (3) replacement of a consummatory belief system by an instrumental one; (4) replacement of a transcendent belief system by an instrumental one; and (5) replacement of an expressive belief system by an instrumental one. In other words, only the replacement of a transcendent ideology by an expressive belief system would not qualify as "decline" because it would lose on the programmatic dimension while gaining in affective intensity.

It is necessary to be quite explicit as to what the hypothesis of decline does *not* mean. The hypothesis does not suggest the total disappearance of ideologies. The notion of an "end" of ideology is simply a euphemism. What the hypothesis does convey is an ending of "apocalyptic," "total," or "extremist" ideologies—that is to say, a decline of ideology. This is one of the key sources of confusion in the literature on the decline of ideology, and it must be attributed in large measure to the decline writers themselves, who have stated their hypothesis in two different ways: (1) a "decline of ideology," and (2) an "end of [extremist] ideology." There is no question that the decline writers consider ideology a permanent factor in human affairs.

The hypothesis of ideological decline is stated within certain explicit limits: specifically, it is both time-bound and space-bound. The hypothesis is time-bound in that it embraces ideological politics in the postwar period only. It is space-bound in that it applies primarily to advanced, industrial, Western societies. The second proposition requires some elaboration.

The decline hypothesis stipulates certain conditions under which it would be fully operative. These conditions have largely materialized in Western industrial societies, are in the process of materialization in selected non-Western (though industrially advanced) countries, and are largely absent in most of the developing areas of the world.

What are some of these conditions? Internationally, two developments have been especially relevant: (1) a relative discreditation of the ideologies of fascism, nazism, and racism; and (2) a relative "thaw" in cold-war policies and attitudes and a relative diminution in crisis world politics. The latter condition is integrally associated with the erosion of Marxist ideologies and a redefinition and modification of their goals and tactics (see Introductory Note, Part II). The most significant overall outcome has been a near-universal disillusionment with war as an instrument of national politics and ideology.

The most important internal changes revolve around economic development and its attendant consequences: an increasing general affluence; an increasing exposure to education and the media of communication; an increasing reliance on science and expertise; an increasing attenuation of class and party conflict; a gradual attainment of political and economic citizenship

by the lower classes; a gradual emergence of a vast, homogeneous, professional-managerial middle class; a gradual transformation of laissez-faire capitalism into the welfare state; and a
gradual institutionalization of stable political processes for resolution of political issues.

A systematic comparative treatment of the decline hypothesis
and its relationship to some of these variables has been undertaken by Lipset. His comments deserve quotation in some detail:

> The linkage between level of industrial development and other
> political and social institutions is obviously not a simple one.
> Greater economic productivity is associated with a more equi-
> table distribution of consumption goods and education—factors
> contributing to a reduction of intra-societal tension. As the
> wealth of a nation increases, the status gap inherent in poor
> countries . . . is reduced. As differences in style of life are
> reduced, so are the tensions of stratification. And increased edu-
> cation enhances the propensity of different groups to "tolerate"
> each other, to accept the complex idea that truth and error are
> not necessarily on one side.
>
> An explanation for the reduction in the appeal of total
> ideologies *(weltanschauungen)* as simply derivative from the social
> concomitants inherent in increasing economic productivity is
> clearly oversimplified. T. H. Marshall has suggested that such
> extreme ideologies initially emerged with the rise of new strata,
> such as the bourgeoisie or the working class, as they sought the
> rights of citizenship, that is, the right to fully participate socially
> and politically. As long as they were denied such rights sizable
> segments of these strata endorsed revolutionary ideologies. In
> turn, older strata and institutions seeking to preserve their ancient
> monopolies of power and status fostered conservative extremist
> ideologies. . . .
>
> Still a third factor related to the general decline in ideological
> bitterness has been the acceptance of scientific thought and
> professionalism in matters which have been at the center of
> political controversy. Insofar as most organized participants in
> the political struggle accept the authority of experts in economics,
> military affairs, interpretations of the behavior of foreign na-
> tions, and the like, it becomes increasingly difficult to challenge
> the views of opponents in moralistic "either/or" terms. Where
> there is some consensus among the scientific experts on specific
> issues, these tend to be removed as possible sources of intense

controversy. As the ideology of "scientism" becomes accepted, the ideologies of the extreme left and right lose much of their impact.[41]

This is perhaps another way of saying that as the economic, technological, and industrial conditions that gave rise to ideologies in the eighteenth and nineteenth centuries undergo transformation, so do the ideologies to which they gave rise. As these conditions transform and stabilize, the ideologies in question undergo corresponding modification and modulation. By the same token, new conditions set the stage for the emergence of new and appropriate ideologies.

The range and variety of criticisms launched against the decline hypothesis are quite impressive. The most important of these are as follows:[42]

1. The decline of ideology hypothesis is unrealistic and far-fetched. It is an elementary fact that all political thought and activity is ideological. Ideologies have not ended in the affluent West, as witness the race and poverty issues, the emergence of the New Left and the radical right, etc. There will be continued clashes over the distribution of national income and opportunities. Nor are ideologies about to disappear in the developing countries, where, it anything, they are on the rise.

2. The decline hypothesis reflects parochialism and provincialism on the part of its exponents, since it limits itself to Western countries only.

3. The decline hypothesis separates domestic and international politics and pays little or no attention to the latter. There will always be contending conceptions of foreign and military policies. International politics will continue to require decisive ideological alignments.

4. The decline hypothesis embraces a value judgment based on vested interest and a commitment to the status quo, the welfare state, "scientism," etc. It represents a posture of "false consciousness" and a "slogan of complacency," since it assumes that there are no longer any issues of great political consequence. It assumes, moreover, that history is moving toward an ultimate

static equilibrium in which, given economic growth, the developing countries will join the sterile rank of Western societies. As such, the decline hypothesis is a philosophy of history, not a social-scientific proposition. The decline of ideology is itself an ideology.

5. The decline hypothesis stands for "a fetishism of empiricism," for a denial of the continued relevance of moral and human ideals.

6. The decline hypothesis confuses an attenuation of ideology for the intellectuals with a decline of ideology among the masses.

7. The decline hypothesis confuses a shift in the arena of ideological conflict with a decline in ideology, even in Western societies. While there has been a reduction of ideological cleavage surrounding old political issues, there has been a sharp increase of ideological disuputes in new areas. The "new democratic Leviathan"—with its centralized, bureaucratized, dehumanized, impersonal, distant mode of operation—will continue to alienate significant segments of the population, particularly the youth and the intellectuals, "not because it is democratic but because, in their view, it is not democratic enough."[43]

On the basis of these and similar analyses, some scholars have foreseen the emergence of new ideologies based on new social and political dynamics. Dahl, believes, for example, that "differences in basic political ideas and evaluations are likely to become more and more important in explaining differences in political behavior and therefore in patterns of [political] opposition. Yet these crucial differences in political ideas and evaluations will probably be less and less traceable to differences in social and economic characteristics. In this sense, political ideologies, far from waning, will be ascendant."[44]

The above criticisms, it will be noted, are of three types: (1) those based on a *misunderstanding* of either the meaning of ideology or of the decline hypothesis, (2) those based on *disagreements* about the meaning of ideology or of the decline hypothesis, and (3) those based on a *misconstruction* of the decline hypothesis. We shall examine these criticisms in turn.

The first criticism reflects a misunderstanding of the issue at hand and a confusion of a relative *decline* in ideology with a literal *ending* of all ideology. No one has suggested that ideologies have ended; rather, the contention is that there has been a relative attenuation in their scope and intensity. Note the confusion in Clifford Geertz, for example, when he writes, on the one hand, that in stable societies "the role of ideology, in any explicit sense, is marginal," while on the other that "We may wait as long for the 'end of ideology' as the positivists have waited for the end of religion."[45]

Similarly, the criticism that ideologies continue to be important in the developing countries is a mark of inattention to the substance of the decline thesis. Surely Friedrich confuses the issue when he insists that the decline hypothesis is "by no means" justified because "ideology is on the increase throughout the non-European world."[46] This, after all, is what the decline thesis is in part about.

The second criticism betrays an apparent desire to universalize the decline hypothesis and extend it to all countries, East and West, developed and underdeveloped. In so doing, it ignores the nature of social-scientific investigation. A social-scientific hypothesis differs from a philosophical or moral argument, for example, by (among other things) its limited scope. The value of a proposition does not lie in whether it explains *all* phenomena but whether it explains what it sets out to explain. One of the most common—and least convincing—of all criticisms is to attack a proposition for what it does *not* purport to do.

The third criticism either misunderstands or misconstrues the hypothesis in question. The decline hypothesis is admittedly not centrally concerned with international politics; its *articulated* primary focus is domestic developments. However, as we have seen, the hypothesis is not oblivious of international relations.

The fourth criticism is part misconstruction and part misunderstanding. The notion of an ultimate movement toward a static equilibrium is a logical implication of an *end* of ideology hypothesis, not of the decline proposition. Such an implication has not been contemplated by any of the decline writers because there is nothing unavoidable about the direction of historical development. The decline hypothesis simply describes a particular state of affairs at a given point in time. It may even express a preference for civil politics in contrast to ideological politics (to use Shils' terminology), but it does not suggest that civil politics is the epitome of human achievement. The decline hypothesis, in other words, permits fluidity and dynamism; it is not closed to change.

Viewed in this light, the criticism that the decline hypothesis is itself ideological loses its force and persuasiveness. The *significant* question is whether or not the hypothesis has any social-scientific value. If it does, then it is by definition empirical rather than ideological. The decline hypothesis, as Aron has aptly put it, "is first and foremost a diagnosis of the historical situation. For this reason, considered as a statement of fact, it requires either confirmation or refutation on that level. In short, the first question concerns the truth or falsity of the analysis, or if you like, its degree of truthfulness or falsehood."[47]

The fifth criticism is in part valid. The decline hypothesis does hope and intend to be empirical, but there is no evidence to suggest that the decline writers are indifferent to human values. It does not seem warranted to confuse an objective, neutral style of analysis with moral indifference.

The sixth criticism is well taken. The literature will certainly leave the reader confused as to whether the hypothesis applies to the intellectuals or to the masses or to both. Though initially directed to the intellectuals, the hypothesis is now understood to embrace the masses as well.

The last criticism is an important one, though one must, once again, recall the relativistic character of the decline hypothesis and insist upon its inapplicability to all situations. Even such a severe critic as Dahl concedes that "the traditional ideologies that have played so great a role in Western politics in the past century show every sign of being well on the way to ultimate extinction."[48] *That* is precisely the point, and *that* is what the decline hypothesis is all about. The point that there has been an emergence of ideology in certain new areas is well taken, to be sure, but it does not contradict the decline hypothesis, *for it is addressed to another question.* Indeed, it helps validate the hypothesis of decline.

So far as the new ideological groupings are concerned (such as the world-wide student movement, the peace and civil rights movements, the New Left, the radical right, etc.), several points need to be borne in mind. To begin with, as suggested earlier, just as the particular conditions of the eighteenth and nineteenth centuries gave rise to a distinct set of ideologies, new conditions logically generate corresponding belief systems. In this context, it might be well to recall Thomas S. Kuhn's hypothesis that scientific paradigms—and perhaps ideological ones as well—undergo revolutionary transformation when their explanatory power fades.[49] Second, these movements—whether left or right—embrace relatively small numbers of people; they have been too elitist to appeal to substantial segments of the general population. Third, these movements—whether left or right—are too seriously fragmented to be able to put forward a convincing, unified, and unifying political-ideological front. Fourth, some observers have suggested that these movements are not even "ideological" in the conventional sense of that term, since they lack an explicit belief system, a statement of objectives and programs, and an appropriate strategy for their realization. Thus Richard Goodwin, one of the foremost spokesmen for the new politics, stated in an interview that, although there is widespread discontent among the new groups, "except for the young, this is a very non-ideological discontent, because people don't have a very clear idea of the direction of the change that they want, except that they know that it ["the system"] isn't working."[50] In this sense, one may say that there has been a resurgence of negative protest movements but not of ideological politics. Edward Shils has found it useful to call such movements "proto-ideological." By this he means "those collectivities—such as adolescent gangs and military and paramilitary units—which, although 'sodalitylike' in structure, do not have the intellectual patterns which are here designated as ideological. Such collectivities are alienated from the prevailing outlook associated with the central institutional and value systems and draw sharply defined boundaries around themselves. Moreover, they insist on a concentration of loyalty to the group and on stringent discipline to the standards of the group and have simplistic criteria of partisanship and enmity. They do not, however, develop or espouse a coherent moral and intellectual doctrine. . . . They have no image of a comprehensive order that would permanently replace the order from which they are alienated."[51]

Indeed, with the exception of such fringe groups as the Maoists and the Birchers, the new politics are the politics of *de*-ideologization. There has been a call, in effect, for the abandonment of all ideologies. There is a demand that men live together harmoniously and cooperatively, with no distinctions, no gradations, and no ideologies (cf. the notion of the "commune"). The new politics, in short, are anti-ideological politics.

The new politics, however anti-ideological, have generated an intensification of feelings among the masses of the people (the "silent majorities") on a range of issues including race, foreign policy, the youth, and the economy. With particular reference to the United States, the politics of polarization practiced by both the extreme left and the extreme right have forced the general population to choose sides—which means, more often than not, strengthening the right-wing groups. Whether this polarization is ideological—in the sense that ideology has been defined in this paper—remains to be determined.

This paper has developed a conception of ideology and has constructed a typology of belief systems as preliminary steps toward the comparative analysis of political ideologies. It has sought to clarify the hypothesis of ideological decline and the many difficulties that surround it. Any definitive resolution of the issues raised in this paper would be contingent on a series of agreements among the concerned scholars. These agreements would extend to: (1) the meaning of ideology, (2) the meaning of the decline hypothesis, (3) the cases or countries in which the hypothesis is to be tested, (4) the methodological operations to be performed, and (5) the interpretive guidelines to be employed. Meanwhile, we can expect the controversy to continue.

## N O T E S

1. For a good example of the sustained confusion of ideology and concept, see Norman Birnbaum, "The Sociological Study of Ideology (1940–60)," *Current Sociology,* IX:2 (1960), 91–117.
2. Giovanni Sartori, "Politics, Ideology, and Belief Systems," *American Political Science Review,* 63:2 (June 1969), 398.
3. For an explicit treatment of this theme see, for example, William E. Connolly, *Political Science and Ideology* (New York: Atherton Press, 1967).
4. For some sociological approaches to ideology, see Daniel Bell, *The End of Ideology* (New York: Free Press, 1960), especially the Epilogue; Bell, "Ideology and Soviet Politics," *Slavic Review,* XXIV:4 (December 1965), 591–603; Birnbaum, "The Sociological Study of Ideology (1940–60)"; Karl Mannheim, *Ideology and Utopia* (New York: Harcourt, Brace & Co., 1936); Talcott Parsons, "An Approach to the Sociology of Knowledge," *Transactions of the Fourth World Congress of Sociology* (Louvain: International Sociological Association, 1959), pp. 25–49.

   Some psychological approaches to ideology may be found in T. W. Adorno et al., *The Authoritarian Personality* (New York: Harper and Brothers, 1950); Erik Erikson, *Young Man Luther: A Study in Psychoanalysis and History* (New York: W. W. Norton & Co., 1962), especially pp. 14, 22, 41–43; Milton Rokeach, *The Open and Closed Mind* (New York: Basic Books, 1960); Francis X. Sutton et al., *The American Business Creed* (Cambridge: Harvard University Press, 1956), especially chap. 15.

   For some psychocultural approaches, see Léon Dion, "Political Ideology as a Tool of Functional Analysis in Socio-Political Dynamics: An Hypothesis," *Canadian Journal of Economics and Political Science,* 25:1 (February 1959), 47–59; Clifford Geertz, "Ideology as a Cultural System," in David E. Apter, ed., *Ideology and Discontent* (New York: Free Press, 1964), pp. 47–76.

   Other important works on ideology include Henry D. Aiken, *The Age of Ideology* (New York: Mentor Books, 1956); Apter "Introduction: Ideology and Discontent," in *Ideology and Discontent,* pp. 15–46; Samuel H. Barnes, "Ideology and the Organization of Conflict," *Journal of Politics,* 28:3 (August 1966), 513–530; Reinhard Bendix, "The Age of Ideology: Persistent and Changing," in Apter, *Ideology and Discontent,* pp. 294–327; Gustav Bergmann,

"Ideology," *Ethics*, LXI (April 1951), 205–218; Philip E. Converse, "The Nature of Belief Systems in Mass Publics," in Apter, *Ideology and Discontent*, pp. 206–261; Carl J. Friedrich, *Man and His Government* (New York: McGraw-Hill, 1963), chaps. 4 and 5; Thomas P. Jenkin, *The Study of Political Theory* (New York: Random House, 1955); Harry M. Johnson, "Ideology and the Social System," in *International Encyclopedia of the Social Sciences* (New York: Macmillan and Free Press, 1968), Vol. 7, pp. 76–85; Robert E. Lane, *Political Ideology* (New York: Free Press, 1962); Harold D. Lasswell and Abraham Kaplan, *Power and Society* (New Haven: Yale University Press, 1950), pp. 116–133; George Lichtheim, "The Concept of Ideology," in *The Concept of Ideology and Other Essays* (New York: Vintage Books, 1967), pp. 3–46; Karl Loewenstein, "The Role of Ideologies in Political Change," *International Social Science Bulletin*, V:1 (1953), 51–74; David W. Minar, "Ideology and Political Behavior," *Midwest Journal of Political Science*, V:4 (November 1961), 317–331; Sartori, "Politics, Ideology, and Belief Systems"; Edward Shils, "The Concept and Function of Ideology," *International Encyclopedia of the Social Sciences*, Vol. 7, pp. 66–76.

5. The first three dimensions are adapted from Talcott Parsons' conception of culture. See Parsons, *The Social System* (New York: Free Press, 1951), especially pp. 15 ff., 51 ff.; Parsons and Edward Shils, "Values, Motives, and Systems of Action," in Parsons and Shils, eds., *Toward a General Theory of Action* (Cambridge: Harvard University Press, 1951), especially p. 163.

6. See Converse, "The Nature of Belief Systems in Mass Publics"; Rokeach, *The Open and Closed Mind;* Sartori, "Politics, Ideology, and Belief Systems."

7. Rokeach, *The Open and Closed Mind*, p. 33.

8. Converse, "The Nature of Belief Systems in Mass Publics," p. 208.

9. Sartoi, "Politics, Ideology, and Belief Systems," pp. 406–407.

10. Rokeach, *The Open and Closed Mind*, p. 50 (italics in original).

11. *Ibid.*, pp. 57, 58.

12. *The German Ideology* (New York: International Publishers, 1947), p. 14.

13. Mannheim, *Ideology and Utopia*, p. 55.

14. MacIver, *The Web of Government*, rev. ed. (New York: Free Press, 1965), p. 4 et passim.

15. Bergmann, "Ideology," p. 210.

16. Lasswell and Kaplan, *Power and Society*, p. 123.

17. Parsons, "An Approach to the Sociology of Knowledge," p. 38.

18. Apter, "Introduction: Ideology and Discontent," pp. 19–20; Jenkin, *The Study of Political Theory*, especially p. 10; Johnson, "Ideology and the Social System," pp. 78–81; Lichtheim, "The Concept of Ideology," p. 3; Shils, "The Concept and Function of Ideology," pp. 73–74.

19. Carl J. Friedrich and Zbigniew K. Brzezinski, *Totalitarian Dictatorship and Autocracy*, 2nd ed. (New York: Frederick A. Praeger, 1965), p. 89.

20. See Michael Walzer, "On the Role of Symbolism in Political Thought," *Political Science Quarterly*, 82:2 (June 1967), 191–204.

28 : *Political Ideology: Theoretical and Comparative Perspectives*

21. Lasswell and Kaplan, *Power and Society*, p. 104.
22. Bell, *The End of Ideology*, p. 371.
23. Shils, "The Concept and Function of Ideology," p. 67.
24. This point was first brought to my attention by Robert L. Fulton.
25. David Easton, *The Political System* (New York: Alfred A. Knopf, 1953); Easton, *A Framework for Political Analysis* (Englewood Cliffs: Prentice-Hall, Inc., 1965); Easton, *A Systems Analysis of Political Life* (New York: John Wiley & Sons, 1965).
26. Clyde Kluckhohn, "Values and Value-Orientations in the Theory of Action," in Parsons and Shils, *Toward a General Theory of Action*, pp. 395, 396.
27. Shils, "The Concept and Function of Ideology," p. 68.
28. Bell, *The End of Ideology*, p. 372.
29. Barnes, "Ideology and the Organization of Conflict."
30. Converse, "The Nature of Belief Systems in Mass Publics," p. 213 et passim.
31. Lane, *Political Ideology*, p. 16.
32. Sartori, "Politics, Ideology, and Belief Systems," p. 407.
33. *Ibid.*, p. 411.
34. Hans Riechenbach, *The Rise of Scientific Philosophy* (Berkeley and Los Angeles: University of California Press, 1952), p. 83.
35. Daniel Lerner, Ithiel de Sola Pool, and Harold D. Lasswell, "Comparative Analysis of Political Ideology: A Preliminary Statement," *Public Opinion Quarterly*, XV (Winter 1951–52), 715, 717.
36. *Ibid.*, pp. 717, 718.
37. *Ibid.*, p. 729.
38. Roy C. Macridis, *The Study of Comparative Government* (New York: Random House, 1954), especially chap. 7.
39. Sartori, "Politics, Ideology, and Belief Systems," pp. 405–406.
40. *Ibid.*, p. 406.
41. Lipset, "The Changing Class Structure and Contemporary European Politics," *Daedalus*, 93 (Winter 1964), 272–273.
42. The most brilliant, unsparing, and polemical critique is C. Wright Mills, "Letter to the New Left," *New Left Review*, 5 (1960), reprinted in Chaim I. Waxman, ed., *The End of Ideology Debate* (New York: Funk & Wagnalls, 1968), pp. 126–140. See also the following essays in the same volume: Henry D. Aiken, "The Revolt Against Ideology," pp. 229–258; Daniel Bell and Henry D. Aiken, "Ideology—A Debate," pp. 259–280; William Delany, "The Role of Ideology: A Summation," pp. 291–314; Robert A. Haber, "The End of Ideology as Ideology," pp. 182–205; Donald Clark Hodges, "The End of 'The End of Ideology,'" pp. 373–388; Irving Louis Horowitz, "Another View from Our Left," pp. 166–181; Stephen W. Rousseas and James Farganis, "American Politics and the End of Ideology," pp. 206–228. See further Reinhard Bendix, "The Age of Ideology: Persistent and Changing," pp. 294–327; Birnbaum, "The Sociological Study of Ideology"; Robert A. Dahl, *Political Oppositions in Western Democracies* (New Haven: Yale University Press, 1966), Epilogue; Carl J. Friedrich, "Ideology in Politics: A Theoretical Comment," *Slavic Review*, 24:4 (December 1965), 612–616; Geertz, "Ideology as a Cultural System"; Morris Janowitz and

David R. Segal, "Social Cleavage and Party Affiliation: Germany, Great Britain, and the United States," *American Journal of Sociology*, 72:6 (May 1967), 601–618.

43. Dahl, *Political Oppositions in Western Democracies,* p. 400.
44. *Ibid.,* p. 401.
45. Geertz, "Ideology as a Cultural System," pp. 63, 51.
46. Friedrich, "Ideology in Politics," p. 613.
47. Raymond Aron, *The Industrial Society: Three Essays on Ideology and Development* (New York: Frederick A. Praeger, 1967), p. 146.
48. Dahl, *Political Oppositions in Western Democracies,* p. 401.
49. Thomas S. Kuhn, *The Structure of Scientific Revolutions* (Chicago: University of Chicago Press, 1962).
50. David Gelman and Beverly Kempton, "New Issues for the New Politics: An Interview with Richard N. Goodwin," *The Washington Monthly,* August 1969, p. 18.
51. Shils, "The Concept and Function of Ideology," p. 72.

# I The Hypothesis

# Introductory Note

Roy Pierce (p. 287 below) identifies Albert Camus as the first person to have used the expression "end of ideology" and analyzes Camus' thoughts in some detail. Seymour Martin Lipset (p. 108 below) refers to two European writers, T. H. Marshall and Herbert Tingsten, who "enunciated the basic thesis without using the term in the late 40's and early 50's."

"The end of political ideology" is a theme also developed by H. Stuart Hughes in a 1951 article surveying the European political scene.[1] Hughes identifies a "process of ideological dissolution" and a "wreckage of political faiths" in which radical ideologies have lost their sway. He approvingly quotes Isaiah Berlin to the effect that "disagreements about political principles" have been replaced by "disagreements, ultimately technical, about method."

Raymond Aron elaborates upon the theme of ideological decline. In a book published in 1955, he emphasizes the passing of fanaticism in political belief and the erosion of ideologies that were at one time sharp, distinct, and explicit.[2] He writes of an increasing awareness that "the political categories of the last cen-

tury—Left and Right, liberal and socialist, traditionalist and revolutionary—have lost their relevance." Having surveyed the ideological scene in Western and non-Western countries, he concludes that "In most Western societies, ideological controversy is
dying down because experience has shown that divergent demands can be reconciled."[3]

The most significant impetus to the spread and acceptance of
the decline thesis was provided by a conference on "The Future
of Freedom," sponsored by the Congress of Cultural Freedom in
September 1955.[4] Held in Milan, the conference was attended
by some 150 intellectuals, scholars, politicians, and journalists
from numerous countries. After five days of discussion and debate, there emerged among the Western representatives a clear
consensus along the following lines: (1) total or extremist ideologies appeared to be in a state of decline; (2) this decline was
due largely to the increasing economic affluence in western countries; and (3) this decline was crystallized in the fact that "over
the past thirty years the extremes of 'right' and 'left' had disclosed identities which were more impressive than their
differences."[5] By contrast, representatives from the non-Western countries found it necessary to insist on the continued relevance of radical ideologies.

Following the Milan conference, some of the American participants (who included Daniel Bell, John Kenneth Galbraith,
Friedrich A. Hayek, Sidney Hook, George F. Kennan, Seymour
Martin Lipset, Arthur M. Schlesinger, Jr., and Edward Shils)
became centrally involved in further exploration and elaboration
of the decline hypothesis. In the two selections reproduced
below, Bell and Lipset develop the theme in some detail. Bell
addresses himself to the "exhaustion" of total ideologies in the
1950s and notes the coalescence on certain issues of traditionally
antagonistic ideologies. Lipset specifically relates the theme of
ideological decline to economic development (among other variables) and develops a hypothesis capable of empirical testing
and verification.

## NOTES

1. H. Stuart Hughes, "The End of Political Ideology," *Measure,* II:2 (Spring 1951), 146–158.
2. *The Opium of the Intellectuals* (New York: W. W. Norton & Co., 1962). The first American edition was published by Doubleday & Co. in 1957; the original French edition *(L'opium des intellectuels)* appeared in 1955.
3. Aron, "Nations and Ideologies," *Encounter,* IV (January 1955), 24, 32.
4. A fairly detailed account of the conference appears in Edward Shils, "The End of Ideology?" *Encounter,* V (November 1955), 52–58. See also Lipset, "The State of Democratic Politics," *Canadian Forum,* 35 (November 1955), 170–171.
5. Shils, "The End of Ideology?" p. 53.

# 1 *The Passing of Fanaticism*

## DANIEL BELL

Men commit the error of not knowing when to limit their hopes—Machiavelli

There have been few periods in history when man felt his world to be durable, suspended surely, as in Christian allegory, between chaos and heaven. In an Egyptian papyrus of more than four thousand years ago, one finds: ". . . impudence is rife . . . the country is spinning round and round like a potter's wheel . . . the masses are like timid sheep without a shepherd . . . one who yesterday was indigent is now wealthy and the sometime rich overwhelm him with adulation." The Hellenistic period as described by Gilbert Murray was one of a "failure of nerve"; there was "the rise of pessimism, a loss of self-confidence, of hope in this life and of faith in normal human effort." And the old scoundrel Talleyrand claimed that only

From Daniel Bell, *The End of Ideology* (New York: Free Press, 1960), pp. 369–375. Copyright © 1960 by the Free Press, a Corporation. Reprinted by permission of The Macmillan Company.

those who lived before 1789 could have tasted life in all its sweetness.[1]

This age, too, can add appropriate citations—made all the more wry and bitter by the long period of bright hope that preceded it —for the two decades between 1930 and 1950 have an intensity peculiar in written history: world-wide economic depression and sharp class struggles; the rise of fascism and racial imperialism in a country that had stood at an advanced stage of human culture; the tragic self-immolation of a revolutionary generation that had proclaimed the finer ideals of man; destructive war of a breadth and scale hitherto unknown; the bureaucratized murder of millions in concentration camps and death chambers.

For the radical intellectual who had articulated the revolutionary impulses of the past century and a half, all this has meant an end to chiliastic hopes, to millenarianism, to apocalyptic thinking —and to ideology. For ideology, which once was a road to action, has come to be a dead end.

Whatever its origins among the French *philosophes,* ideology as a way of translating ideas into action was given its sharpest phrasing by the left Hegelians, by Feuerbach and by Marx. For them, the function of philosophy was to be critical, to rid the present of the past. ("The tradition of all the dead generations weighs like a nightmare on the brain of the living," wrote Marx.) Feuerbach, the most radical of all the left Hegelians, called himself Luther II. Man would be free, he said, if we could demythologize religion. The history of all thought was a history of progressive disenchantment, and if finally, in Christianity, God had been transformed from a parochial deity to a universal abstraction, the function of criticism—using the radical tool of alienation, or self-estrangement—was to replace theology by anthropology, to substitute Man for God. Philosophy was to be directed at life, man was to be liberated from the "specter of abstractions" and extricated from the bind of the supernatural. Religion was capable only of creating "false consciousness." Philosophy would reveal "true consciousness." And by placing Man, rather than God, at the center of consciousness, Feuerbach sought to bring the "infinite into the finite."[2]

If Feuerbach "descended into the world," Marx sought to transform it. And where Feuerbach proclaimed anthropology, Marx, reclaiming a root insight of Hegel, emphasized History and historical contexts. The world was not generic Man, but men; and of men, classes of men. Men differed because of their class position. And truths were class truths. All truths, thus, were masks, or partial truths, but the real truth was the revolutionary truth. And this real truth was rational.

Thus a dynamic was introduced into the analysis of ideology, and into the creation of a new ideology. By demythologizing religion, one recovered (from God and sin) the potential in man. By the unfolding of history, rationality was revealed. In the struggle of classes, true consciousness, rather than false consciousness, could be achieved. But if truth lay in action, one must act. The left Hegelians, said Marx, were only *littérateurs*. (For them a magazine was "practice.") For Marx, the only real action was in politics. But action, revolutionary action as Marx conceived it, was not mere social change. It was, in its way, the resumption of all the old millenarian, chiliastic ideas of the Anabaptists. It was, in its new vision, a new ideology.

Ideology is the conversion of ideas into social levers. Without irony, Max Lerner once entitled a book "Ideas Are Weapons." This is the language of ideology. It is more. It is the commitment to the consequences of ideas. When Vissarion Belinsky, the father of Russian criticism, first read Hegel and became convinced of the philosophical correctness of the formula "what is, is what ought to be," he became a supporter of the Russian autocracy. But when it was shown to him that Hegel's thought contained the contrary tendency, that dialectically the "is" evolves into a different form, he became a revolutionary overnight. "Belinsky's conversion," comments Rufus W. Mathewson, Jr., "illustrates an attitude toward ideas which is both passionate and myopic, which responds to them on the basis of their immediate relevances alone, and inevitably reduces them to tools."[3]

What gives ideology its force is its passion. Abstract philosophical inquiry has always sought to eliminate passion, and the person, to rationalize all ideas. For the ideologue, truth arises in action, and meaning is given to experience by the "transforming moment." He comes alive not in contemplation, but in "the deed." One might say, in fact, that the most important, latent, function of ideology is to tap emotion. Other than religion (and war and nationalism), there have been few forms of channelizing emotional energy. Religion symbolized, drained away, dispersed emotional energy from the world onto the litany, the liturgy, the sacraments, the edifices, the arts. Ideology fuses these energies and channels them into politics.

But religion, at its most effective, was more. It was a way for people to cope with the problem of death. The fear of death—forceful and inevitable—and more, the fear of violent death, shatters the glittering, imposing, momentary dream of man's power. The fear of death, as Hobbes pointed out, is the source of conscience; the effort to avoid violent death is the source of law. When it was possible for people to believe, really believe, in heaven and hell, then some of the fear of death could be tempered or controlled; without such belief, there is only the total annihilation of the self.[4]

It may well be that with the decline in religious *faith* in the last century and more, this fear of death as total annihilation, unconsciously expressed, has probably increased. One may hypothesize, in fact, that here is a cause of the breakthrough of the irrational, which is such a marked feature of the changed moral temper of our time. Fanaticism, violence, and cruelty are not, of course, unique in human history. But there was a time when such frenzies and mass emotions could be displaced, symbolized, drained away, and dispersed through religious devotion and practice. Now there is only this life, and the assertion of self becomes possible—for some even necessary—in the domination over others.* One can challenge death by emphasizing the omnipotence of a movement (as in the "inevitable" victory of communism), or overcome death (as did the "immortality" of Captain Ahab) by bending others to one's will. Both paths are taken, but politics, because it can institutionalize power, in the way that religion once did, becomes the ready avenue for domination. The modern effort to transform the world chiefly or solely through politics (as contrasted with the religious transformation of the self) has meant that all other institutional ways of mobilizing emotional energy would necessarily atrophy. In effect, sect and church became party and social movement.

A social movement can rouse people when it can do three things: simplify ideas, establish a claim to truth, and, in the union of the two, demand a commitment to action. Thus, not only does ideology transform ideas, it transforms people as well. The nineteenth-century ideologies, by emphasizing inevitability and by infusing passion into their followers, could compete with religion. By identifying inevitability with progress, they linked up with the positive values of science. But more important, these ideologies were linked, too, with the rising class of intellectuals, which was seeking to assert a place in society.

The differences between the intellectual and the scholar, without being invidious, are important to understand. The scholar has a bounded field of knowledge, a tradition, and seeks to find his place in it, adding to the accumulated, tested knowledge of the past as to a mosaic. The scholar, qua scholar, is less involved with his "self." The intellectual begins with *his* experience, *his* individual perceptions of the world, *his* privileges and deprivations, and judges the world by these sensibilities. Since his own status is of high value, his judgments of the society reflect the

---

* The Marquis de Sade, who, more than any man, explored the limits of self-assertion, once wrote: "There is not a single man who doesn't want to be a despot when he is excited . . . he would like to be alone in the world . . . any sort of equality would destroy the despotism he enjoys then." De Sade proposed, therefore, to canalize these impulses into sexual activity by opening universal brothels which could serve to drain away these emotions. De Sade, it should be pointed out, was a bitter enemy of religion, but he understood well the latent function of religion in mobilizing emotions.

treatment accorded him. In a business civilization, the intellectual felt that the wrong values were being honored, and rejected the society. Thus there was a "built-in" compulsion for the free-floating intellectual to become political. The ideologies, therefore, which emerged from the nineteenth century had the force of the intellectuals behind them. They embarked upon what William James called "the faith ladder," which in its vision of the future cannot distinguish possibilities from probabilities, and converts the latter into certainties.

Today, these ideologies are exhausted. The events behind this important sociological change are complex and varied. Such calamities as the Moscow Trials, the Nazi-Soviet pact, the concentration camps, the suppression of the Hungarian workers, form one chain; such social changes as the modification of capitalism, the rise of the Welfare State, another. In philosophy, one can trace the decline of simplistic, rationalistic beliefs and the emergence of new stoic-theological images of man, e.g. Freud, Tillich, Jaspers, etc. This is not to say that such ideologies as communism in France and Italy do not have a political weight, or a driving momentum from other sources. But out of all this history, one simple fact emerges: for the radical intelligentsia, the old ideologies have lost their "truth" and their power to persuade.

Few serious minds believe any longer that one can set down "blueprints" and through "social engineering" bring about a new utopia of social harmony. At the same time, the older "counter-beliefs" have lost their intellectual force as well. Few "classic" liberals insist that the State should play no role in the economy, and few serious conservatives, at least in England and on the Continent, believe that the Welfare State is "the road to serfdom." In the Western world, therefore, there is today a rough consensus among intellectuals on political issues: the acceptance of a Welfare State; the desirability of decentralized power; a system of mixed economy and of political pluralism. In that sense, too, the ideological age has ended.

And yet, the extraordinary fact is that while the old nineteenth-century ideologies and intellectual debates have become exhausted, the rising states of Asia and Africa are fashioning new ideologies with a different appeal for their own people. These are the ideologies of industrialization, modernization, Pan-Arabism, color, and nationalism. In the distinctive difference between the two kinds of ideologies lies the great political and social problems of the second half of the twentieth century. The ideologies of the nineteenth century were universalistic, humanistic, and fashioned by intellectuals. The mass ideologies of Asia and Africa are parochial, instrumental, and created by political leaders. The driving forces of the old ideologies were social equality and, in the largest sense, freedom. The impulsions of the new ideologies are economic development and national power.

And in this appeal, Russia and China have become models. The fascination these countries exert is no longer the old idea of the free society, but the new one of economic growth. And if this involves the wholesale coercion of the population and the rise of new elites to drive the people, the new repressions are justified on the ground that without such coercions economic advance cannot take place rapidly enough. And even for some of the liberals of the West, "economic development" has become a new ideology that washes away the memory of old disillusionments.

It is hard to quarrel with an appeal for rapid economic growth and modernization, and few can dispute the goal, as few could ever dispute an appeal for equality and freedom. But in this powerful surge—and its swiftness is amazing—any movement that instates such goals risks the sacrifice of the present generation for a future that may see only a new exploitation by a new elite. For the newly risen countries, the debate is not over the merits of Communism—the content of that doctrine has long been forgotten by friends and foes alike. The question is an older one: whether new societies can grow by building democratic institutions and allowing people to make choices—and sacrifices —voluntarily, or whether the new elites, heady with power, will impose totalitarian means to transform their countries. Certainly in these traditional and old colonial societies where the masses are apathetic and easily manipulated, the answer lies with the intellectual classes and their conceptions of the future.

Thus one finds, at the end of the fifties, a disconcerting caesura. In the West, among the intellectuals, the old passions are spent. The new generation, with no meaningful memory of these old debates, and no secure tradition to build upon, finds itself seeking new purposes within a framework of political society that has rejected, intellectually speaking, the old apocalyptic and chiliastic visions. In the search for a "cause," there is a deep, desperate, almost pathetic anger. The theme runs through a remarkable book, *Convictions,* by a dozen of the sharpest young Left Wing intellectuals in Britain. They cannot define the content of the "cause" they seek, but the yearning is clear. In the U.S. too there is a restless search for a new intellectual radicalism. Richard Chase, in his thoughtful assessment of American society, *The Democratic Vista,* insists that the greatness of nineteenth-century America for the rest of the world consisted in its radical vision of man (such a vision as Whitman's), and calls for a new radical criticism today. But the problem is that the old politico-economic radicalism (preoccupied with such matters as the socialization of industry) has lost its meaning, while the stultifying aspects of contemporary culture (e.g., television) cannot be redressed in political terms. At the same time, American culture has almost completely accepted the avant-garde, particularly in art, and the older academic styles have been driven out completely. The irony, further, for those who seek "causes" is that the workers, whose grievances were once the driving energy for social change, are more satisfied with the society than the intellectuals. The workers have not achieved utopia, but their expectations were less than those of the intellectuals, and the gains correspondingly larger.

The young intellectual is unhappy because the "middle way" is for the middle-aged, not for him; it is without passion and is deadening.[5] Ideology, which by its nature is an all-or-none affair, and temperamentally the thing he wants, is intellectually devitalized, and few issues can be formulated any more, intellectually, in ideological terms. The emotional energies—and needs —exist, and the question of how one mobilizes these energies is a difficult one. Politics offers little excitement. Some of the younger intellectuals have found an outlet in science or university pursuits, but often at the expense of narrowing their talent into mere technique; others have sought self-expression in the arts, but in the wasteland the lack of content has meant, too, the lack of necessary tension that creates new forms and styles.

Whether the intellectuals in the West can find passions outside of politics is moot. Unfortunately, social reform does not have any unifying appeal, nor does it give a younger generation the outlet for "self-expression" and "self-definition" that it wants. The trajectory of enthusiasm has curved East, where, in the new ecstasies for economic utopia, the "future" is all that counts.

And yet, if the intellectual history of the past hundred years has any meaning—and lesson—it is to reassert Jefferson's wisdom (aimed at removing the dead hand of the past, but which can serve as a warning against the heavy hand of the future as well), that "the present belongs to the living." This is the wisdom that revolutionists, old and new, who are sensitive to the fate of their fellow men, rediscover in every generation. "I will never believe," says a protagonist in a poignant dialogue written by the gallant Polish philosopher Leszek Kolakowski, "that the moral and intellectual life of mankind follows the law of economics, that is by saving today we can have more tomorrow; that we should use lives now so that truth will triumph or that we should profit by crime to pave the way for nobility."

And these words, written during the Polish "thaw," when the intellectuals had asserted, from their experience with the "future," the claims of humanism, echo the protest of the Russian writer Alexander Herzen, who, in a dialogue a hundred years ago, reproached an earlier revolutionist who would sacrifice the present mankind for a promised tomorrow: "Do you truly wish to condemn all human beings alive today to the sad role of caryatids . . . supporting a floor for others some day to dance on? . . . This alone should serve as a warning to people: an end that is infinitely remote is not an end, but, if you like, a trap; an end must be nearer—ought to be, at the very least, the laborer's wage or pleasure in the work done. Each age, each generation, each life has its own fullness. . . ."[6]

# NOTES

1. Karl Jaspers has assembled a fascinating collection of laments by philosophers of each age who see their own time as crisis and the past as a golden age. These — and the quotations from the Egyptian papyri as well as the remark of Talleyrand—can be found in his *Man in the Modern Age* (rev. ed., London, 1951), Chapter II. The quotation from Gilbert Murray is from *Five Stages of Greek Religion* (2d ed.; New York, 1930), Chapter IV.

2. The citation from Marx from the celebrated opening passages of *The Eighteenth Brumaire of Louis Napoleon* has a general discussion of alienation, but I have followed here with profit the discussion by Hans Speier in his *Social Order and the Risks of War* (New York, 1952), Chapter XI.

3. Rufus W. Mathewson, Jr., *The Positive Hero in Russian Literature* (New York, 1958), p. 6.

4. See Leo Strauss, *The Political Philosophy of Hobbes* (Chicago, 1952), pp. 14–29.

5. Raymond Aron, *The Optium of the Intellectuals* (New York, 1958); Edward Shils, "Ideology and Civility," *Sewanee Review,* Vol. LXVI, No. 3, Summer, 1958, and "The Intellectuals and the Powers," in *Comparative Studies in Society and History,* Vol. I, No. 1, October, 1958.

6. To see history as changes in sensibilities and style or, more, how different classes or people mobilized their emotional energies and adopted different moral postures is relatively novel; yet the history of moral temper is, I feel, one of the most important ways of understanding social change, and particularly the irrational forces at work in men. The great model for a cultural period is J. H. Huizinga's *The Waning of the Middle Ages,* with its discussion of changing attitudes toward death, cruelty, and love. Lucien Febvre, the great French historian, long ago urged the writing of history in terms of different sensibilities, and his study of Rabelais and the problem of covert belief *(Le problème de L'incroyance du XVIème siécle)* is one of the great landmarks of this approach. Most historians of social movements have been excessively "intellectualistic" in that the emphasis has been on doctrine or on organizational technique, and less on emotional styles. Nathan Leites' *A Study of Bolshevism* may be more important, ultimately, for its treatment of the changing moral temper of the Russian intelligentsia than for the formal study of Bolshevik behavior. Arthur Koestler's novels and autobiography are a brilliant mirror of the changes in belief of the European intellectual. Herbert Leuthy's study of the playwright Bert Brecht *(Encounter,* July, 1956) is a jewel in its subtle analysis of the changes in moral judgment created by the acceptance of the image of "the Bolshevik." The career of Georg Lukacs, the Hungarian Marxist, is instructive regarding an intellectual who has accepted the soldierly discipline of the Communist ethic; other than some penetrating but brief remarks by Franz Borkenau (see his *World Communism* [New York, 1939], pp. 172–175), and the articles by Morris Watnick *(Soviet Survey* [London, 1958], Nos. 23–25), very little has been written about this extraordinary man. Ignazio Silone's "The Choice of Comrades" (reprinted in *Voices of*

*Dissent* [New York, 1959]) is a sensitive reflection of the positive experiences of radicalism. An interesting history of the millenarian and chiliastic movements is Norman Cohn's *The Pursuit of the Millennium.* From a Catholic viewpoint, Father Ronald Knox's study, *Enthusiasm,* deals with the "ecstatic" movements in Christian history.

# 2 The End of Ideology?

## SEYMOUR MARTIN LIPSET

A basic premise of this book[1] is that democracy is not only or even primarily a means through which different groups can attain their ends or seek the good society; it is the good society itself in operation. Only the give-and-take of a free society's internal struggle offers some guarantee that the products of the society will not accumulate in the hands of a few power-holders, and that men may develop and bring up their children without fear of persecution. And democracy requires institutions which support conflict and disagreement as well as those which sustain legitimacy and consensus. In recent years, however, democracy in the Western world has been undergoing some important changes as serious intellectual conflicts among groups representing different values have declined sharply.

The consequences of this change can perhaps be best illustrated by describing what happened at a world congress of intel-

From Seymour Martin Lipset, *Political Man: The Social Bases of Politics* (New York: Doubleday, 1960), pp. 403–417. Copyright © 1960 by Seymour Martin Lipset. Reprinted by permission of Doubleday & Company, Inc.

lectuals on "The Future of Freedom" held in Milan, Italy, in September 1955. The conference[2] was attended by 150 intellectuals and politicians from many democratic countries, and included men ranging in opinions from socialists to right-wing conservatives. Among the delegates from Great Britain, for example, were Hugh Gaitskell and Richard Crossman, socialists, and Michael Polanyi and Colin Clark, conservatives. From the United States came Sidney Hook, then the vice-chairman of the Union for Democratic Socialism, Arthur Schlesinger, Jr., of Americans for Democratic Action, and Friedrich A. Hayek, the arch-conservative economist. The French representatives included André Philip, a left-socialist leader, Raymond Aron, once active in the Gaullist movement, and Bertrand de Jouvenal, the conservative philosopher. Similar divergencies in political outlook were apparent among the delegates from Scandinavia, Germany, Italy, and other countries.

One would have thought that a conference in which so many important political and intellectual leaders of socialism, liberalism, and conservatism were represented would have stimulated intense political debate. In fact, nothing of the sort occurred. The only occasions in which debate grew warm were when someone served as a "surrogate Communist" by saying something which could be defined as being too favorable to Russia.

On the last day of the week-long conference, an interesting event occurred. Professor Hayek, in a closing speech, attacked the delegates for preparing to bury freedom instead of saving it. He alone was disturbed by the general temper. What bothered him was the general agreement among the delegates, regardless of political belief, that the traditional issues separating the left and right had declined to comparative insignificance. In effect, all agreed that the increase in state control which had taken place in various countries would not result in a decline in democratic freedom. The socialists no longer advocated socialism; they were as concerned as the conservatives with the danger of an all-powerful state. The ideological issues dividing left and right had been reduced to a little more or a little less government ownership and economic planning. No one seemed to believe that it really made much difference which political party controlled the domestic policies of individual nations. Hayek, honestly believing that state intervention is bad and inherently totalitarian, found himself in a small minority of those who still took the cleavages within the democratic camp seriously.

A leading left-wing British intellectual, Richard Crossman, has stated that socialism is now consciously viewed by most European socialist leaders as a "Utopian myth . . . often remote from the realities of day-to-day politics."[3] Few socialist parties still want to nationalize more industry. This objective has been largely given up by the socialist parties of the more industrialized states like Scandinavia, Britain, and Germany. The Labor party premier of the Australian state of Queensland, defending the retention of socialization as an objective at the party's 1950 convention, clearly acknowledged that its significance was largely ritualistic when he said:

> I point out that there are serious implications in any way altering our platform and objectives. In the first place it is a bad thing to break ground in attack if we can avoid it, and I think we should not duck around corners and pretend we do not want socialization of industry. It is a long term objective in the Labor movement, exactly in the same way that there is a long term objective in the Christian movement. The people who espouse Christianity have been struggling for over 2,000 years and have not arrived at it.[4]

The rationale for retaining long-term objectives, even those which may not be accomplished in 2,000 years, was well stated by Richard Crossman:

> A democratic party can very rarely be persuaded to give up one of its central principles, and *can never afford to scrap its central myth*. Conservatives must defend free enterprise even when they are actually introducing state planning. A Labour Government must defend as true Socialism policies which have very little to do with it. The job of party leaders is often to persuade their followers that the traditional policy is still being carried out, even when this is demonstrably not true.[5]

The fact that the differences between the left and the right in the Western democracies are no longer profound does not mean that there is no room for party controversy. But as the editor of one of the leading Swedish newspapers once said to me, "Politics is now boring. The only issues are whether the metal workers should get a nickel more an hour, the price of milk should be raised, or old-age pensions extended." These are important matters, the very stuff of the internal struggle within stable democracies, but they are hardly matters to excite intellectuals or stimulate young people who seek in politics a way to express their dreams.

This change in Western political life reflects the fact that the fundamental political problems of the industrial revolution have been solved: the workers have achieved industrial and political citizenship; the conservatives have accepted the welfare state; and the democratic left has recognized that an increase in overall state power carries with it more dangers to freedom than solutions for economic problems. This very triumph of the democratic social revolution in the West ends domestic politics for those intellectuals who must have ideologies or utopias to motivate them to political action.

Within Western democracy, this decline in the sources of serious political controversy has even led some to raise the question as to whether the conflicts that are so necessary to democracy will continue. Barrington Moore, Jr., a Harvard sociologist, has asked whether

> as we reduce economic inequalities and privileges, we may also eliminate the sources of contrast and discontent that put drive into genuine political alternatives. In the United States today, with the exception of the Negro, it is difficult to perceive any section of the population that has a vested material interest on behalf of freedom. . . . There is, I think, more than a dialectical flourish in the assertion that liberty requires the existence of an oppressed group in order to grow vigorously. Perhaps that is the tragedy as well as the glory of liberty. Once the ideal has been achieved, or is even close to realization, the driving force of discontent disappears, and a society settles down for a time to a stolid acceptance of things as they are. Something of the sort seems to have happened to the United States.[6]

And David Riesman has suggested that "the general increase of wealth and the concomitant loss of rigid distinctions make it difficult to maintain the Madisonian [economic] bases for political diversity, or to recruit politicians who speak for the residual oppressed strata."[7] The thesis that partisan conflict based on class differences and left-right issues is ending is based on the assumption that the "the economic class system is disappearing . . . that redistribution of wealth and income . . . has ended economic inequality's political significance."[8]

Yet one wonders whether these intellectuals are not mistaking the decline of ideology in the domestic politics of Western society with the ending of the class conflict which has sustained democratic controversy. As the abundant evidence on voting patterns in the United States and other countries indicates, the electorate as a whole does not see the end of the domestic class struggle envisioned by so many intellectuals. A large number of surveys of the American population made from the 1930s to the 1950s report that most people believe that the Republicans do more for the wealthy and for business and professional people and the Democrats do more for the poor and for skilled and unskilled workers.[9] Similar findings have been reported for Great Britain.

These opinions do not simply represent the arguments of partisans, since supporters of both the left and the right agree on the classes each party basically represents—which does not mean the acceptance of a bitter class struggle but rather an agreement on the representation functions of the political parties similar to the general agreement that trade unions represent workers, and the Chamber of Commerce, businessmen. Continued class cleavage does not imply any destructive consequences for the system; a stable democracy requires consensus on the nature of the political struggle, and this includes the assumption that different groups are best served by different parties.

The predictions of the end of class politics in the "affluent society" ignore the relative character of any class system. The decline of objective deprivation—low income, insecurity, malnutrition—does reduce the potential tension level of a society, as we have seen. But as long as some men are rewarded more than others by the prestige or status structure of society, men will feel *relatively* deprived. The United States is the wealthiest country in the world, and its working class lives on a scale to which most of the middle classes in the rest of the world aspire; yet a detailed report on the findings of various American opinion surveys states: "The dominant opinion on polls before, during, and after the war is that the salaries of corporation executives are too high and should be limited by the government." And this sentiment, prevalent even among prosperous people, finds increasing support as one moves down the economic ladder.[10]

The democratic class struggle will continue, but it will be a fight without ideologies, without red flags, without May Day parades. This naturally upsets many intellectuals who can participate only as ideologists or major critics of the *status quo.* The British socialist weekly, *The New Statesman,* published a series of comments through 1958–59 under the general heading "Shall We Help Mr. Gaitskell?" As the title suggests, this series was written by various British intellectuals who are troubled by the fact that the Labor party is no longer ideologically radical but simply the interest organization of the workers and the trade unions.

The decline of political ideology in America has affected many intellectuals who must function as critics of the society to fulfill their self-image. And since domestic politics, even liberal and socialist politics, can no longer serve as the arena for serious criticism from the left, many intellectuals have turned from a basic concern with the political and economic systems to criticism of other sections of the basic culture of American society, particularly of elements which cannot be dealt with politically. They point to the seeming growth of a concern with status ("keeping up with the Joneses"), to the related increase in the influence of advertisers and mass media as the arbiters of mass taste, to the evidence that Americans are overconformist—another side of keeping up with the Joneses. Thus the critical works about American society in the past decades which have received the most attention have been sociological rather than political, such books as David Riesman's *The Lonely Crowd,*

William H. Whyte's *The Organization Man,* Max Lerner's *America as a Civilization,* and Vance Packard's *The Status Seekers.*

Yet many of the disagreeable aspects of American society which are now regarded as the results of an affluent and bureaucratic society may be recurring elements inherent in an equalitarian and democratic society. Those aspects of both American and socialist ideology which have always been most thoroughly expressed in the United States make a concern with status and conformity constant features of the society.

The patterns of status distinction which Lloyd Warner, Vance Packard, and others have documented have been prevalent throughout America's history, as the reports of various nineteenth-century foreign travelers plainly show. These visitors generally believed that Americans were *more* status-conscious than Europeans, that it was easier for a *nouveau riche* individual to be accepted in nineteenth-century England than in nineteenth-century America; and they explained the greater snobbery in this country by suggesting that the very emphasis on democracy and equalitarianism in America, the lack of a well-defined deference structure, in which there is no question about social rankings, make well-to-do Americans place more emphasis on status background and symbolism than do Europeans.

It may seem a paradox to observe that a millionaire has a better and easier social career open to him in England than in America. . . . In America, if his private character be bad, if he be mean or openly immoral, or personally vulgar, or dishonest, the best society may keep its doors closed against him. In England great wealth, skillfully employed, will more readily force these doors to open. For in England great wealth can, by using the appropriate methods, practically buy rank from those who bestow it. . . . The existence of a system of artificial rank enables a stamp to be given to base metal in Europe which cannot be given in a thoroughly republican country.[11]

The great concern with family background (which generation made the money?) that many observers, from Harriet Martineau (one of the most sophisticated British commenters on American

life in the 1820s) to the contemporary American sociologist
Lloyd Warner, have shown to be characteristic of large parts of
American society may be a reaction to the feelings of uncertainty
about social position engendered in a society whose basic values
deny anyone the inherent right to claim higher status than his
neighbor. As the sociologist Howard Brotz has pointed out in
comparing the status systems of Britain and the United States:

> In a democracy snobbishness can be far more vicious than in
> an aristocracy. Lacking that natural confirmation of superiority
> which political authority alone can give, the rich and particularly
> the new rich, feel threatened by mere contact with their inferiors.
> This tendency perhaps reached its apogee in the late nineteenth
> century in Tuxedo Park, a select residential community com-
> posed of wealthy New York businessmen, which, not content
> merely to surround itself with a wire fence, posted a sentry at
> the gate to keep nonmembers out. Nothing could be more fan-
> tastic than this to an English lord living in the country in the
> midst, not of other peers, but of his tenants. His position is such
> that he is at ease in the presence of members of the lower classes
> and in associating with them in recreation. For example, farmers
> [that is, tenants] ride to the hounds in the hunts. It is this
> "democratic" attitude which, in the first instance, makes for an
> openness to social relations with Jews. One cannot be declassed,
> so to speak, by play activities.[12]

The problem of conformity which so troubles many Americans
today has been noted as a major aspect of American culture
from Tocqueville in the 1830s to Riesman in the 1950s. Analysts have repeatedly stressed the extent to which Americans (as
compared to other peoples) are sensitive to the judgments of
others. Never secure in their own status, they are concerned with
"public opinion" in a way that elites in a more aristocratic and
status-bound society do not have to be. As early as the nineteenth century foreign observers were struck by the "other-directedness" of Americans and accounted for it by the nature of
the class system. This image of the American as "other-directed"
can, as Riesman notes, be found in the writing of "Tocqueville
and other curious and astonished visitors from Europe."[13] Har-

riet Martineau almost seems to be paraphrasing Riesman's own description of today's "other-directed" man in her picture of the early nineteenth-century American:

> Americans may travel over the world, and find no society but their own which will submit [as much] to the restraint of perpetual caution, and reference to the opinions of others. They may travel over the whole world, and find no country but their own where the very children beware of getting into scrapes, and talk of the effect of actions on people's minds; where the youth of society determines in silence what opinions they shall bring forward, and what avow only in the family circle; where women write miserable letters, almost universally, because it is a settled matter that it is unsafe to commit oneself on paper; and where elderly people seem to lack almost universally that faith in principles which inspires a free expression of them at any time, and under all circumstances.[14]

It may be argued that in an open democratic society in which people are encouraged to struggle upward, but where there are no clearly defined reference points to mark their arrival, and where their success in achieving status is determined by the good opinion of others, the kind of caution and intense study of other people's opinions described by Martineau is natural. Like Riesman today, she notes that this "other-directed" type is found most commonly in urban centers in the middle and upper classes, where people live in "perpetual caution." Nowhere does there exist "so much heart-eating care [about others' judgments], so much nervous anxiety, as among the dwellers in the towns of the northern states of America."[15] Similarly, Max Weber, who visited the United States in the early 1900s, noted the high degree of "submission to fashion in America, to a degree unknown in Germany," and explained it as a natural attribute of a democratic society without inherited class status.[16]

A society which emphasizes achievement, which denies status based on ancestry or even long-past personal achievements, must necessarily be a society in which men are sensitively oriented toward others, in which, to use Riesman's analogy, they employ a radar to keep their social equilibrium. And precisely as we become more equalitarian, as the lower strata attain citizenship, as more people are able to take part in the status race, to that extent do we, and other peoples as well, become more concerned with the opinions of others, and therefore more democratic and more American in the Tocquevillian sense.

The politics of democracy are to some extent necessarily the politics of conformity for the elite of the society. As soon as the masses have access to the society's elite, as soon as they must consider mass reaction in determining their own actions, the freedom of the elite (whether political or artistic) is limited. As Tocqueville pointed out, the "most serious reproach which can be addressed" to democratic republics is that they "extend the practice of currying favor with the many and introduce it into all classes at once," and he attributed "the small number of distinguished men in political life to the ever increasing despotism of the majority in the United States."[17]

The same point has been made in regard to much of the discussion about the negative consequences of mass culture. Increased access by the mass of the population to the culture market necessarily means a limitation in cultural taste as compared to a time or a country in which culture is limited to the well to do and the well educated.

The current debates on education reflect the same dilemma—that many who believe in democracy and equalitarianism would also like to preserve some of the attributes of an elitist society. In England, where the integrated "comprehensive" school is seen as a progressive reform, the argument for it is based on the assumption that the health of the society is best served by what is best for the largest number. This argument was used in this country when liberal educators urged that special treatment for the gifted child served to perpetuate inequality and that it rewarded those from better home and class environments at the expense of those from poorer backgrounds. Educators in Britain today argue strongly that separate schools for brighter children (the so-called "grammar schools") are a source of psychic punishment for the less gifted. Many of us have forgotten that liberals in this country shared similar sentiments not too long ago; that, for example, Fiorello La Guardia, as Mayor of New York, abolished Townsend Harris High School, a special school for gifted boys in which four years of school work were completed in three, on the ground that the very existence of such a school was undemocratic, that it gave special privileges to a minority.

What I am saying is simply that we cannot have our cake and eat it too. We cannot have the advantages of an aristocratic *and* a democratic society; we cannot have segregated elite schools in a society which stresses equality; we cannot have a cultural elite which produces without regard to mass taste in a society which emphasizes the value of popular judgment. By the same token we cannot have a low divorce rate and end differentiation in sex roles, and we cannot expect to have secure adolescents in a culture which offers no definitive path from adolescence to adulthood.

I do not mean to suggest that a democratic society can do nothing about reducing conformity or increasing creativity. There is considerable evidence to suggest that higher education, greater economic security, and higher standards of living strengthen the level of culture and democratic freedom. The market for good books, good paintings, and good music is at a high point in American history.[18] There is evidence that tolerance for ethnic minorities too is greater than in the past. More people are receiving a good education in America today than ever before, and regardless of the many weaknesses of that education, it is still true that the more of it one has, the better one's values and consumption patterns from the point of view of the liberal and culturally concerned intellectual.

There is a further point about the presumed growth of conformity and the decline in ideology which has been made by various analysts who rightly fear the inherent conformist aspects of populist democracy. They suggest that the growth of large bureaucratic organizations, an endemic aspect of modern industrial society, whether capitalist or socialist, is reducing the scope of individual freedom because "organization men" must conform to succeed. This point is sometimes linked to the decline in the intensity of political conflict, because politics is seen as changing into administration as the manager and expert take over in government as well as in business. From James Burnham's *Managerial Revolution* to more recent restatements of this thesis by Peter Drucker and others, this trend has been sometimes welcomed, but more often in recent years deplored.

The growth of large organizations may, however, actually have the more important consequences of providing new sources of continued freedom and more opportunity to innovate. Bureaucratization means (among other things) a decline of the arbitrary power of those in authority. By establishing norms of fair and equal treatment, and by reducing the unlimited power possessed by the leaders of many nonbureaucratic organizations, bureaucracy may mean less rather than greater need to conform to superiors. In spite of the emergence of security tests, I think that there is little doubt that men are much less likely to be fired from their jobs for their opinions and behavior today than they were fifty or even twenty-five years ago. Anyone who compares the position of a worker or an executive in a family-owned corporation like the Ford Motor Company when its founder was running it to that of comparably placed people in General Motors or today's Ford Motor Company can hardly argue that bureaucratization has meant greater pressure to conform on any level of industry. Trade unions accurately reflect their members' desires when they move in the direction of greater bureaucratization by winning, for example, seniority rules in hiring, firing, and promotion, or a stable three-year contract with detailed provisions for grievance procedures. Unionization, of both manual and white-collar workers, increases under conditions of large-scale organization and serves to free the worker or employee from subjection to relatively uncontrolled power. Those who fear the subjection of the workers to the organizational power of unionism ignore for the most part the alternative of arbitrary management power. In many ways the employee of a large corporation who is the subject of controversy between two giant organizations—the company and the union—has a much higher degree of freedom than one not in a large organization.

Although the pressures toward conformity within democratic and bureaucratic society are an appropriate source of serious concern for Western intellectuals, my reading of the historical evidence suggests that the problem is less acute or threatening today than it has been in the past, if we limit our analysis to domestic threats to the system. There is reason to expect that stable democratic institutions in which individual political freedom is great and even increasing (as it is, say, in Britain or Sweden) will continue to characterize the mature industrialized Western societies.

The controversies about cultural creativity and conformity reflect the general trend discussed at the beginning of the chapter —the shift away from ideology towards sociology. The very growth of sociology as an intellectual force outside the academy in many Western nations is a tribute, not primarily to the power of sociological analysis but to the loss of interest in political inquiry. It may seem curious, therefore, for a sociologist to end on a note of concern about this trend. But I believe that there is still a real need for political analysis, ideology, and controversy within the world community, if not within the Western democracies. In a larger sense, the domestic controversies within the advanced democratic countries have become comparable to struggles within American party primary elections. Like all nomination contests, they are fought to determine who will lead the party, in this case the democratic camp, in the larger political struggle in the world as a whole with its marginal constituencies, the underdeveloped states. The horizon of intellectual political concerns must turn from the new version of local elections— those which determine who will run national administrations—to this larger contest.

This larger fight makes politics much more complex in the various underdeveloped countries than it appears within Western democracies. In these states there is still a need for intense political controversy and ideology. The problems of industrialization, of the place of religion, of the character of political institutions are still unsettled, and the arguments about them have become

intertwined with the international struggle. The past political relations between former colonial countries and the West, between
colored and white peoples, make the task even more difficult. It
is necessary for us to recognize that our allies in the underdeveloped countries must be radicals, probably socialists, because
only parties which promise to improve the situation of the masses through widespread reform, and which are transvaluational
and equalitarian, can hope to compete with the Communists.
Asian and African socialist movements, even where they are
committed to political democracy (and unfortunately not all of
them are, or can be even if they want to), must often express
hostility to many of the economic, political, and religious institutions of the West.

Where radicals are in power—in India, Ghana, Ceylon,
Burma, and other countries—they must take responsibility for
the economic development of the country, and hence must suffer
the brunt of the resentments caused by industrialization, rapid
urbanization, bad housing, and extreme poverty. The democratic
leftist leader must find a scapegoat to blame for these ills—domestic capitalists, foreign investors, or the machinations of the
departed imperialists. If he does not, he will lose his hold on the
masses who need the hope implicit in revolutionary chiliastic
doctrine—a hope the Communists are ready to supply. The socialist in power in an underdeveloped country must continue,
therefore, to lead a revolutionary struggle against capitalism, the
Western imperialists, and, increasingly, against Christianity as
the dominant remaining foreign institution. If he accepts the arguments of Western socialists that the West has changed, that
complete socialism is dangerous, that Marxism is an outmoded
doctrine, he becomes a conservative within his own society, a
role he cannot play and still retain a popular following.

The leftist intellectual, the trade-union leader, and the socialist politician in the West have an important role to play in this
political struggle. By virtue of the fact that they still represent
the tradition of socialism and equalitarianism within their own
countries, they can find an audience among the leaders of the

non-Communist left in those nations where socialism and trade-unionism cannot be conservative or even gradualist. To demand that such leaders adapt their politics to Western images of responsible behavior is to forget that many Western unions, socialist parties, and intellectuals were similarly "irresponsible and demagogic" in the early stages of their development. Today Western leaders must communicate and work with non-Communist revolutionaries in the Orient and Africa at the same time that they accept the fact that serious ideological controversies have ended at home.

Concern with making explicit the conditions of the democratic order reflects my perhaps overrationalistic belief that a fuller understanding of the various conditions under which democracy has existed may help men to develop it where it does not now exist. Although we have concluded that Aristotle's basic hypothesis of the relationship of democracy to a class structure bulging toward the middle is still valid, this does not encourage political optimism, since it implies that political activity should be directed primarily toward assuring economic development. Yet we must not be unduly pessimistic. Democracy has existed in a variety of circumstances, even if it is most commonly sustained by a limited set of conditions. It cannot be achieved by acts of will alone, of course, but men's wills expressed in action can shape institutions and events in directions that reduce or increase the chances for democracy's development and survival. Ideology and passion may no longer be necessary to sustain the class struggle within stable and affluent democracies, but they are clearly needed in the international effort to develop free political and economic institutions in the rest of the world. It is only the ideological class struggle within the West which is ending. Ideological conflicts linked to levels and problems of economic development and of appropriate political institutions among different nations will last far beyond our lifetime, and men committed to democracy can abstain from them only at their peril. To aid men's actions in furthering democracy in then absolutist Europe was in some measure Tocqueville's purpose in studying the operation of

American society in 1830. To clarify the operation of Western democracy in the mid-twentieth century may contribute to the political battle in Asia and Africa.

## N O T E S

1. I have taken the chapter heading from the title of Edward Shils' excellent report on a conference on "The Future of Freedom" held in Milan, Italy, in September 1955, under the auspices of the Congress for Cultural Freedom. See his "The End of Ideology?" *Encounter,* 5 (November 1955), 52–58; for perceptive analyses of the nature and sources of the decline of ideology see Herbert Tingsten, "Stability and Vitality in Swedish Democracy," *The Political Quarterly,* 2 (1955), 140–151; and Otto Brunner, "Der Zeitalter der Ideologien," in *Neue Wege der Sozialgeschichte* (Göttingen: Van den Hoeck and Ruprecht, 1956), pp. 194–219. For a prediction that the "age of ideology" is ending see Louis S. Feuer, "Beyond Ideology," *Psychoanalysis and Ethics* (Springfield: Charles C. Thomas, 1955), pp. 126–130. Many of these topics are discussed in detail by Daniel Bell in *The End of Ideology* (Glencoe: The Free Press, 1960) and by Ralf Dahrendorf in *Class and Class Conflict in Industrial Society* (Stanford: Stanford University Press, 1959).

2. My original report on this conference which I attended was published as "The State of Democratic Politics," *Canadian Forum,* 35 (November 1955), 170–171. It is interesting to note the similarities of the observations in it and the report by Edward Shils, *op. cit.*

3. Richard Crossman, "On Political Neurosis," *Encounter,* 3 (May 1954), 66.

4. Cited in T. C. Truman, "The Pressure Groups, Parties and Politics of the Australian Labor Movement" (unpublished M.A. thesis, Department of Political Science, University of Queensland, 1953), Chap. II, p. 82.

5. Richard Crossman, *op. cit.,* p. 67. (My emphasis) And in Sweden, Herbert Tingsten reports: "The great controversies have thus been liquidated in all instances. As a result the symbolic words and the stereotypes have changed or disappeared. . . . Liberalism in the old sense is dead, both among the Conservatives and in the Liberal party; . . . and the label of socialism on a specific proposal or a specific reform has hardly any other meaning than the fact that the proposal or reform in question is regarded as attractive. The actual words 'socialism' or 'liberalism' are tending to become mere honorifics, useful in connection with elections and political festivities." Tingsten, *op. cit.,* p. 145.

6. Barrington Moore, Jr., *Political Power and Social Theory* (Cambridge: Harvard University Press, 1958), p. 183.

7. David Riesman, "Introduction," to Stimson Bullitt, *To Be a Politician* (New York: Doubleday & Co., Inc., 1959), p. 20.
8. S. Bullitt, *ibid.,* p. 177.
9. See Harold Orlans, *Opinion Polls on National Leaders* (Philadelphia: Institute for Research in Human Relations, 1953), pp. 70–73. This monograph contains a detailed report on various surveys conducted by the different American polling agencies from 1935–53.
10. *Ibid.,* p. 149. The one exception is among the very poor who are somewhat less intolerant of high executive salaries than those immediately above them.
11. James Bryce, *The American Commonwealth,* Vol. II (New York: Macmillan, 1910), p. 815. Cf. D. W. Brogan, *U.S.A.* (London: Oxford University Press, 1941), pp. 116 ff.; see Robert W. Smuts, *European Impressions of the American Worker* (New York: King's Crown Press, 1953), for a summary of comments by many visitors in the 1900s and the 1950s who reported that "social and economic democracy in America, far from mitigating competition for social status, intensified it" (p. 13).
12. Howard Brotz, "The Position of the Jews in English Society," *The Jewish Journal of Sociology,* 1 (1959), 97.
13. David Riesman, *et. al., The Lonely Crowd: A Study of the Changing American Character* (New Haven: Yale University Press, 1950), pp. 19–20.
14. Harriet Martineau, *Society in America,* Vol. II (New York: Saunders and Otley, 1837), pp. 158–159.
15. *Ibid.,* pp. 160–161.
16. Max Weber, *Essays in Sociology* (New York: Oxford University Press, 1946), p. 188.
17. Alexis de Tocqueville, *Democracy in America,* Vol. I (New York: Vintage Books, 1954), pp. 276, 277. Of course, Plato made the same points 2500 years ago when he argued that in a democracy, the father "accustoms himself to become like his child and to fear his sons, and the son in his desire for freedom becomes like his father and has no fear or reverence for his parent. . . . The school master fears and flatters his pupils . . . while the old men condescend to the young and become triumphs of versatility. . . . The main result of all these things, taken together, is that it makes the souls of the citizens . . . sensitive." *The Republic of Plato,* ed. by Ernest Rhys (London: J. M. Dent and Co., 1935), pp. 200–226.
18. See Daniel Bell, "The Theory of Mass Society," *Commentary,* 22 (1956), p. 82, and Clyde Kluckhohn, "Shifts in American Values," *World Politics,* 11 (1959), 250–261, for evidence concerning the growth rather than the decline of "genuine individuality in the United States."

# II Empirical and Comparative Perspectives

# Introductory Note

During the past two decades, a number of scholars have sought to verify the hypothesis of decline in advanced industrial societies. In a 1957 study of European parliamentary regimes, Otto Kirchheimer identifies the most significant changes in Europe as a temporizing of ideological formulations together with the emergence of a vast, homogenized, prosperous, and consumption-oriented middle class. He writes: "The rise of the consumption-oriented individual of mass society . . . sets the stage for the shrinking of the ideologically oriented nineteenth-century party. . . . By and large, European parliamentary parties are reducing their special ideological . . . offering." The parliamentary party, he notes, has become a "harmonizing agency." The increasing consensus on the desired ends has led to the "transformation of political problems into administrative and technical routines."[1]

In a subsequent study some years later, Kirchheimer examines the evolution of traditional European political parties into "catch-all parties." He identifies the major characteristic of such parties as a "drastic reduction of [their] . . . ideological baggage" in an effort to broaden their electoral appeal, to "catch" all categories of voters. He notes: "Released from their previous unnecessary fears as to the ideological propensities and future intentions of the class-mass party . . . the catch-all party's role as consensus purveyor [has been assured]."[2]

A wide-ranging study of postwar developments in European politics was undertaken recently by Lipset (pp. 76–115 below). Relying on massive empirical data from many parts of Europe, he reaffirms the conclusion that ideological polarization is disappearing from the canvas of European politics. The increasing affluence in Western societies, he notes, has transformed domestic politics into the "politics of collective bargaining."

The hypothesis of ideological decline has been examined in a number of individual countries as well. As early as 1955, Herbert Tingsten noted a direct relationship between economic development and the "leveling" of party and ideological conflicts in Swedish democracy. Having considered the major areas of traditional ideological cleavage in Swedish politics (such as defense, public ownership, social welfare), he concludes: "The great [ideological] controversies have . . . been liquidated in all instances. . . . Liberalism in the old sense is dead, both among the Conservatives and in the Liberal Party; Social Democrat thinking has lost nearly all its traits of doctrinaire Marxism, and the label of socialism on a specific proposal or a specific reform has hardly any other meaning than the fact that the proposal or reform in question is regarded as attractive. The actual words 'socialism' or 'liberalism' are tending to become mere honorifics, useful in connection with elections and political festivities." The political parties have changed character: "In place of conflicting ideas we are faced with competing bureaucracies." The emergence of "a community of values" between widely divergent parties and groups has reduced the importance of ideology to a point where "one can speak of a movement from politics to administration, from principles to techniques."[3]

Tingsten's findings were verified a decade later by Nils Stjernquist. In fact, the latter's description of the situation in

Sweden is a model of the decline thesis in operation. Stjernquist's comments deserve quotation at length:

> Before the introduction of universal suffrage the socioeconomic and ideological cleavages were very deep, and the society was in fact a class society. As democracy was gradually accepted these differences were modified. Considerable further leveling took place when the Socialists abandoned their demand for nationalization and all the nonsocialist parties accepted a social welfare policy. Universal suffrage gave political power, in principle, to the "little man," whose interests, by and large the nonsocialists as well as Socialist parties tended to look after. To a large extent he achieved the same income and the same standard of living as the middle class. . . . The concept of class is in fact not very useful in politics today. The socialists do not appeal only to wage earners, nor does the Center Party [until 1959, the Farmers' Party] appeal only to farmers. The Conservatives have used the idea of "the common citizen" as a political slogan. The political parties often appeal to all groups in society, and modern mass-media have certainly made people feel less like members of a particular class.[4]

Stjernquist adds that the increasing complexity of political issues and decisions has magnified the role of "bureaucracy and technocracy" at the expense of parties and politicians.

Ulf Torgersen's analysis of the Norwegian scene reveals strikingly similar results. Having examined recent developments in Norwegian politics, Torgersen notes: "If in one short word one wants to characterize the political situation in present-day Norway, *depoliticization* seems to be the one that fits best" (italics in original). His more specific findings include the following: (1) Party politics have been moving in the direction of decreasing political polarization: The Labor party "has largely dropped its plan for nationalization"; the Conservative party has been stressing an "essentially reformist and welfare state-accepting character." Overall, there has been an unmistakable "development toward the political center." (2) Among the intellectuals, there has been a "general pattern of decline of excitement about what is usually called the 'old' issues of politics." There is "almost complete unanimity about the outdated character of the distinction" between "bourgeois" and "socialist." (3) Within the Parliament, Torgersen agrees with Kirchheimer, the opposition has been waning. (4) There has been a general decline of party political activity due to a general absence of citizen interest in ideological politics.[5]

A 1965 study of Dutch politics yields analogous findings (pp. 140–159 below). A. Hoogerwerf's comparative analysis of the election programs of the four major Dutch political parties for the years 1948 and 1963, together with analysis of survey data, reveals a growing agreement on previously intense political issues. Ideological disputes, Hoogerwerf concludes, are becoming increasingly blurred. Political leaders have shifted focus "from the choice of ends to the choice of means."

Erik Allardt treats Finland as "a deviant case with many qualifications" (pp. 116–139 below). Finland deviates from the pattern, Allardt notes, primarily because of the continuing strength of the Communist party. And yet, he shows, the Communists have been fully integrated into the Finnish political system—to the point even of having attained formal representation in the Cabinet. As such, Allardt finds it useful to characterize the situation in Finland as one of "institutionalized radicalism." Moreover, he notes, there is "strong consensus" in all ideological quarters regarding Finland's foreign policy, in itself "a rather clear-cut case of decline of ideology." The decline hypothesis, Allardt concludes, has been particularly operative in party politics and party organization. Although there has been some ideological revitalization in Finland in recent years, this "has occurred outside the institutionalized political organizations and channels."

Robert E. Lane's secondary analysis (pp. 160–206 below) of a wide range of public-opinion data from the United States and other Western countries over a number of years shows that the "Age of Affluence" has everywhere led to an increasing reduction of ideological tensions. The age of affluence, Lane finds, is marked by the disappearance of "sense of crises," "sense of alarm," and "high stakes" in partisan politics. With particular reference to the United States, his data shows that only 5 percent of the population agrees with the proposition that "Republicans probably endanger welfare," while only 3 percent believes that "Democrats probably endanger welfare." Lane thus concludes that in the age of affluence politics "becomes more a discussion of means than ends."

A subsequent study by Robert A. Dahl substantiates Lane's findings. Having examined recent trends in American politics, Dahl concludes that "the tendency for opinions and beliefs to converge will probably continue. The center will then continue to dominate political life, and dissenters will continue to be frustrated and alienated."[6]

Given the hypothesized link between economic development and ideological decline, one would expect the pattern to be repeated in all advanced industrial societies—Western as well as non-Western. One would expect to find a relative decline in ideological politics, for example, in Japan. And this, indeed, appears to be the case. In a study of economic growth and the "end of ideology" in Japan (pp. 207–220 below), Masaaki Takane finds a partial substantiation of the decline hypothesis and a trend toward depoliticization in Japanese politics. In a separate study Robert A. Scalapino reports similar findings, though not without qualification. Scalapino documents the decline of both the radical left and the radical right in contemporary Japan. He adds: "The old tendency to conceive of ideology as a total way of life or an abstract cosmic theory into which all phenomena should be fitted has begun to fade away. . . . In this sense, it is possible to speak of the decline of ideology in Japan, as elsewhere in the 'advanced' world." Scalapino believes, however, that recent changes in Japan are "more properly viewed as adaptation to new stages of development."[7] He does not make clear why he considers "adaptation" as necessarily inconsistent with the decline hypothesis. In fact, decline of ideology *is* a form of adaptation to changing conditions.

The most remarkable phenomenon in connection with the hypothesis of ideological decline, however, is not its empirical relevance for European or Japanese politics but its application even to such a country as the U.S.S.R. Writing on the "cumulative effect" of recent social, political, and economic developments in the Soviet Union, Zbigniew Brzezinski identifies one of the most important consequences of these developments as "the reduced importance of both ideological issues and personalities." He goes so far as to write: "Indeed, the effort to maintain a doctrinaire dictatorship over an increasingly modern and industrial society has already contributed to a reopening of the gap that existed in prerevolutionary Russia between the political system and the society, thereby posing the threat of the degeneration of the Soviet system."[8]

The erosion of ideology in the Soviet Union is a theme identified also by Daniel Bell (pp. 221–238 below), who perceives the overall direction of recent changes in that country as "the breakup, on all levels, of a monolithic society." Marxism-Leninism, Bell argues, has been on the defensive in the Soviet Union, and for the following reasons: (1) its antiscientific character in an age of science; (2) its inadequate economic and social theories; (3) its incompatibility with contemporary conditions, as manifested in the wide-ranging modification of doctrine after Stalin's death; and (4) the gradual disillusionment of Soviet intellectuals with utopian formulations.

Adam B. Ulam argues persuasively that Marxism-Leninism has in effect become irrelevant to the Soviet system. He writes: "Marxism . . . has concluded its main work in Russia. From now on, its further aims and formulas are likely to appear increasingly artificial to the majority of Soviet citizens and even to party members. It remains as the official rationale of the totalitarian regime, and, as such, it will continue to be useful in official incantations and declamations. But its two points of historical significance—the ability to catalyze human energies for revolution and for industrialization—are no longer relevant under Russian conditions." He thus raises the possibility that "the Soviet Union, in its professed attempt to 'catch up with and overcome' the West in material culture, will discover that in the process it has left Marxism behind."[9]

Some provocative comments on the condition of Marxist-Leninist ideologies were offered recently by Milovan Djilas. Djilas sees a general movement "toward the death of all ideologies." He specifically characterizes Marxism as "outdated" and "old-fashioned." He adds: "All versions of Communism are becoming decadent. They must inevitably change into a democratic society. This is absolutely inevitable. Communism is a combative, warrior concept and organization. Society cannot bear to live indefinitely in such a tense atmosphere."[10]

A broader theme of deradicalization of Marxist movements —orthodox as well as revisionist—has been developed by Robert C. Tucker.[11] He perceives the deradicalization of orthodox Marxism as chiefly a post-Stalinist phenomenon. Tucker emphasizes Khrushchev's revision of a number of orthodox Leninist-Stalinist theses: (1) substitution of "peaceful coexistence" and "peaceful competition" for the Leninist thesis of the inevitability of war with capitalism; (2) doctrine of "peaceful transition" and parliamentary path to communism; (3) policy of rapprochement with social-democratic parties and with nationalist movements in the developing countries; and (4) doctrine that in the U.S.S.R. the dictatorship of the proletariat has been replaced by a "dictatorship of the whole people." In other words, Tucker shows, "neo-Communist Marxism" has drastically modified both its domestic and international beliefs.

Tucker traces the deradicalization of democratic socialism to the doctrinal revisions undertaken by the German social democratic party at the turn of the century. In fact, he points out, most European social democratic parties have turned reformist and gradualist. He concludes that deradicalization is the "general fate of radical movements."

The far-reaching revisions in democratic socialism are currently substantiated not only in some of the Scandinavian countries discussed above but also in the British Labour Party. Labour M.P. Crosland has argued forcefully that, if it is to survive, democratic socialism must re-examine and revise some of its basic ideological premises. The old ideology, he states, is irrelevant; the failure to update has been the chief source of weakness in democratic socialism. The "overriding aim" of the Labour Party should be to adapt itself to changing conditions and "to present itself to the electorate in a mid-twentieth century guise." In particular, Crosland insists, Labour must revise its position on nationalization. He stresses the need for a mixed economy and an explicit recognition of a private sector. In short, according to Crosland, democratic socialism is moving toward the right, just as conservatism has moved toward the left. He writes: "A Socialist . . . will seldom totally repudiate the theoretical validity of *all* Conservative principles, or vice versa; but each will rate the other's values much lower than his own, and hence will choose to act quite differently in any given situation. It follows, however, . . . that there must inevitably be *some* common ground between a statement of Socialist and one of progressive Conservative beliefs."[12]

To sum up, an impressive array of studies carefully documents a decline of ideology in both Western and non-Western countries, a reduction of ideological passion in politics, and a shift of focus from principle to technique.

## N O T E S

1. Otto Kirchheimer, "The Waning of Opposition in Parliamentary Regimes," *Social Research,* 24 (Summer 1957), 149, 150–151, 153.
2. Otto Kirchheimer, "The Transformation of the Western European Party Systems," in Joseph LaPalombara and Myron Weiner, eds., *Political Parties and Political Development* (Princeton: Princeton University Press, 1966), pp. 190, 199.
3. Herbert Tingsten, "Stability and Vitality in Swedish Democracy," *Political Quarterly,* 26 (1955), 145–148.
4. Nils Stjernquist, "Sweden: Stability or Deadlock?" in Robert A. Dahl, ed., *Political Oppositions in Western Democracies* (New Haven: Yale University Press, 1966), pp. 129–130.
5. Ulf Torgersen, "The Trend Towards Political Consensus: The Case of Norway," *Acta Sociologica,* VI (1962), 160 ff., 165 ff., Analogous conclusions are reached in Stein Rokkan, "Geography, Religion, and Social Class: Crosscutting Cleavages in Norwegian Politics," in

Seymour Martin Lipset and Stein Rokkan, eds., *Party Systems and Voter Alignments* (New York: Free Press, 1967), especially pp. 434–435.

6. Robert A. Dahl, "The American Opposition: Affirmation and Denial," in Dahl, *Political Oppositions in Western Democracies,* p. 69.
7. Robert A. Scalapino, "Ideology and Modernization: The Japanese Case," in David E. Apter, ed., *Ideology and Discontent* (New York: Free Press, 1964), pp. 123, 127.
8. Zbigniew Brzezinski, "The Soviet Political System: Transformation or Degeneration," *Problems of Communism,* XV (January-February 1966), 8, 14.
9. Adam B. Ulam, *The Unfinished Revolution* (New York: Vintage Books, 1964), pp. 288, 299.
10. Quoted in C. L. Sulzberger, "A Conversation with Yugoslavia's Djilas: 'We Are Going Toward the Death of All Isms,' " *The New York Times Magazine,* June 9, 1968, p. 114.
11. Robert C. Tucker, "The Deradicalization of Marxist Movements," *American Political Science Review,* 61 (June 1967), 343–358.
12. C. A. R. Crosland, "The Future of the Left," *Encounter,* 14 (March 1960), 3–12. For a vigorous attack on Crosland's position, see R. H. S. Crossman, "The Spectre of Revisionism: A Reply to Crosland," *Encounter,* 14 (April 1960), 24–28.

# 3

## *Europe: The Politics of Collective Bargaining*

### SEYMOUR MARTIN LIPSET

During the 1950's commentators on both sides of the Atlantic began to depict western society by terms such as "The End of Ideology," "the post-industrial society," and the "post-bourgeois society."[1] While emphasizing different themes, these commentators agreed that the growth of bureaucracy and "affluence" in western industrial democratic society has made possible a social system in which class conflict is minimized. Domestic politics has become the politics of collective bargaining. True, an argument does remain as to the relative income at any given moment of the rural sector, of different groups of workers,

Seymour Martin Lipset, "The Changing Class Structure and Contemporary European Politics," *Daedalus,* 93:1 (Winter 1964), 271–303. Reprinted by permission of the American Academy of Arts and Sciences, Boston, Massachusetts. *Author's note:* I would like to express my thanks to Joseph Strotgen and Ruth Ann Pitts for assistance. This paper has been written as part of the program of the Research and Training Group on Comparative Development of the Institutes of International Studies and Industrial Relations of the University of California at Berkeley.

of private corporations, and so forth. But each group accepts the others' right to legitimate representation within the structure of representation and discussion.

Such a pattern in European society is relatively new. Much of the history of industrial society was a story of class-conscious politics and violent controversy between proletarian and bourgeois ideologists. Marxists viewed such tensions as inherent in a capitalist culture. That the United States, the most powerful capitalist state, lack a strong socialist movement was viewed as a cultural lag, an inheritance of the period of an open land frontier that served as a "safety valve" for the tensions of industrialism. Presumably once this safety valve was gone, the European model of class-conscious politics would emerge.

In fact, history has validated a basic premise of Marxist sociology at the expense of Marxist politics. Marxist sociology assumes that cultural superstructures, including political behavior and status relationships, are a function of the underlying economic and technological structure. Hence, the most developed industrial society should also have the most developed set of political and class relationships. Since the United States is the most advanced society technologically, its superstructure should be more likely to correspond to the social structure of a modern industrial society than the "less" developed economies of Europe. In addition, one might argue that the absence of a traditional feudal past should mean that the United States has been most likely to develop the pure institutions of a capitalist industrial society. Hence, as an unpolitical Marxist sociology would expect, instead of European class and political relationships holding up a model of the United States' future, the social organization of the United States has presented the image of the European future.

The linkage between level of industrial development and other political and social institutions is obviously not a simple one.[2] Greater economic productivity is associated with a more equitable distribution of consumption goods and education—factors contributing to a reduction of intra-societal tension.[3] As the wealth of a nation increases, the status gap inherent in poor countries, where the rich perceive the poor as vulgar outcasts, is reduced. As differences in style of life are reduced, so are the tensions of stratification. And increased education enhances the propensity of different groups to "tolerate" each other, to accept the complex idea that truth and error are not necessarily on one side.

An explanation for the reduction in the appeal of total ideologies *(weltanschauugen)* as simply derivative from the social concomitants inherent in increasing economic productivity is clearly oversimplified. T. H. Marshall has suggested that such extreme ideologies initially merged with the rise of new strata, such as the bourgeoisie or the working class, as they sought the rights of citizenship, that is, the right to fully participate socially and politically. As long as they were denied such rights sizable segment of these strata endorsed revolutionary ideologies. In turn, older strata and institutions seeking to preserve their ancient monopolies of power and status fostered conservative extremist doctrines.

The history of changes in political ideologies in democratic countries, from this point of view, can be written in terms of the emergency of new strata, and this eventual integration in society and polity. The struggle for such integration took the form of defining the place in the polity of the old preindustrial upper classes, the church, the business strata, and the working class. The variation in the intensity of "class conflict" in many European nations has been in large measure a function of the extent to which the enduring economic struggle among the classes overlapped with the issues concerning the place of religion and the traditional status structure. Such controversies usually were perceived in "moral" terms involving basic concepts of right versus wrong, and hence they were much more likely than economic issues to result in sharp ideological cleavage and even civil war. The continuance of extremist movements in nations such as Germany and the Latin countries of southern Europe may be traced to the force of moral sentiments inherent in concerns for tradi-

tional status or religious privileges. Where such issues were resolved without becoming identified with the economic class
struggle, then as Marshall suggests intense ideological controversy declined almost as soon as the new strata gained full citizenship rights.

Still a third factor related to the general decline in ideological
bitterness has been the acceptance of scientific thought and professionalism in matters which have been at the center of political
controversy. Insofar as most organized participants in the political struggle accept the authority of experts in economics, military affairs, interpretations of the behavior of foreign nations,
and the like, it becomes increasingly difficult to challenge the
views of opponents in moralistic "either/or" terms. Where there
is some consensus among the scientific experts on specific issues,
these tend to be removed as possible sources of intense controversy. As the ideology of "scientism" becomes accepted, the
ideologies of the extreme left and right lose much of their impact.

But whatever the long-run sources of the reduction of the appeal of total ideologies (and there are short-run factors as well,
such as the impact of wars both hot and cold), the fact remains
that there has been a reduction in the intensity of class-linked
political struggles in most of Europe. This paper surveys developments in the economies, social structures and political parties
of European societies which are relevent to an analysis of such
trends. Within the context of a broad comparative analysis it
also deals with the sources of deviations from these trends. The
analysis thus seeks to define the elements in the changing structures which make for a lessening or persistence of class ideologies in different parts of Europe.

## CLASS AND POLITICAL CONSENSUS AFTER 1945

The "miracle" of the postwar economic growth of Europe has
been well documented. A combination of circumstances—the

depression crises, prolonged experience with state economic intervention and planning under fascism or wartime regimes, the sharp increase in approval of socialist or welfare state concepts during and immediately following the war and the need for some years after the conflict to plan for and even furnish the capital for capital investment—resulted in a far greater amount of planning and government involvement in spurring economic growth than had existed in any democratic state before 1939.[4] The nationalization of businesses in France under the first de Gaulle regime surpassed the most grandiose ambitions of Third Republic Socialists, and systematic planning emerged in the early fifties.[5] The Austrian economy is characterized by large-scale government ownership. Italy retained and even expanded the considerable government economic sector developed under Fascism. In Germany, the numerous dependent war victims and the presence of refugees from the East, comprising more than one quarter of the population of West Germany, involved the state in welfare and other expenditures that took a large share of the gross national product for many years.[6] And in Britain, the Labour government undertook an elaborate program of nationalization and welfare expenditures.

In almost all of these nations, therefore, two general events of considerable significance for class behavior have occurred. On the one hand, many of the political-economic issues that occasioned deep conflict between representatives of the left and of the right were resolved in ways compatible with social-democratic ideology. On the other hand, the dominant strata, business and other, discovered that they could prosper through economic reforms that they regarded a decade earlier as the rankest socialist measures. The socialists and trade unionists found that their formal structural objectives, in many cases, had been accomplished with the cooperation of their political rivals. The need for government planning for economic growth and full employment was generally accepted; the obligation of the state to provide welfare services for the ill, the aged, and other dependent groups was viewed as proper by all parties; and the right of the trade union and political representatives of the workers to participate in decisions affecting industry and politics also was increasingly coming to be accepted. Domestic politics in most of these societies became reduced to the "politics of collective bargaining," that is, to the issue of which groups should secure a little more or less of the pie.

The transformation in class attitudes as reflected in political and interest group behavior is most noticeable in northern non-Latin Europe and among the socialist and Roman Catholic political parties. Large-scale extremist or avowedly authoritarian parties have almost completely disappeared north of France and Italy, with the exception of Finland and Iceland. The Norwegian and Austrian socialists who subscribed to a relatively left-wing Marxist view before World War II are now clearly moderate social-democratic parties.[7] The latter take part in what has become a stable coalition regime with the bourgeois People's party. The parties of the three German-speaking nations, Switzerland, Austria, and Germany, have given up any adherence to Marxism or class war doctrines and are little concerned with any further expansion of the area of state ownership of industry.[8] The 1959 Godesberg Program of the German party explicitly revoked the traditional policy of public ownership of the means of production.[9] An indication of the mood of European socialism may be found in a description of an international socialist conference:

In July, 1958, the socialist international held a congress in Hamburg. The name of Karl Marx was mentioned exactly once. The old slogans of the class struggle and exploitation had disappeared. But the words "liberty," "democracy," "human dignity" came up again and again. . . . The principal theoretical speech was made by Oscar Pollack [famed theoretician of prewar Austro-Marxism]. His theme was, "Why is it that we cannot get the working classes excited about socialism any longer?" The answer that Pollack gave is that their lot is so improved, in a way which would have been incredible to nineteenth-century Socialists of any variety, that they are no longer easily moved by the slogans of class struggle and socialism.[10]

On the right, one finds that those parties which still defend traditional European liberalism *(laissez-faire)* or conservatism (social hierarchy) are extremely weak. The Scandinavian Liberals and Agrarians now accept much of the welfare state. Many Scandinavian bourgeois politicians, in fact, propose that their countries adopt Swiss and Austrian political practice, a permanent coalition of all parties in which collective bargaining issues are fought out and compromised within the cabinet.[11] The Roman Catholic parties, on the whole, have accepted the welfare state and economic planning, and have even supported increases in government ownership. They willingly participate in coalitions with socialist parties in many countries. Roman Catholic trade unions, once the bitter rivals of the so-called free or socialist unions in most Roman Catholic countries, either participate in the same unions as the socialists, as in Germany and Austria, or cooperate closely with the socialist unions, as in the Benelux nations. Issues concerning the relationship of church and state, particularly as they affect education and family legislation, still separate the left wing of the Roman Catholic parties from the Socialists, but these are not of grave moment as compared to their agreement on economic and class matters. In Germany the traditional base of the opposition to a democratic regime, the regions beyond the Elbe, the homeland of the Junkers and feudal social relationships, is no longer part of the nation.[12] West Germany today is physically and socially largely comprised of regions and classes which historically have shown a willingness to sustain modern socio-economic and political systems. Although once playing a major role in politics, the civil service, and the army, the old aristocracy today participate little in these institutions.

Reactionary parties in postwar Europe have tended on the whole to be peripheral movements based on the outlying regions and strata which have not shared in the rapid economic growth, which find themselves increasingly outside of the new cosmopolitanism, and which have lost out in the relative struggle for influence and status.*[13] Thus in Norway the Christian party, which seeks to further traditional values, is clearly a provincial party based on the lower middle classes of the rural and provincial communities. Poujadism was the classic case of a movement appealing to the *resentments* of declining strata; its base was the backward parts of France which had been losing population, and the petit bourgeoisie whose relative position in French economy and society had worsened with the growth of the metropolis and large business and government. In Italy, the Monarchists and

---

* Parenthetically, it may be noted that similar processes are operative on the left. The only significant exceptions within European socialism to increased political moderation have been the enhanced strength of "radical wings" within the socialist and labor movements of Great Britain and Belgium. These movements have long been among the most moderate in the European left, and their dominant tendency has not changed, so that the growth in left strength is not very important. However, it should be noted that the growth in "militancy" within these parties and unions seems to constitute a form of proletarian Poujadism. Both nations lag behind the other industrialized nations of Europe in their growth rate, their standards of living have increased more slowly than those of most other European countries, and the felt need to renovate their economies—these are the two oldest industrial countries on the continent—by building new plants or changing policies in old ones poses serious threats to the established way of life of many workers and union leaders. In Wallonia, the ancient industrial section of Belgium, the socialists and unions waged a major general strike in 1960–1961 designed basically to stop the shutdown of marginal coal mines, and the location of new and efficient factories in Flanders. Since the strike, the "left-wing" socialists have formed the Walloon Popular Movement seeking to divide Belgium into a federal state with two autonomous regions, an action which would enable a Walloon government to defend the Walloon economy. Similar Poujadist processes have occurred in Britain, although their impact is not as visible, since the backward sections of the British economy are not concentrated within one ethnic-linguistic region as they are in Belgium. The powerful resistance among many British union leaders and members to Britain's entry into the Common Market is, to a considerable extent, motivated by their fear of the possible effects on their jobs and unions resulting from the modernization of the national economy which would be necessitated by the need to compete within the Market. As in Wallonia, this essentially Poujadist reaction has taken the form of an alliance between trade union leaders and "left-wing" intellectuals who formulate the opposition on traditional left socialist grounds.

Neo-Fascists have recruited strength from roughly comparable groups, a pattern that has also characterized the support of the Austrian Freedom party.[14]

Not unexpectedly, studies of the attitudes and behavior of the entrepreneurial strata in various parts of Europe suggest that the managerial groups in the traditionally less developed countries of Europe, such as France and Italy, have been the most resistant to yielding their historic autocratic and paternalistic view of the role of management. "In general, France and Italy have been characterized by a large number of small enterprises, looked on by the family as a source of personal security and conducted in an atmosphere of widespread absence of trust."[15] The resistance to accepting trade unions as a legitimate part of the industrial system is greater in these nations than anywhere else in democratic western Europe. And consequently, the presence of extreme views of class and industrial relations among leaders of workers and management has contributed to resisting the pressures inherent in industrialization to stabilize such relationships. The available evidence would suggest that Italian industrialists may be more resistant to accepting a *modus vivendi* with trade unions and the planning-welfare state than are the French, although, as shall be noted, the relative situation is reversed among the worker-based Communist parties of these countries.[16] It is difficult to account for these variations other than to suggest that Fascism as practiced in Italy for two decades conditioned many Italian businessmen to a pattern of labor-management relations that they still long for. Conversely, however, Fascism spared the Italian Communists the experience of having to repeatedly purge the various levels of leadership of a mass party. The party could emerge after World War II with close intellectual links to its pre-Fascist, and more significantly pre-Stalinist, past and with a secondary leadership and rank-and-file whose major formative political experience was the Resistance rather than the Comintern.*

---

* The differences between Italian and French Communism are discussed in more detail below.

Class conflict ideologies have become less significant components of the political movements supported by the middle classes in Germany, Italy, and France. In Germany and in Italy, the Christian-Democratic type parties, with their efforts to retain the support of a large segment of the unionized working classes, have made a trans-class appeal in favor of moderate changes. As compared to pre-Fascist days, they have gained considerably at the expense of older, more class-oriented, more conservative parties. The classically liberal Free Democratic and Liberal parties receive about 7 per cent of the vote in each country. In France, the Christian Democrats (MRP) were not able to retain the massive upper and middle class conservative vote which the party inherited in the first elections of the Fourth Republic, as a result of the traditional right's being discredited by its involvement with Vichy. And large-scale anti-labor and anti-welfare state parties arose in the late forties and fifties. The Gaullism of the Fifth Republic, however, has replaced such parties in the affections of the conservative and business part of the electorate. Gaullism is oriented to a trans-class appeal designed to integrate the lower strata into the polity, and it supports economic and social reforms which foster economic growth and reduce class barriers.

Looking at the policies of business toward workers and their unions, it would appear that Germany first, and much more slowly and reluctantly, France and Italy, in that order, have been accepting the set of managerial ideologies characteristic of the more stable welfare democracies of northern and western Europe.[17] Curiously, the one country for which research data exist which bear on the relationship between degrees of modernization and bureaucratization of industry and the attitudes of industrial managers is contemporary Spain. An as yet unpublished study of the Spanish businessman by Juan Linz indicates clearly that the larger and more modern a factory, the more likely is its manager to believe in, or accept, modern personnel policies with their denigration of the particularistic rights of *patrons* and their assumptions concerning universalistic treatment of subordinates. It is interesting to note that whether a manager is an owner or not seems to have little bearing on his attitudes on such issues. If the Spanish pattern occurs in the other Latin countries as well, it would suggest that those who argue that significant changes are occurring among managers in France and Italy are correct. As yet, however, little systematic comparative data exist on the subject, and many of the available analyses rely heavily on published statements of, or interviews with, the officials, that is, ideologues, of business associations. The latter tend to mouth, and probably even believe, the traditional *laissez-faire* and anti-labor ideologies which many of their members no longer follow in practice.

## THE INTEGRATION OF THE WORKING CLASS

But if the evidence drawn from developments in various parts of the continent suggests that the secular trends press for political moderation, for the politics of collective bargaining, it is also important to note that these trends do not imply a loss of electoral strength for working class-based parties. In fact, in all European countries varying majorities of the manual workers vote for parties which represent different shades of socialism. As the workers have become integrated into the body politic, they have not shifted from voting socialist to backing bourgeois parties. If anything, the opposite seems to have occurred. In the Scandinavian nations, for example, "all evidence indicates that social class explains more of the variation in voting and particularly more of the working class voting than some decades ago. This has occurred simultaneously with the disappearance of traditional class barriers. As equality has increased the working class voters have been more apt to vote for the worker's own parties than before."[18]

A comparative look at the pattern of working class voting in contemporary Europe reveals that with the exception of Holland and Germany, the leftist parties secure about two thirds or more of the working-class vote, a much higher percentage than during the depression of the 1930's.[19] The two exceptions are largely a by-product of the Roman Catholic-Protestant cleavage in their countries. The traditionally minority German and Dutch Roman Catholics have considerable group solidarity, and the Christian Democratic and Roman Catholic parties in these countries secure a larger working class vote than occurs anywhere else on the continent. Close to 70 per cent of German Protestant workers vote Socialist, as do "humanist" and moderate Calvinist Dutch workers, as opposed to the conservative Duth Calvinists, who are more like the Roman Catholics. The leftist working class-oriented parties have increased their strength in much of Europe during the 1960's. It is clear, therefore, that the easy assumption made by many, concerning American as well as European politics, that greater national affluence would mean a weakening of the electoral support for the left is simply wrong. Regardless of how wealthy a nation may be compared to its past, all democratic countries, from the still impoverished lands of the Mediterranean basin to Sweden, Australia, or the United States, remain highly stratified societies in which access to education, economic opportunity, culture, and consumption goods is grossly unequal. The nature of such inequalities varies greatly; in general the poorer a country, the greater the gap in the standard of consumption between the classes. However, in all countries the more deprived strata, in income and status terms, continue to express their resentments against the stratification system or perhaps simply their desire to be represented by politicians who will seek to further redistribute the goods of the society, by voting for parties which stand for an increase in welfare state measures and for state intervention in the economy to prevent unemployment and increase their income vis-à-vis the more privileged strata.

Greater national wealth and consequent lower visible class differentials, therefore, do not weaken the voting strength of the left as compared with the right; rather, their effects become most evident in the decline of ideological differences, in changes in the policies advocated by different parties. The leftist parties have become more moderate, less radical, in the economic reforms which they espouse. A look at the political history of Europe indicates that no mass lower class-based political party, with the single exception of the German Communists, has ever disappeared or significantly declined through losing the bulk of its votes to a party on its right.*

The loyalites once created in a *mass* left-wing party are rarely lost. The most striking testimony to this has been the ability of the Finnish Communist party to retain mass support and even to grow since World War II, in spite of the Russian invasion of the country in 1940, the subsequent war of 1941–1945, and the Russian annexation of Karelia. The Communists are able to secure a quarter of the vote even though 10 per cent of the population are refugees from the Russian-annexed territory. The support for the Communist party goes back to the Finnish Civil War, which followed the Russian revolution, when the Social-Democratic party, the largest party under Czarist rule, divided into two roughly equal groups in reacting to Bolshevism. And although the Communist party was illegal for much of the period between the wars, it seemingly lost little backing. In recent years, it has grown somewhat during a period of rapid economic development and a sharply rising standard of living.

But if workers have remained loyal to the parties of their class on election day, they show much less commitment to these parties the rest of the year. All over Europe, both socialist and Communist parties have complained about losses in membership, in attendance at party meetings, and in the reading of party newspapers. Such changes attest to the growth of what French intellectuals are increasingly coming to describe as the problem of *dépolitisation*.[20] Another phenomenon illustrating these trends is the growing tendency of all the working class organizations to place less emphasis on traditional *political* doctrines and to put more stress on representation of concrete interests. Roman Catholic trade unions also are increasingly reluctant to intervene directly in politics.

* Although the German Communists secured about 16 per cent of the vote in 1932, they were never as large as the Social-Democrats. The latter always retained their status as the predominant party of the workers. Hence even the German case is not a real exception.

In discussing the implications of changes such as these, a number of French political analysts have argued that what is occurring in France, and presumably in some other countries as well, is not so much a decline in political interest *(dépolitisation),* as of ideology *(déideologisation).* Thus René Rémond, in introducing a general symposium on these issues, points out that while political parties have suffered a considerable decline in membership, this has not been true of other French associations; that in fact there has been a considerable increase in the number of voluntary associations in France. Such groups, while nonpartisan, play important roles in politics in representing the specific interests of their members. André Philip has even suggested that contemporary France finally is developing the social infrastructure recommended by Tocqueville as a condition for stable democracy, widespread support for secondary associations. He suggests that this is another consequence of modernization, since the pattern of commitment to one group which represents the individual totally is a characteristic of the early phase of development. In a modernized society, any given group or party will report a relatively low level of direct participation by their members or supporters since the segmentalized individual involved in many roles must support diverse groups, and hence seemingly takes on the role of spectator in most of them.[21]

It would seem as if much of France has taken the plunge of finally dropping its historic commitments to total *weltanschauungen* and seeing the problem of progressive social change as a pragmatic and gradual one. And insofar as Frenchmen are able to see some of the changes and policies which they advocate being adopted, even by a government which many of them distrust, their motivation to continue to participate in such pragmatic parapolitical activity continues.

There are many ways in which the more pragmatic orientation of Europeans manifests itself, but the changes in trade union behavior are most noticeable. As already noted, in a number of countries socialist and Roman Catholic unionists are cooperating as they never did before World War II. The fact of such cooperation reflects the extent to which both have moved away from ideological or political unionism toward pragmatic or even, in the American sense of the term, "business unionism." In Italy and France, the trend toward a *syndicalisme de controle* is furthered by the emerging patterns of plant unions and supplementary factory contracts.[22] Such organization and negotiation for the first time involve the unions in dealing with the concrete problems of the factory environment such as job evaluation, rates, productivity, and welfare.[23] The pressures in this direction have come primarily from the non-Communist unions, though the Communist unions have also increasingly come to accept such institutions, more in Italy than in France.[24] The increase in economic strikes as distinct from political ones, though often resulting in an overall increase of the strike rate, has been interpreted by some observers as reflecting the integration of the workers into the industrial system; an economic strike is part of a normal bargaining relationship with one's employer. Some have suggested that the Italian strike wave of 1961 and 1962 was perhaps the first of this type since the war in that country.[25]

The two major strikes of 1963, those of the coal miners in France and of the metal workers in Germany, are also notable for the extent to which each resembled a typical American strike flowing from a breakdown in collective bargaining. Each strike was ended by a negotiated settlement in which the unions secured more than they had been offered initially. Neither turned into a political strike, though the governments were directly involved in the negotiations. Essentially there was general recognition on both sides that the strike was a normal part of the collective bargaining process, although de Gaulle showed some initial reluctance to concur. Note further that in France the Communist-controlled CGT initially called for a two-day protest strike, while much less politicized miners' unions affiliated to the Socialist Force Ouvrière and the Roman Catholic CFTC called a trade union strike, one that would last until settled by negotiation. The Communists were forced to change their tactics, to shift from a political protest to an economic strike. These strikes in Italy, Germany, and France may signify the beginning of a new era in labor relations—one in which strikes are recognized as part of the normal bargaining relationship rather than an embryonic civil war the outbreak of which is threatening to leadership on both sides.[26]

The relative weakness of traditional leftist ideology in western and southern Europe is suggested also by various attitude surveys. These studies indicate that the actual sentiment favoring a "socialist solution" to economic or social problems is much lower than the Socialist or Communist vote. It again demonstrates that people will vote for such parties without commitment to the once basic ideological values of these parties.

In Britain today, where public opinion polls and local election results indicate that the Labour party has an overwhelming lead over the Conservatives, only 18 per cent of the electorate say that they favor more nationalization. Among Labour party voters, 39 per cent support increased nationalization, 46 per cent would leave things as they are, and 15 per cent would actually favor some denationalization. Conversely, only 43 per cent of the Conservatives advocate denationalization.[27]

A comparative analysis of attitudes toward ownership of industry in seven European countries based on interviews in the spring of 1958 reported strong sentiment favoring public ownership of industry only in Italy, the nation which has the largest support for radical ideologies in the form of large Communist and left-Socialist parties.[28]

In France, where about half the workers have voted Communist in most postwar elections, with another 20 per cent going to the Socialists, and a large majority voting for the Communist-controlled CGT trade union federation in Social Security Board elections, opinion data suggest that the workers are not as hostile to the existing institutions as this record might imply. A detailed survey of French workers in 1956 reported that 53 per cent thought there was "confidence" in the relations between employees and management, as contrasted to 27 per cent who said there was "distrust." Over four-fifths believed their employer was doing his job well; nine-tenths thought the quality of the work done at their plant was good; only 13 per cent thought there was a great deal of waste in their firm; 57 per cent stated that they had a chance for a promotion at their work; and 86 per cent reported they liked their jobs. Though the Communists had secured the vote of a majority of French workers shortly before this survey, only 12 per cent of those interviewed stated they were very much interested in politics, about the same percentage as that which reported strong interest in trade union activities.[29] And when asked in which country "the workers are best off," 54 per cent said the United States as compared with 14 per cent who answered the Soviet Union.[30]

How many of the French Communist voters actually adhere to a class war perspective and a generally Communist view of politics is a question that is impossible to answer. French experts who have examined the available evidence from studies of workers' attitudes differ in their interpretations. Thus Raymond Aron suggests that the polls indicate that about two thirds of French Communist supporters are "convinced Communists," while Mattei Dogan believes that less than half of them think of political action and the class struggle in the Marxist sense of the term.[31]

The weakness of a sharp class conflict view of politics in Germany is borne out by a 1960 opinion study which asked a sample of the electorate their opinions concerning class solidarity and party voting. Less than one-fifth took a purely class view of voting behavior, that is, that workers should always vote for the Socialists, and middle class people always for the non-socialist parties.[32] The majority agreed with the statement that workers or middle class people might vote for either tendency, depending on the political situation and the issues involved. Over three-fifths of those in middle class occupations, although predominantly non-socialist in their voting habits, agreed with the opinion that the division between the bourgeoisie and the workers was no longer strong and that a doctor or a professor might vote either Christian Democratic or Social Democratic, depending on the particular issues of a campaign. Conversely, only 30 per cent of the workers thought that a worker must always vote for the Social-Democrats, while half of the worker respondents agreed with the statement that a worker should choose between the parties according to the issues.[33]

The ideology of the "open society" in which competent individuals can succeed seems to have permeated much of Europe, a phenomenon which may also contribute to a reduction of class tension. Thus surveys in a number of countries which inquired as to the chances of capable individuals rising socially in their country found large majorities which reported their belief that the chances were good. The percentages of respondents saying that chances were good were 90 in Norway, 88 in England, 72 in West Germany, and 70 in Belgium. The one European country covered in this study in which the proportion of those who were optimistic about mobility was less than half was Austria, but even there the positive answers outweighed the pessimistic ones, 49 per cent to 34 per cent. Italy and France were not covered in this comparative study. However, another set of surveys which inquired as to careers one would recommend to a young man found that the Italians ranked second only to the English in suggesting high status professional occupations (62 per cent). The strongest French preference seemed to be for careers in the civil service, an orientation which distinguished them from all other European nations except the Belgians. It should be noted also that the Italians and the French were least likely among the citizens of eleven European countries to recommend a career as a skilled worker or artisan to a young man.[34]

There is some direct evidence that modernization results in a positive attitude by workers toward their occupational situation. A French study of the consequences of modernization in textile factories in northern France brings this out clearly. The author notes that the workers view the effects of technological innovation as a "good thing," that they see it as resulting in an increase in employment, greater possibilities for social mobility and increased earnings.[35] The findings of French factory surveys with respect to worker reaction to modernization are paralleled in a report on the comparative strength of the Communist party in five large Italian factories which varied in their degree of modernization. The less modernized the plants the larger the proportion of workers who belonged to the Communist party, holding size of plant constant.[36]

But if workers react positively to working in modernized, more bureaucratic work environments, if they see these as offering greater opportunity for higher earnings and mobility, if job satisfaction is actually higher in many of these, the fact remains that when one looks at the sources of left-wing strength, either in voting or in union membership, and in the extent to which men agree with "anti-capitalist" attitudes, such strength is to be found disproportionately in the larger factories and the larger cities.[37] This seeming contradiction points up an interesting relation between the variables linked to the overall characteristics of a national political class culture and the same variables operating within a given society. As noted above, nations with a high level of industrialization and urbanization tend to have a low level of ideological conflict. But within nations, whatever the level of intensity of political controversy, larger factories and cities tend to be the strongholds of the left politics dominant in the country, Communist, Socialist, or Democratic.[38] Trade unions also are generally stronger in large factories in large cities. It would seem that while greater industrialization and urbanization with consequent greater national wealth make for a more stable polity, *within* any system these social factors are conducive to fostering working class political and trade union strength.

How might we account for this? In part it may be related to the fact that the large factory environment sustains fewer informal relations between members of different classes, reducing the possibility that the members of the lower class will be influenced personally by the more conservative and more prestigeful members of middle and higher classes such as owners, managers, and supervisors. And the more concentrated the members of a lower class are in a social environment, the easier it is for common class attitudes to spread among them and for representatives of class-oriented parties or other organizations to reach them and activate their anti-elitist sympathies.[39]

But though the emergence of large social environments that are class homogeneous facilitates the spread of lower class-based movements, the same factors operating in the social structure as a whole become linked with other tendencies operating to reduce class friction. On the working class level these involve a rise in standards of living, educational levels, and opportunity for upward social mobility within industry. In all countries with large Communist movements (Italy, France, and Finland), within any given structural environment, the better-paid workers are more moderate in their political views than the poorer ones. Modernization reduces the sources of worker hostility to management by altering the sources of managerial behavior. These trends involve a decline in the family-owned corporation and in the domination of the economy by the *patron* type who sees himself as all powerful, and the rise within the management strata of a corporate leadership characterized by a division of labor and by the requisite of formal higher education. Accompanying the growth in large systems is a consequent increased emphasis on universalistic and achievement values, on judging individuals on the basis of their specific roles as worker or manager. As management's resistance to formalizing the labor-management relationship gradually declines, union labor's commitment to an ideological view of unionism, as distinct from a business or pragmatic view, is also reduced.

## THE NEW MIDDLE CLASS—THE BASE FOR EMPLOYEE POLITICS

The emergence of the new middle class—the increasingly large layer of clerks, salesmen, technicians, middle management, civil servants—has served to introduce as a major factor in the European polity a group which itself is so exposed to conflicting pressures from the left and the right that it can contribute to stabilizing class tensions. A broad middle class has a mitigating position because it can give political rewards to moderate parties and penalize extreme parties on both sides—right and left. Its members wish to obtain more for themselves and their offspring; they advocate universalistic equality in the educational and other aspects of the status-allocating mechanisms; they often uphold the extension of the welfare state. Yet their position among the relatively privileged in status and possession terms makes them supporters of political and social stability, of the politics of collective bargaining. And the larger a proportion of the electorate and the labor force formed by the new middle class, the more both the left and the right must take this group into account in determining their own policies. The political and trade union influence of the new middle class is largely thrown on the side of pressing for greater opportunity, not greater social equality. The unions of the middle class are interested in maintaining, or even extending, the income gap existing between themselves and the manual workers. They often abstain from affiliating to the same central federation as the manual unions, and many of them are led by men who back "liberal" rather than labor parties. In some countries of Europe, and in Israel in recent years, there have been strikes by unions of salaried professionals in order to widen the gap between themselves and manual workers.[40] However, interest in income differences apart, these rapidly growing new middle classes press the political system toward consensus because as employees they favor many of the same statist policies that were long pressed by the representatives of the manual workers. Otto Kirchheimer in fact has argued that it is the very growth of these strata, who form the mass base of the "bourgeois" parties, that is largely responsible for the decline of ideology.[41]

It is important to recognize that the bourgeois parties are no longer bourgeois in the classic sense of the term. That is, the proportion of those who are self-employed, or who have close ties to the self-employed on the land or in the town, is an increasingly small part of the electorate. Most large parties now represent employees, manual or nonmanual. And while these strata differ in their orientations to many issues, they are also united on many welfare concerns. Recent Swedish political history is an apt illustration of this point. The dominant Social-Democrats were experiencing a secular decline in support, largely, according to survey analyses, because the white-collar segment of the population was growing relative to the manual sector. The party introduced a major reform, an old age pension of 65 per cent of salary, in large part because their electoral researches had suggested such a proposal would be popular not only with their traditional manual supporters but with many white-collar workers. The proposal ultimately carried in referendum, and the party increased its national vote substantially. Even more significant, perhaps, is the fact that the Liberal party, which accepted the general principle of the enlarged pension, gained enormously at the expense of the Conservatives, who took a traditional position against high taxes and against increases in the functions of the state. This suggests that the political struggles of the future will increasingly take place between parties representing the status concerns and economic interests of the two employee strata, and that the parties drawing heavily from the self-employed will continue to lose influence.[42]

## COMMUNISM RESISTS THE TREND

The dominant structural trend in Europe involves the final triumph of the values of industrial society, the end of rigid status classes derivative from a pre-industrial world, and increasing emphasis on achievement rather than ascription, on universalism rather than particularism, and on interaction among individuals in terms of the specific roles played by each rather than in terms of their diffuse generalized statuses. The heightening standard of living of the masses gives them greater market power and enables them to affect much of culture and societal taste. All these changes imply the emergence of a somewhat similar social and political culture, one which increasingly resembles the first advanced industrial society to function without institutions and values derivative from a feudal past, the United States. And as has been indicated earlier, this should mean the end of class-linked severely ideological politics.

Yet there is one major force which in a number of countries has rejected this view of European social change and which has done its best to block these trends—the Communist party. It is clear that the very existence of powerful Communist movements in countries like France and Italy has been a major force perpetuating the institutions and values of the old society. In countries in which the Communists are the largest working class party, in which they secure around a quarter of all votes, it has been difficult to elect a progressive government to office. If governments must secure a majority from the non-Communist three quarters of the population, they have to rely in large part on the conservative and traditionalist elements. The fact that one quarter of the electorate, constituting one half of more of the social base of the "left," have been outside of the political game inevitably gives a considerable advantage to the conservatives. In effect, by voting Communist, French and Italian workers have disfranchised themselves. Thus not only does a mass Communist party serve to fossilize the ideological orientations characteristic of a pre-industrial society among the working class, it contributes to preserving pre-modern orientations on the right.

A series of political developments—the revival of French Communist support recouping most of the electoral losses it suffered between 1956 and 1958 as a result of the Hungarian revolution and the Gaullist coup, the continued massive strength of Finnish Communism and the fairly continuous slow growth in the vote of the Italian Communists—each of which has occurred during long periods of prosperity and economic growth—would seem to contradict the thesis that economic growth and an improvement in social conditions enhance the prospects for political stability.[43] In these countries economic modernization has seemingly not been followed by a reduction in ideological tensions.

The countries with large Communist parties, however, remain among the less modernized of the big nations; their industry tends to be less centralized in large plants. Thus in the mid-1950's the proportion of German employees in plants with more than 1000 workers was twice as high (38.9 per cent) as it was in France (17.6 per cent), while only 12 per cent of the employed Germans were in plants with fewer than 50 workers, in contrast to 37 per cent of the French.[44] Note too that the European countries in which Communism is strongest are among those with a relatively small proportion of their total population living in metropolitan areas.[45] The rank-order correlation between the proportion of Communist votes in a nation and urbanization as of the early 1950's was −.61, while the comparable correlation between left extremist voting and an index of industrialization was −.76.[46] Insofar as the general pattern of politics, class relations, and other social attitudes is affected by the degree of bureaucratization of industrial and community life, it is clear that the nations with large Communist movements are on the whole among the less developed in these respects of the nations of Europe.

The comparative analysis of the consequences of economic growth on class relationships in relatively industrialized societies is further complicated by the fact that processes endemic in such improvement affect those workers who are accustomed to the industrial system differently from those who are drawn into it. For the former, increased bureaucratization of industry should make for improvement in income and the conditions of work, and thus should serve to moderate their propensity toward extremist politics. For the latter, the experiences of dislocation inherent in social and geographic mobility, particularly the shift from rural or small-town background to crowded urban slums, and from the pace and discipline of rural work to that of the factory, may increase their potential for support of political radicalism.[47] The need to adjust quickly to new social conditions and cultural norms makes individuals receptive to new values and ideologies which explain the sources of their discontent in revolutionary terms.[48] It should also be noted that the decline in the number of the chronically unemployed—from 2,500,000 in 1950–1951 to around 800,000 in 1962—in Italy may have increased rather than decreased the vote available to the extreme left. There are two empirical generalizations about the political behavior of the jobless and the formally unemployed that hold true in a number of countries. First, the unemployed are much more likely than those regularly employed to be uninformed and apathetic about politics. Their insecurity would seem to reduce their availability for any "outside" interest, including the act of voting. Second, employed individuals who report a past experience of unemployment, or areas which were once centers of high rates of unemployment, are much more likely to exhibit leftist voting propensities than those with more fortunate economic histories.[49]

The most comprehensive analysis of the sources of, and changes in, the support of a mass European Communist party, that of Erik Allardt in Finland, strongly suggests that economic growth in the less industrialized regions of a rapidly developing nation heightens the possibilities for extremist class-conscious politics. He points out that the characteristics of Communist strength in regions in which Communism has gained greatly since World War II, the north and east, are quite different from those in the areas in which it has always been strong, the south and west. The latter are the original industrialized sections of the country. His detailed statistical analyses point to the conclusion that *"increase in Communist strength in all areas is related to changes which in one way or another are likely to uproot individuals."*[50] Ecological analysis indicates that increases in the per capita income of the poorer regions are correlated highly with gains in Communist support. Allardt's analysis also suggests some of the factors underlying the continuation of Communist strength once attained. Stable Communist strength, that is, little fluctuations up or down, is associated with the older industrial areas in which the party has been strong since the Russian revolution and which also give strong support to the Social-Democrats. In such regions, the Communists have erected an elaborate network of party-linked voluntary associations and leisure activities, so that, as in parts of France and Italy, one almost has a functioning Communist subculture unaffected by political events.

As already noted, it is doubtful that structural changes alone will result in the decline of a mass Communist party.[51] Where the party is strong, it endeavors, as in Finland, to isolate its base from serious influence by non-Communist sources. There are plenty of social strains inherent in the situation of the worker or poor peasant to reinforce acceptance of leftist doctrine, and a mass movement can claim that any improvements are the result of its agitation. The Communist sector of the electorate will join the democratic political game in the foreseeable future only if their party, as a party, does it. There is little doubt that if the various European Communist parties were genuine national parties—that is, if their behavior were largely determined by experiences within their own countries—they would have evolved in much the same way as the European Socialist parties. And consequently, it is necessary to recognize that any predictions about their future behavior must be part of an analysis of developments within the Communist-controlled nations. If the break between the Soviet Union and China permits genuine autonomy for all national Communist parties, then the pattern of independence from Russian control emerging in Italy will probably occur elsewhere as well.

The doctrinal base for such a change in the role of Communist parties has already been advanced by various Yugoslav and Italian Communists.[52] The former have argued that there is a world-wide pressure for socialist innovations which is inherent in the nature of large-scale capitalist economic institutions. They accept the proposition that Communist movements and ideologies as they emerged in eastern Europe and Russia are appropriate for underdeveloped countries which have not had the experience of large and legally instituted labor, political, and union movements nor the experience of political freedom.[53] The more developed nations not only can avoid the experiences of the less developed Communist societies, but they can and are moving toward socialism while preserving political freedom. It has even been suggested that in the United States, socialist adjustments and institutions exist even though Americans refuse to accept the term socialism to describe the changes occurring within their society. Co-existence is possible, say these Yugoslavs, not only because war is impossible in an atomic age, but because there is no basic cleavage between the Communist and the capitalist world, since the latter is ceasing to be capitalist in any traditional meaning of the term. Hence Communists in the developed countries will not have to make a revolution or come to power in their own right. By collaborating with other "progressive forces," they can hasten the emergence of socialist institutions.

The Italian Communist party has gradually modified its ideology so that some sophisticated observers would now describe it as a left social-democratic rather than a Communist party. Like the Yugoslav party, it no longer sees a fundamental dichotomy between capitalism and socialism, but rather argues that "there exists in the capitalist world today an urge towards structural reforms and to reforms of a socialist nature, which is related to economic progress and the new expansion of the productive forces."[54] And its leader, Palmiro Togliatti, has gone on to argue the need to "correct" Lenin's position that "bourgeois state apparatus cannot be used for building a socialist society," in the light of "the changes which have taken place and which are still in the process of being realized in the world."[55] It denies the need for one-party dictatorship in Italy, and it has accepted Italian membership in the Common Market. Communist municipal office-holders work closely with business groups in fostering the interests of their cities, and party-controlled labor unions play a somewhat more responsible role in collective bargaining and Italian life generally than has been true for Communist unions in the past.[56] The Chinese Communists correctly point to the Italian party as the foremost example of reformist heresies among the non-governing parties. If the Italian electorate has not turned away from the Communists, the Communists have moved to the right. Thus the effect of a reduction in social strains among sections of the Italian workers may be reflected in the changed behavior of their party and unions.[57]

But if the experiences and the behavior of the Italian party suggest an adaptation to the emergence of stable political institutions and economic modernization in Italy, the French Communist party simply has not behaved in the same way and its policies seemingly challenge the underlying interpretation here.[58] The French party also had to react to the end of Soviet domination of party life and to economic modernization in France. But where the Italian party and its union federation, the CGIL, modified their programs and explicitly decided to cooperate "with what they termed the representatives of neo-capitalism," the French party refused. It continued to insist that capitalism could not reform itself, that the workers could not make long-term improvements in their social situation, and that the unions must remain primarily political instruments. The Italian party decided to join forces with modernization, the French party to resist it.[59] The reasons for the differences between the parties are complex and I cannot detail them here.[60] Briefly, they would seem to relate to the fact that the French party was Stalinized and proletarianized in its leadership and membership during the 1930's and 1940's, while Fascism enabled the Italian party to escape some of these consequences; after 1944 it recruited and retained many non-Stalinist intellectuals in its organizations. Palmiro Togliatti, the leader of the Italian party, though an official of the Comintern during the 1930's, more closely resembles the pre-Stalin leaders of Communism than those like Maurice Thorez, who won and maintained leadership as a result of following Stalin's every turn.[61] The variations in the Italian and French political systems have meant that elected local Communists have had more real power and involvement in running municipalties and other institutions in Italy than in France.[62] The Italian Socialists, in part because of their long and mutual Fascist experience, have been much less hostile to the Communists than have been the French Socialists. Hence the Italian party has never been as isolated from non-Communists as the French. These differences between the French and Italian Communist parties may be related to the facts that the Italian party has lost fewer members than the French (both parties have lost a considerable portion of their membership as compared with their post-war high point), and that the Italian party has done better at the polls.[63]

Communist parties without a Moscow-centered world party would be like national Roman Catholic churches without a pope, without the need to follow a dogma decreed from a single source. And many observers predict that the individual parties will follow the road of Protestantism, of deviation, of variation, of adjustment to particular national conditions, much as the Social-Democrats did half a century or more earlier. Those parties which operate within democratic societies will be under constant pressure to modify their totalitarian structures, as in fact the Italian party seems to be beginning to do.[64]

Given the history of the Communist movement, the training which its leaders have received in totalitarian methods and the use of conscious deception, the acceptance (even though now critical) of the experiences of one-party regimes as a positive model, no one who cares about freedom can accept a Communist party as an equal player in a parliamentary game. On the other hand, the possibility that changes in the Communist world are permitting sufficient independence and variations among Communist parties to allow some of them to react to the forces which press them to act as regular participants within political democracies should not be ignored. The more positively involved are Communists and their *followers* in a political system which in fact is paying off socially and economically, the more difficult it will be for a given Communist party to renew an alienated stance among its supporters should the leadership decide to do so. Hence the possibility may be held out that the vicious circle of Communist-reactionary resistance to modernization in Latin-Europe may be breaking down, not only as a result of the decline of the reactionary groups, but because of changes within Communism. Even Communism may be yielding to the pressures making for a decline of ideology and of class war.

## CONTINUING SOURCES OF STRAIN

There are many sources of political strain within stable democratic societies. The stratification systems of all inherently involve a grossly inequalitarian distribution of status, income, and power. Even the very "affluent" United States contains a large minority living in poverty by its own standards.[65] A look at consumption standards for Europe finds that very large minorities or majorities in different European countries still lack many items which are available to all but a few in the United States.[66] Status inequality would seem to be experienced as punitive by the lower classes in all systems. But while all societies present some ideological justification for enduring consumption and status inequalities, the concept of mass citizenship that arose with the industrial revolution undermines the stability of class systems because it implies, as T. H. Marshall put it, that "all are equal with respect to the rights and duties with which the status is endowed."[67] Hence he argues that modern democratic industrial society is historically unique in seeking to sustain a system of contradictory stratification values. All previous societies had class systems that assumed inequality, but they also denied citizenship to all except a small elite. Once full and equal political (manhood suffrage) and economic (trade union organization) citizenship was established, the equalitarian emphasis inherent in the concept sustains a successful and continuing attack on many aspects of inequality. Much of democratic politics involves the efforts of the lower strata to equalize the conditions of existence and opportunity.

The tension between equality and inequality is endemic in modern industrial democratic society. The dominant strata will continue the attempt to institutionalize their privileges, to find means to pass on to their kin and offspring the privileges they have gained. This conflict, however, does not mean that one or the other tendency must triumph, or that the strain will destroy or even necessarily weaken the social fabric. The predominant character of modern industrial democracy, as a free and evolving society, is in part a result of the chronic tensions between the inherent pressures toward inequality and the endemic emphasis in democracy on equality.

The current wave of writings that somehow see in the growth of affluence in the western world the emergence of a peaceful social utopia—which will not require continued political struggle between representatives of the haves and of the have-nots—ignores the extent to which the content of these very concepts changes as society evolves. As Marshall has pointed out, ever since the beginning of the industrial revolution almost every generation proclaimed a social revolution to elevate the lower strata.

"From the 1880's to the 1940's people were constantly expressing amazement at the social transformation witnessed in their
lifetime, oblivious of the fact that, in this series of outbursts of
self-congratulation, the glorious achievements of the past became
the squalid heritage of the present."[68]

But in spite of the progress leading one generation to proclaim
the significance of recent social improvements, only a few years
later others are arguing that the present conditions of the poor,
of the lowly, are intolerable, that they cannot possibly be tolerated by free men who believe in equality.[69] And as Marshall indicates, such phenomena do not "mean that the progress which
men thought they made was illusory. It means that the standards
by which that progress was assessed were constantly rising, and
that ever deeper probing into the social situation kept revealing
new horrors which had previously been concealed from view."[70]
One may ask with Marshall whether the concept of the affluent
society will have any longer life than some of its predecessors.

In large measure, the problem of the lower strata is now seen
as that of "cultural deprivation." It is clear that in all countries,
variation in participation in the intellectual culture serves to ne-
gate the dream of equal opportunity for all to mount the educational ladder; consequently, access to the summits of the occupational structure is still grossly restricted. In Sweden, for example,
in spite of thirty years of Social-Democratic government providing free access to universities together with state bursaries, the
proportion of working class children taking advantage of such
opportunities has hardly risen. Few commodities are distributed
as unequally in Europe as high school and university education.
The simple improvement in economic standards of living, at
least at its present pace, does little to reduce the considerable advantages held by the culturally privileged strata to perpetuate
their families in an equally advantaged position.[71] And socialist
parties in a number of countries are beginning to look for ways
to enhance the educational and cultural aspirations of lower class
youth. Here, then, is the most recent example of the conflict between the principles of equality inherent in citizenship and the
forces endemic to complex stratified society that serve to main-

tain or erect cultural barriers between the classes. The latter operate as a consequence of the differential distributions of rewards and access to culture, and must be combatted continually if they are not to dominate.[72]

In conclusion, this survey of economic and social developments accompanying the modernization of European society has shown compelling evidence for the moderation of ideological differences in Europe as a consequence of the increasing affluence of European nations, the attainment of economic as well as political citizenship by the workers, the gradual absorption and assimilation of the remnants of European society still living in feudal or otherwise underdeveloped economic and social conditions. The changes in parties of the left, especially Communist parties, to a more moderate orientation toward capitalist society and class conflict have been shown to be also related to broad changes in the international Communist world, as exemplified by the thesis of polycentrism and the reinterpretation of Marxism concerning the possibility of a rapprochement with capitalism. But it has also been pointed out that industrialization does not automatically remove sources of tension. These sources are endemic to an industrial society which permits a relatively open struggle for the fruits of individual effort and which does not automatically give access to opportunity for individual advancement to those on the lower rungs of the status ladder. Finally, it has been shown that much of the anachronistic ideological politics of the "Poujadist" left and right is a response to anachronistic orientations and forms of industrial organization still present in some sectors of European society, as among some peasants and small businessmen in France, or a result of the preservation of outmoded forms of production and extraction, as in Britain and Belgium. In the latter two nations ideological left working class politics, in part, has taken the form of opposition to modernization which might threaten the present security of some categories of workers and their unions in the interests of improvement of the total economy. In the long run, however, the remaining bases of ideologically intransigent politics will continue to decline due to the contradictions between reality and their definition of the situation, and because of the irrelevance of their call to action in terms of a situation which will no longer exist.

As a final comment, I would note that not only do class conflicts over issues related to division of the total economic pie, influence over various institutions, symbolic status, and opportunity, continue in the absence of *weltanschauungen,* but that the decline of such total ideologies does *not* mean the end of ideology. Clearly, commitment to the politics of pragmatism, to the rules of the game of collective bargaining, to gradual change whether in the direction favored by the left or the right, to opposition both to an all powerful central state and to *laissez-faire* constitutes the component parts of an ideology. The "agreement on fundamentals," the political consensus of western society, now increasingly has come to include a position on matters which once sharply separated the left from the right. And this ideological agreement, which might best be described as "conservative socialism," has become *the* ideology of the major parties in the developed states of Europe and America. As such it leaves its advocates in sharp disagreement with the relatively small groups of radical rightists and leftists at home, and at a disadvantage in efforts to foster different variants of this doctrine in the less affluent parts of the world.

## NOTES

1. It is difficult to establish credit for the origin of this concept. Raymond Aron certainly deserves recognition for having presented it in the form which was widely followed by other writers in the West. See Raymond Aron, "Fin de l'age ideologique?" in Theodore W. Adorno and Walter Dirks (eds.), *Sociologica* (Frankfurt: Europaische Verlaganstalt, 1955), pp. 219–233, and *L'Opium des intellectuals* (Paris: Calmann-Levy, 1955), pp. 315–334. However, it should be noted that two major European scholars, T. H. Marshall and Herbert Tingsten, enunciated the same basic thesis without using the term in the late 40's and early 50's. Tingsten's early writings on the subject were presented in various articles in the Stockholm newspaper, *Dagens Nyheter,* while Marshall elaborated on the theme in his now almost classic essay, "Citizenship and Social Class," first presented in 1949 and recently reprinted in his volume

*Sociology at the Crossroads* (London: Heinemann, 1963), pp. 67–127. See also Edward Shils, "The End of Ideology?" *Encounter,* 5 (November, 1955), 52–58; Herbert Tingsten, "Stability and Vitality in Swedish Democracy," *The Political Quarterly,* 26 (1955), 140–151; S. M. Lipset, "The State of Democratic Politics," *Canadian Forum,* 35 (1955), 170–171; Otto Brunner, "Der Zeitalter der Ideologien," in *Neue Wege der Sozialgeschichte* (Gottingen: Van den Hoeck und Ruprecht, 1956), pp. 194–219; Lewis Feuer, *Psychoanalysis and Ethics* (Springfield: Charles C. Thomas, 1955), pp. 126–130; Otto Kirchheimer, "The Waning of Opposition in Parliamentary Regimes," *Social Research,* 24 (1957), 127–156; Stein Rokkan, *Sammenlignende Politisksosilogi* (Bergen: Chr. Michelsens Institutt, 1958); Daniel Bell, *The End of Ideology* (Glencoe: The Free Press, 1960), especially pp. 369–375; and S. M. Lipset, *Political Man* (Garden City: Doubleday, 1960), especially pp. 403–417. Daniel Bell has written of the "post-industrial society." See his "The Post Industrial Society" (mimeographed, 1962). Ralf Dahrendorf describes comparable phenomena as the "post-capitalist society." See his *Class and Class Conflict in Industrial Society* (Stanford: Stanford University Press, 1959), especially pp. 241–318, and Gunnar Myrdal, *Beyond the Welfare State* (New Haven: Yale University Press, 1960). George Lichtheim has commented on many of these ideas under the heading of the "postbourgeois" society. See his *The New Europe* (New York: Frederick A. Praeger, 1963), especially pp. 175–215; see p. 194.

2. For an excellent article on this subject see Val Lorwin, "Working Class Politics and Economic Development in Western Europe," *American Historical Review,* 63 (1958), 338–351.

3. See Simon Kuznetz, "Economic Growth and Income Inequality," *American Economic Review,* 45 (1955), 4.

4. For systematic data on government ownership generally in Europe, see John O. Coppock, "Government Expenditures and Operations," in J. Frederick Dewhurst, John O. Coppock, P. Lamartine Yates, and Associates, *Europe's Needs and Resources: Trends and Prospects in Eighteen Countries* (New York: Twentieth Century Fund, 1961), pp. 436–442. See also Massimo Salvadori, "Capitalism in Postwar Europe," in *ibid,* pp. 746–758.

5. On the nature and extent of planning in postwar France see Pierre Bauchet, *La planification française: Quinze ans d'expérience* (Paris: Editions du Seuil, 1962).

6. In "Germany in 1952, something like 37 per cent of the stock of industry was State-owned." Roy Lewis and Rosemary Stewart, *The Managers: A New Examination of the English, German, and American Executives* (New York: Mentor Books, 1961), p. 233. The figure is probably lower now.

7. See Hubert Ferraton, *Syndicalisme ouvrier et social-democratie en Norvège* (Paris: Armand Colin, 1960) for a detailed analysis of the transformation of the Norwegian Labor party from a radical oppositionist to a moderate governmental party. For a detailed account of the general changes in Norway see Ulf Torgensen, "The Trend Towards Political Consensus: The Case of Norway," *Acta Sociologica,* 6, Nos. 1–2 (1962), pp. 159–172. For analysis of the

changes in the Austrian parties, see Alexander Vodopivec, *Wer regiert in Osterreich?* (Vienna: Verlag für Geschichte und Politik, 1961).

8. For a detailed account of the changes in the approach of the Swiss Socialist party, a movement rarely discussed in social science political analysis, see Francois Masmata, "Le parti socialiste suisse" (thesis for the Doctor of Research degree, Ecole Politique, mimeographed, Paris: Foundation Nationale des Sciences Politiques, Cycle Superieur d'Etudes Politiques, 1963).

9. See Jossleyn Hennessy, "Productive Unrest in Germany," *New Society,* 1, No. 15 (January 10, 1963), 21–23. For the text of the new program which favors competition, see *Die Zeit,* 22 (June 7, 1963), 14.

10. Bertram D. Wolfe, "A Century of Marx and Marxism," in Henry L. Plaine (ed.), *Darwin, Marx, and Wagner* (Columbus: Ohio State University Press, 1962), pp. 106–107.

11. See Dankwart A. Rustow, *The Politics of Compromise* (Princeton: Princeton University Press, 1955), pp. 219–223.

12. Theodore Schieder, *The State and Society in Our Times* (London: Thomas Nelson and Sons, 1962), p. 121.

13. Discussions of the problems of British and Belgian economies may be found in Michael Shanks, *The Stagnant Society* (London: Penguin Books, 1961); A. Lamfalussy, *The United Kingdom and the Six* (London: Macmillan, 1963); A. Lamfalussy, *Investment and Growth in Mature Economics: The Case of Belgium* (London: Macmillan, 1961). On recent trends in British politics see C. A. R. Crosland, *The Conservative Enemy* (London: Jonathan Cape, 1962), and Norman Birnbaum, "Great Britain: The Reactive Revolt," in M. A. Kaplan (ed.), *The Revolution in World Politics* (New York: John Wiley and Sons, 1962), pp. 31–68. On Belgium see Val Lorwin, " 'All Colors But Red': Interest Groups and Political Parties in Belgium" (mimeographed paper: Center for Advanced Study in the Behavioral Sciences, Stanford, California, 1962); Marcel Bolle de Bal, "Les sociologues, la conscience de classe et la grand grève belge de l'hiver 60–61," *Revue de l'institut de Sociologie,* 34 (1961–63), pp. 541–579; and Ernest Mandel, "The Dialectic of Class and Region in Belgium," *New Left Review,* 20 (Summer 1963), 5–31.

14. On Norway see Stein Rokkan and Henry Valen, "The Mobilization of the Periphery," *Acta Sociologica,* 6, Nos. 1–2 (1962), 111–141. On France and Italy, see Mattei Dogan, "Les Bases sociales des partis politique en France et en Italie" (mimeographed paper presented at the Fifth World Congress of Sociology, September, 1962), pp. 13–14.

15. See the various studies reported in Frederick Harbison and Charles A. Myers, *Management in the Industrial World: An International Analysis* (New York: McGraw-Hill, 1959). On Italy see also Joseph LaPalombara, "La Confindustria e la politica in Italia," *Tempi Moderni,* 4 (October-December, 1961), 3–16; on France see Francois Bourricaud, "Le 'Jeune Patron' tel qu'il se voit et tel qu'il voudrait être," *Revue Economique,* 6 (1958), 896–911; Lewis and Stewart, *op. cit.,* especially pp. 165–187; Harbison and Myers, *op. cit.,* p. 123.

16. See LaPalombara, *op. cit.*, and Bourricaud, *op. cit.*, pp. 901, 903.

17. "Paradoxes of the French Political Community," in Stanley Hoffman, et al., *In Search of France* (Cambridge: Harvard University Press, 1963), pp. 61–62; see also Laurence Wylie, "Social Change at the Grass Roots," in *ibid.*, p. 184. For a detailed analysis of the problems of analyzing the complexity of French economic life see Raymond Aron, *France Steadfast and Changing* (Cambridge: Harvard University Press, 1960), "Myths and Realities of the French Economy," pp. 45–77.

18. Erik Allardt, "Traditional and Emerging Radicalism" (mimeographed paper), p. 5.

19. See Mattei Dogan, "Le Vote ouvrier en Europe occidentale," *Revue Française de sociologie*, 1 (1960), 25–44.

20. See especially the various articles in Georges Vedel (ed.), *La Dépolitisation, mythe ou réalité?* (Paris: Armand Colin, 1962).

21. Colloque "France Forum," *La Démocratic à refaire* (Paris: Editions Ouvrières, 1963), "La Dépolitisation de l'opinion publique," pp. 15–74. The relevant comments of Rémond are on pp. 26–27; Philip's statements are on pp. 38–39.

22. See Jean Maynaud, "Apatia e responsibilita dei cittadini," *Tempi Moderni*, New Series 5, No. 9 (April-June, 1962), 30–38.

23. See Arthur M. Ross, "Prosperity and Labor Relations in Western Europe: Italy and France," *Industrial and Labor Relations Review*, 16 (1962), 63–85; see also Vera Lutz, *Italy, A Study in Economic Development* (London: Oxford University Press, 1962), pp. 222–223; and Joseph A. Raffaele, *Labor Leadership in Italy and Denmark* (Madison: University of Wisconsin Press, 1962), pp. 291–293.

24. See Serge Moscovici, *Reconversion industrielle et changements sociaux* (Paris: Armand Colin, 1961), pp. 127–128.

25. E. A. Bayne, "Italy's Seeds of Peril, Part IV," *American Universities Field Staff Reports Service*, Southeast Europe Series, 10, No. 4 (July, 1962).

26. See Club Jean Moulin, *L'Etat et le citoyen* (Paris: Editions du Seuil, 1961), "Vers le syndicalisme d'enterprise," pp. 271–279, for an analysis of the structural pressures changing the nature of French unionism.

27. *Gallup Political Index*, Report No. 38, March, 1963, p. 34.

28. See studies completed by Affiliates of International Research Associates and reported in DIVO Institut, *Umfragen: Ereignisse und Probleme der Zeit im Urteil der Bevölkerung* (Frankfurt: Europaische Verlagsanstalt, 1959), p. 77.

29. "The French Worker: Who he is, how he lives, what he thinks, what he wants." *Réalités*, 65 (April, 1956), 8–18.

30. The findings of a study conducted for *Réalités* by IFOP, the French Gallup Poll; see also Charles Micaud, *Communism and the French Left* (New York: Frederick A. Praeger, 1963), pp. 138–139.

31. Aron, *France Steadfast and Changing*, pp. 39–40; Mattei Dogan, "Il compartamento politico delgi operai francesi," *Tempi Moderni*, 9 (April, 1962), 26–27. Dogan reports that in 1952 the majority of workers supporting the Communists told interviewers that "the doctrine of this party was not the main reason for their vote" *(op. cit.,* p. 25). See also Micaud, *op. cit.*, pp. 140–141.

32. The most recent German opinion polls (March, 1963) indicate a large Social-Democratic lead (47%) over the Christian Democrats (41%). Quincy Howe, "World Press Comment," *Atlas,* 5 (1963), 324.

33. Viggo Graf Blucher, *Der Prozess der Meinungsbildung dargestellt am Beispiel der Bundestagswahl 1961* (Bielefeld: Emnid Institut, 1962), pp. 73–75. See also Heinrich Popitz, Hans Paul Bahrdt, Ernst August Jures and Hanno Kesting, *Das Gesellschaftsbild des Arbeiters* (Tubingen: Mohr-Siebeck, 1957), p. 233. Similar findings are reported in Alfred Willener, *Images de la société et classes sociales* (Berne: Stämpfli, 1957), pp. 153, 206. See also Ralf Dahrendorf, "Burger und Proletarier: Die Klassen und ihr Schicksal," in his *Gesellschaft und Freiheit* (Munich: Pieper, 1961), pp. 133–162, especially p. 175; Rainer M. Lepsius, "Zum Wandel der Gesellschaftsbilder in der Gegenwart," *Koelner Zeitschrift für Soziologie,* 14 (1962), 450; Hansjurgen Daheim, "Die Vorstellungen vom Mittelstand," *ibid.,* 12 (1960), 252; and Renate Mayntz, *Soziale Schichtung und Soziale Wandel in einer Industriegemeinde* (Stuttgart: Ferdinand Emke, 1958), p. 103. For a poll of workers, see Institut für Demoskopie, *Jahrbuch der Offentlichen Meinung, 1947–1955* (Allensbach: Verlag für Demoskopie, 1956), pp. 265, 267.

34. DIVO Institut, *op. cit.,* pp. 120, 124.

35. Claude Durand, "Positions syndicales et attitudes ouvrières à l'égard du progrès technique," *Sociologie du travail,* 4 (1960), 351.

36. Mario Einaudi, J. Domenach and A. Garoschi, *Communism in Western Europe* (Ithaca: Cornell University Press, 1951), pp. 43–44.

37. Dogan, *op. cit.,* p. 26. For reports of opinion data on characteristics of working class vote, data on traits of union members and their attitudes drawn from a secondary analysis of the IBM cards on a survey of French workers completed by the French Institute of Public Opinion (IFOP) in 1956, see Richard Hamilton, "The Social Bases of French Working-Class Politics" (unpublished Ph.D. thesis, Department of Sociology, Columbia University, 1963).

38. See Lipset, *Political Man,* pp. 263–267.

39. German data indicate that the larger the plant a man works in the more likely he is to discuss politics with his fellow workers in the factory. Wolfgang Hartenstein and Gunther Schubert, *Mitlaufen oder Mitbestimmen* (Frankfurt: Europaische Verlanganstalt, 1961), p. 25. Conversely, the larger the size of the work unit, the fewer the workers who report that they chat informally with a higher-up. See Juan Linz, "The Social Bases of West German Politics" (unpublished Ph.D. thesis, Department of Sociology, Columbia University, 1959), p. 397.

40. On the behavior of white-collar workers in various countries of Europe see Michel Crozier, "Les attitudes politiques des employés et des petits fonctionnaires," in M. Duverger (ed.), *Partis politiques et Classes sociales en France* (Paris: Armand Colin, 1955), pp. 85–99; *Petits Fonctionnaires au Travail* (Paris: Centre National de la recherche scientifique, 1955); "L'ambiguité de la conscience de classe chez les employés et les petits fonctionnaires," *Cahiers Internationaux de sociologie,* 28 (1955), 78–97; "Les relations de pouvoir dans un système d'organisation bureaucratique," *Sociologie du*

*Travail,* 1 (1960), 61–75; "Classes sans conscience ou préfiguration de la société sans classes," *European Journal of Sociology,* 1 (1960), 233–245; "Le rôle des employés et des petits fonctionnaires dans la structure française contemporaine," *Transactions of the Third World Congress of Sociology* (Amsterdam: International Sociological Association, 1956), III, 311–319; "White Collar Unions, The Case of France" (to be published, 1964); Roger Girod, *Etudes sociologiques sur les couches salariées* (Paris: Marcel Rivière, 1961); Fritz Croner, *Die Angestellten in der modernen Gesellschaft* (Frankfurt: Humbolt, 1954); John Bonham, *The Middle Class Vote* (London: Faber and Faber, 1954); David Lockwood, *The Black-coated Worker* (London: Allen and Unwin, 1958); E. Dahlstrom, *Tjanstemännen, Naringlivet och sämhallet* (Stockholm: Studieförbundet näringsliv och Samhälle, 1954).

41. Kirchheimer, *op. cit.,* p. 148.
42. It is interesting to note that a similar pattern has emerged within the United States. See Herbert J. McClosky, Paul J. Hoffman, and Rosemary O'Hara, "Issue Conflict and Consensus Among Party Leaders and Followers," *American Political Science Review,* 54 (June, 1960), 406–427.
43. Source: E. A. Bayne, "Italy's Seeds of Peril," I, *American Universities Field Staff Reports Service,* Southeast Europe Series, 10, no. 1 (June, 1962), 7; and "Unions on the March Again," *The Economist,* April 13, 1963, 137.
44. For Germany see the *Statistisches Jahrbuch,* 1959, p. 179, and for France in 1954 see Institut national de la statistique et des études economiques, *Mouvement Economique en France de 1944 à 1957* (Paris: Presses Universitaires, 1958), p. 42.
45. See Jack P. Gibbs and Kingsley Davis, "Conventional Versus Metropolitan Data in the International Study of Urbanization," in Jack P. Gibbs (ed.), *Urban Research Methods* (Princeton: D. Van Nostrand Co., 1961), pp. 422–424.
46. William Kornhauser, *The Politics of Mass Society* (Glencoe: The Free Press, 1959), pp. 143, 150. The degree of urbanization was measured by the proportion of the population living in cities with over 20,000 population, while industrialization was measured by the proportion of the labor force in nonagricultural occupations.
47. The change in the Italian occupational structure has been dramatic. See Bayne, "Italy's Seeds of Peril," II, no. 2 (June, 1960), 6.
48. See Edvard Bull, Jr., *Arbeidermilje under det industrielle gjennombrudd. Tre norske industristrok* (Oslo: 1958), as cited in Stein Rokkan and Henry Valen, "Parties, Elections and Political Behavior in the Northern Countries: A Review of Recent Research," in Otto Stammer (ed.), *Politische Forschung* (Koln: Westdeutscher Verlag, 1960), pp. 107–108, 110; Lipset, *Political Man,* pp. 68–71. See also John C. Leggett, "Uprootedness and Working-Class Consciousness," *American Journal of Sociology,* 68 (1963), 682–692. Leggett also cites various historical studies which point to the link between "uprootedness" and radicalism.
49. Lipset, *Political Man,* pp. 187, 198, 236; see also S. M. Lipset, *Agrarian Socialism* (Berkeley: University of California Press, 1950), pp. 176–177.

50. Allardt, "Traditional and Emerging Radicalism," p. 21. In an earlier study Allardt has demonstrated that areas with the highest proportions of unemployed during the depression gave the highest support to the Communists in 1951–1954. See Erik Allardt, *Social Struktur och Politisk Aktivitet* (Helsingfors: Söderstrom and Co., 1956), p. 84.

51. Greece may be an exception to this generalization. See Marcello Dell' Omodarme, "Greece Moves Toward Dictatorship," *Atlas*, 3 (1962), 301–305 (translated from *Communitá*, December, 1961).

52. An analysis of the similarities in the approaches of the Yugoslav and Italian Communists may be found in Francois Fejto, "Le parti communiste francais et le 'polycentrisme,'" *Arguments*, 6 (1962), 69–70.

53. See Walter Z. Laqueur, "The End of the Monolith: World Communism in 1962," *Foreign Affairs*, 40 (1962), 362.

54. Quoted in The Editorial Department of Hongqi, *More on the Differences Between Comrade Togliatti and Us* (Peking: Foreign Languages Press, 1963), p. 13.

55. Togliatti's report, *op. cit.*, p. 130. (Emphasis mine.) For a discussion of some of the issues underlying the question of Marx and Engels' original position, the influence of the Paris Commune on them, and Communist revisionism, see S. M. Lipset, "The Sociology of Marxism," *Dissent*, 10 (1963), 59–69. This is a review article on George Lichtheim, *Marxism: An Historical and Critical Study* (New York: Frederick A. Praeger, 1961). This book must also be read in this context. Lichtheim argues that Marxism as a revolutionary doctrine is appropriate only to countries in the period of early industrialization.

56. In Italy see Giorgio Galli, "Italy," in Walter Laqueur and Leopold Labedz (eds.), *Polycentrism: The New Factor in International Communism* (New York: Frederick A. Praeger, 1962), pp. 127–140; and Giorgio Galli, "Italy: The Choice for the Left," in Leopold Labedz (ed.), *Revisionism* (New York: A Praeger, 1962), pp. 324–336.

57. For an indication of the diversity of opinion and level of open debate which exists among the leadership of the Italian Communist party, see the translations of the report published in *L'Unità*, the organ of the party, of a two-day debate within the central committee. Perry Anderson, "Debate of the Central Committee of the Italian Communist Party on the 22nd Congress of the C.P.S.U.," *New Left Review*, Nos. 13–14 (January-April, 1962), 151–192. For the history of open debate within the Italian party, see Guglielmo Negri and Paolo Ungari, "La vita dei partito," in Alberto Spreafico and Joseph LaPalombara (eds.), *Elezioni e comportamento politico in Italia* (Cremona: Edizioni di Communitá, 1963, pp. 175–180.

58. But for a different interpretation, see Lichtheim, *op. cit.*, p. 180.

59. See Pierre Fougeyrollas, "France," in Laqueur and Labedz, *op. cit.*, pp. 141–151.

60. An excellent analysis of the differences between the Italian and French parties may be found in Fejto, *op. cit.*, pp. 66–72. A similar point is made by Laqueur, *op. cit.*, p. 369.

SEYMOUR MARTIN LIPSET : 115

61. See Ignazio Silone's essay in R. Crossman (ed.), *The God That Failed* (New York: Harper and Bros., 1949), pp. 106–112, and Antonio Gambino, "Togliatti's Balancing Act," *Atlas,* 3 (1962), 126–127 (translated from *L'Espresso,* December 31, 1961).
62. See Michel Crozier, "La France, terre de commandement," *Esprit,* 25 (1957), 790–792.
63. See Hamilton, "The Social Bases of French Working-Class Politics," p. 59. See also Crozier, "La France, terre de commandement."
64. Richard Lowenthal, "The Rise and Decline of International Communism," *Problems of Communism,* 12 (March-April 1963); see also Laqueur, *op. cit.,* pp. 371–373.
65. See S. M. Lipset, *The First New Nation* (New York: Basic Books, 1963), pp. 321–335.
66. A quick glance at any statistical table reporting on income or consumption standards in Europe suggests the extent to which European affluence is considerably below that of the United States. See J. Frederick Dewhurst, "Consumption Levels and Patterns," in Dewhurst, et al., *op. cit.,* pp. 146–147, 161–162; P. Lamartine Yeates, "Household Operations," in Dewhurst, et al., *op. cit.,* pp. 266, 267, 1005; Report of DOXA, XV, No. 16, August, 1961, 2; and "Tableau général de la consommation des français de 1950 à 1960," *Consommation,* 8 (July-December, 1961), 5–174.
67. T. H. Marshall, *op. cit.,* p. 87.
68. *Ibid.,* p. 268.
69. See Howe, *op. cit.,* pp. 325–326. See also John Goldthorpe and David Lockwood, "Not So Bourgeois After All," *New Society,* 1, No. 3 (October 18, 1962), 19.
70. Marshall, *op. cit.,* pp. 269–270.
71. See H. Bouterline Young, "Detection and Encouragement of the Talented in Italian Schools," *The British Yearbook of Education, 1962* (London: Evans Brothers, 1962), pp. 275–280. See also Christiane Peyre, "L'Origine sociale des élèves de l'enseignement secondaire en France," in Jean Floud, et al., *Ecole et société* (Paris: Marcel Rivière, 1959), p. 10.
72. See Mark Abrams, "Social Class and Political Values" (paper presented to the British Sociological Association, Scottish Branch, Conference in Edinburgh, May 3–4, 1963), pp. 13–14.

# 4 Finland: Institutionalized Radicalism

## ERIK ALLARDT

During the period between 1955 and 1965 the new Europe emerging after World War II was often characterized as a society of affluence with a decreasing amount of ideological conflicts. Technology, so to say, had wiped out ideology. After the student riots in a multitude of American and European universities there has been a rush to declare that the notion of "the end of ideology" was all wrong or at best a bold misinterpretation of the situation. This tendency to be in tune with the times may be understandable but it is hardly theoretically fruitful. Whatever the phrases "the end of ideology" or "decline of ideology" are taken to mean they can be considered as broad sensitizing notions about certain tendencies emerging in postwar in-

Prepared especially for this volume, this chapter is an abridged, thoroughly revised, and updated version of the author's "Patterns of Class Conflict and Working Class Consciousness in Finnish Politics," which was published in E. Allardt and Y. Littunen, eds., *Cleavages, Ideologies, and Party Systems* (Helsinki: Academic Bookstore, 1964), pp. 97–131.

dustrialized societies. Data about the new upsurge of interest in ideology can be used to specify and pinpoint what the phenomena subsumed under the concept of the end of ideology actually amounted to.

Many difficulties in the discussions have arisen from the fact that "decline of ideology" actually is a kind of misnomer. Ideology may be regarded as a system of evaluative principles about the ends of human action, about the means of attaining these ends, and about the nature of social and physical reality. Human beings can hardly live without such evaluative principles, and the writers on the theme of the decline of ideology have not denied that such evaluative principles still are part of political organizations. As other sensitizing concepts the decline of ideology is multidimensional or denotes different things loosely related to each other. In a perceptive analysis Ulf Himmelstrand has shown that this notion has meant at least three different things: (1) that there is a development toward an ideological consensus, (2) that the impact of ideology on practical politics has become weaker, and (3) that there is a decreasing saliency of ideological statements.[1]

The theme of the decline of ideology, however, has also been used in a more specific sense. It has been used to describe a trend toward decreasing class conflicts in modern industrialized societies. It is in this specific sense that S. M. Lipset used the term in a paper in 1964,[2] and it is in the same sense that the term will be used in this paper.

## DECLINE OF IDEOLOGY—FINLAND AS A DEVIANT CASE

In the above-mentioned paper, Lipset also shows that there are exceptions or deviant cases to the general trend toward decreasing class conflicts. Deviant cases are not only matters of curiosity but also genuinely interesting theoretically. At least, this is the theoretical reason for treating the deviant case of Finland at some length. This is also the rationale for the importance of considering specific countries in discussions focusing on comparative analysis.

Just as the whole theme of the decline of ideology cannot be presented without many qualifications, so Finland and Finnish politics cannot be presented as a deviant case without many and specific qualifications. The most obvious sign of remaining class conflicts in Finnish society is the strength of the Communist party, appearing in elections under the name of the Finnish People's Democratic League. During the period after World War II, the Communists have received between 18 and 24 percent of the total vote, whereas in the 1920s their support was never higher than 15 percent. However, as will be shown in this paper, there are strong and almost conventional elements in Finnish Communism. Since the elections of 1966 the Communists have been represented in the Cabinet together with the Social Democrats and the Agrarians. Today the Communists have access to political power, and they cannot be regarded as politically disenfranchised in any sense. The Communists have become more and more integrated into the Finnish party system, and, as will be shown, they have in fact integrated some sectors of the population into the political system. At the same time it is apparent that the Communist vote is still more of a protest vote than the votes for other parties. To put it briefly, Finland is a deviant case with many qualifications.

## Finnish Politics as a History of Both Class Conflicts and Consensus

Finnish political history is a curious mixture of class conflicts, other cleavages, and national consensus. During the first quarter of the twentieth century, Finland experienced events which approximated two-class situations several times. Socialism gained a hold in Finland in the 1890s and spread rapidly. Large groups of the Finnish working class were politically conscious before they had the right to vote and participate in the Finnish political system. In 1905, Finland experienced the same general strike which had spread like wildfire all over the Russian empire. When Finland introduced universal suffrage for both men and women in 1906, the Social Democratic Party received 37 percent of the total vote in the first elections and become in one stroke the biggest Socialist party in Europe. Socialist traditions have been strong in Finland ever since. The dependence on tsarist Russia made it hard to modernize and initiate social change, and grave inequalities existed. At the same time, the pressure from the tsarist Russia made for national unity and consensus.

The only genuine two-class situation occurred in 1918, when, soon after Finland's declaration of independence in December 1917, the bitterness of Finnish labor culminated in a cruel civil war, often called the Liberation War, between Whites and Reds. During this war about 20,000 Reds were either killed in battle, executed, or died of hunger and disease in prison camps. In spite of the fact that the war in 1918 was related to the goal of furthering and strengthening national independence, it also had the character of a class war. On the Red side, an overwhelming majority of those who were killed or died in the war were recruited from the working class.

The first half of the 1920s was by and large a period of reconstruction after the civil war. Large-scale land reforms in 1918 and 1922 created independent farmers out of a rural proletariat that had come into existence in the nineteenth century. The second half of the 1920s was a period of intensive political debate. Strongly nationalist movements with a religious, fundamentalist background and a semifascist bent put the government under heavy pressure, and the Communist party was outlawed in 1930. The latter part of the 1930s was a period of particularly rapid economic development and social reconstruction. Other cleavages than those related to social class came into the foreground, and at least publicly the most important cleavage existed between the Finnish-speaking majority and the Swedish-speaking minority. In the so-called Winter War between Finland and Soviet Russia in 1939–40 Finland displayed an almost total national unity.

From 1941 to 1944 the country fought what in Finland is labeled the Continuation War against the Soviet Union. Throughout the war Finland accepted that it was co-belligerent with Germany but it was never formally allied to Germany, and it was often asserted that Finland was engaged in an entirely separate war. Finland made a separate peace in 1944, and had by fighting to force the German troops in Northern Finland to leave Finnish territory. The period between 1944–48 was a time of both internal struggles and rapid national reconstruction. Heavy war reparations demanded by the U.S.S.R. were paid. In 1944 the Communists reentered the political arena and became one of the biggest parties in the first postwar elections in 1945. They have been represented in the Cabinet from 1944 to 1948, and again from 1966 onward. It seems reasonable to state that they have become more and more integrated into the Finnish party system.

One of the most decisive factors in bringing about this integration is the strong consensus regarding Finland's foreign policy. The relationship to the Soviet Union is of course one of the most crucial factors influencing the formulation of goals in Finnish politics. If by goals is meant aims that are consciously promoted by those in the polity who make major decisions, there is strong consensus regarding the goals of promoting friendly relations with Soviet Union while at the same time retaining national independence. In Finland these two goals together are usually associated with the label of "neutrality." Finland has a pact of friendship and mutual aid with the Soviet Union but Finland has the right to remain neutral in conflicts between the great powers unless the Soviet Union is attacked through Finnish territory. The friendly relation with Soviet Union and the right to remain neutral are also constant themes in public declarations by Finnish politicians. Survey studies indicate that this Finnish conception of neutrality has almost unanimous support in the population. According to a nationwide survey in 1964, 91 percent of all respondents expressed their approval of Finland's particular brand of neutrality, while only 2 percent were opposed to it. In the same fashion Finland's line in foreign policy is strongly approved in all sectors of the population. As many as 88 percent of the respondents approved of Finland's handling of foreign affairs, whereas, again, a very negligible minority thought that they had been handled badly. For these crucial parts of the goal structure in Finnish politics there is consensus and almost unanimous support, and the Communist voters accept the same goals as voters of other parties. In many resepcts this consensus represents a rather clear-cut case of decline of ideology. Attitudes in foreign policy matters are strongly instrumental and largely unrelated to ideological differences.

## CLASS-BASED VOTING AND WORKING-CLASS CONSCIOUSNESS: RESULTS BASED ON SURVEY STUDIES

Although there is a strong consensus regarding some goals in Finland, ideology related to social class is still very important in Finnish politics. The working-class vote is divided between the Communists and the Social Democrats. In the elections of 1945–1962 the Social Democrats and the Communists got about equal shares of the working-class vote, but in the most recent elections of March 1966 the Social Democratic vote surpassed the Communist. A total of 80 percent of those working-class voters who actually vote in the elections support either the Social Democrats or the Communists. Accordingly, one may say that class-based voting is high in Finland but it should be pointed out that class-based voting in itself is by no means something rare or unusual in the Scandinavian countries. This is clearly seen from Table 1, in which voting by social class in Finland and Sweden are compared.

There are some differences in the classifications used, and the table can hardly be used for very detailed comparison. However, if class-based voting is defined either by the proportion of working-class voters who vote for a working-class party or by the proportion of middle- and upper-class voters who do not vote for a working-class party, it is obvious that class-based voting is by no means higher in Finland than in Sweden. The most striking dif-

TABLE 1: *Party Preference by Social Class in National Samples in Finland Immediately after the Elections in 1966, and in Sweden Immediately after the Elections in 1964*

| Parties or Combination of Parties | Social Class by Occupation | | | | | | | |
|---|---|---|---|---|---|---|---|---|
| | Farmers | | Working Class | | Middle Class | | Upper Class | |
| | Finland (384) % | Sweden (297) % | Finland (652) % | Sweden (1397) % | Finland (232) % | Sweden (995) % | Finland (133) % | Sweden (160) % |
| Communists (in Finland in coalition with a small group of dissenting Social Democrats) | 7 | | 26 | 4 | 7 | 2 | 4 | |
| Social Democrats | 11 | 6 | 45 | 61 | 32 | 35 | 13 | 7 |
| Agrarians (in both Finland and Sweden called the Center Party) | 57 | 58 | 6 | 8 | 9 | 7 | 8 | 3 |
| Bourgeois parties | 16 | 25 | 12 | 11 | 49 | 40 | 73 | 77 |
| Nonvoters, or information lacking | 9 | 11 | 11 | 16 | 3 | 16 | 2 | 13 |
| TOTALS | 100 | 100 | 100 | 100 | 100 | 100 | 100 | 100 |

SOURCE: The Finnish data are from a poll by Finnish Gallup in April 1966. The Swedish data are from *Official Statistics of Sweden. The Elections to the Riksdag during the Years 1961–64*, Stockholm, 1965.

ference, however, is that the Communists are much stronger in Finland than in Sweden and that the working class in Finland is divided between a more radical and less radical alternative.

There are some findings about the effects of status crystallization on voting patterns in Finland, and it is instructive to contrast them with American data.[3] The American findings are not entirely consistent, but at least they suggest that there are several and distinct status dimensions in American society. It seems reasonable to assume that poor status crystallization under such circumstances will lead to dissatisfaction, withdrawal, and extremism. On the other hand, if dissatisfaction, withdrawal, etc. are found primarily among the highly crystallized, it can be taken as an indication of the fact that different status dimensions tend to merge into one. Accordingly, one may assume that the more dissatisfied the highly crystallized individuals, the more the stratification system tends to develop into a two-class situation.

In Finland, low status crystallization tends to make the Finnish worker support the Social Democrats, while the highly crystallized individuals both in the working and the middle class are more often politically passive. This is evident from Table 2, in which the party preferences of working- and middle-class (upper-class included) voters with high or low status crystallization are compared. In the working class, a status will be defined as highly crystallized only if an individual has no high-school education, an income less than 4,000 marks [about $1,000] per year, and a working-class father. In the middle and upper classes, a status is both high and highly crystallized only if the individual has at least a high-school education, an income larger than 4,000 marks per year, and a middle- or upper-class father.

Within both the working and the middle class low status crystallization is apt to increase the support for the Social Democrats. In Finnish politics today the Social Democrats represent a middle way between the Communists and the bourgeoisie. The picture we get is very different from the one which is presented in American studies. In Finland high status crystallization combined with low status is apt to increase the tendency to political radicalism, whereas high status crystallization combined with

TABLE 2: *Party Preference among Working- and Middle- (and Upper-) Class\* Voters, by Status Crystallization in a Finnish National Sample, 1958*

| Party Preference | Working Class | | Middle (& Upper) Class | |
|---|---|---|---|---|
| | *Highly Crystallized Status* (262) % | *Poorly Crystallized Status* (159) % | *Poorly Crystallized Status* (94) % | *Highly Crystallized Status* (39) % |
| Communists | 37 | 30 | 7 | |
| Social Democrats | 25 | 48 | 18 | 2 |
| Agrarians | 7 | 2 | 5 | 5 |
| Bourgeois (three parties) | 11 | 11 | 59 | 67 |
| No Preference | 20 | 9 | 11 | 26 |

\* Defined by occupation.

high status makes for conservatism. This is, at least to a certain extent, an indication of the tendency to class polarization in Finnish politics.

The results concerning status crystallization show that the Communists tend to be deprived more often than the Social Democrats. Survey data, moreover, indicate that Communist voters have a lower average income than Social Democratic voters even when the comparisons are restricted to the working class defined by occupation, as seen in Table 3.

The proportion of workers preferring the Communists clearly decreases when income increases. On the basis of the same data it can be shown that more Communist supporters have experienced unemployment than Social Democratic supporters. The same is true for education: the Social Democratic supporters have on the average a higher educational level.

It has been assumed in the foregoing that the Communists have a higher degree of class consciousness than the Social Democrats. This assumption corresponds to popular conceptions among Communists as well as among their opponents. The assumption is also in accordance with Marx's theory on working-

TABLE 3: *Party Preference by Yearly Income in the Working Class in a Finnish National Sample, 1958*

| Party Preference | Less than 2000 Marks (88) % | 2000 – 3999 Marks (152) % | 4000 – 5999 Marks (93) % | 6000 Marks or more (57) % | Don't know (31) % |
|---|---|---|---|---|---|
| Communists | 40 | 33 | 32 | 26 | 42 |
| Social Democrats | 28 | 28 | 49 | 44 | 13 |
| Agrarians | 2 | 10 | 2 | 4 | 6 |
| Bourgeois (three parties) | 13 | 11 | 8 | 16 | 10 |
| No preference | 17 | 18 | 9 | 10 | 29 |
| TOTALS | 100 | 100 | 100 | 100 | 100 |

class consciousness. The more all divisions such as occupation, education, wealth, etc., coincide, so that all lines of cleavage merge into one superimposed cleavage, the more class consciousness will be felt by the workers. Marx also clearly implies that class consciousness presupposes some kind of organization: the more the workers are organized, the more class conscious they are. Both conditions are well met by the Finnish Communists. They are well organized, and they are able to recruit voters among those who have a highly crystallized but low status. However, some additional information is needed about how class consciousness is actually felt.

In fact, it can be shown that the Social Democratic voters actually have a stronger sense of division into strata than the Communist voters. This was studied by asking the respondents to which one of the following three groups—farmers, workers, or white-collar—they felt they belonged.

According to Table 4, the Social Democratic voters classify themselves more often as workers than do the Communist voters. This is a reflection of the fact that the Communists get a heavy vote from small farmers who also work as lumbermen. Nevertheless, it is remarkable that a considerable portion of the Communist voters consider themselves farmers, not workers. However, some other types of questions reveal that the Communist voters have a higher sense of class consciousness than the Social Democratic voters. When asked what is wrong with Finnish society, the Communist respondents refer more often than the Social Democrats to inequalities of an economic nature.

A fuller understanding of working-class consciousness in Finland requires that regional variations be accounted for. Communist support is strongest in the poorer parts, notably in the northern and eastern parts of the country. This can be seen from Table 5, in which region and income have been cross-tabulated.

The Social Democrats have their strongest backing among high-income workers in the South and West and their weakest support among low-income workers in the North and East. The Communists have a stronger backing in the North and East than

TABLE 4: *Self-Identification with Social Strata, by Party Preference, in a Finnish National Sample, 1958*

| | Communists (178) % | Social Democrats (171) % | Agrarians (195) % | Bourgeois (181) % | No Preference (137) % |
|---|---|---|---|---|---|
| Farmers | 16 | 5 | 89 | 30 | 42 |
| Workers | 81 | 87 | 8 | 23 | 45 |
| Middle class | 2 | 8 | 3 | 42 | 12 |
| Don't know | 1 | | | 5 | 1 |

TABLE 5: *Party Preference by Income\* in the Working Class in the South and West and North and East in a Finnish National Sample, 1958*

| Party Preference | South and West | | North and East | |
|---|---|---|---|---|
| | Less than 4,000 Marks Yearly (150) % | More than 4,000 Marks Yearly (122) % | Less than 4,000 Marks Yearly (90) % | More than 4,000 Marks Yearly (28) % |
| Communists | 33 | 28 | 40 | 39 |
| Social Democrats | 33 | 50 | 21 | 36 |
| Agrarians | 4 | 2 | 11 | 7 |
| Bourgeois (three parties) | 14 | 11 | 7 | 7 |
| No Preference | 16 | 9 | 21 | 11 |
| TOTALS | 100 | 100 | 100 | 100 |

\* Workers with unknown income are not included in the table.

in the South and West. Actually very few workers belong to the higher income category in the North and East, where the majority of the working class lives in rural areas. Thus, Communism in Finland is partly a rural phenomenon.

Although the dividing line between the South and West and the North and East is drawn so that the northern and eastern half comprises about two-thirds of the total area of the country, the North and East have a much smaller population than the South and West. In 1958 the electoral districts in the South and West elected 126 members and the electoral districts in the North and East 74 members to the Parliament. Therefore, the Communists, in spite of their especially strong backing in the North and East, have more representatives in the Finnish Parliament (29 out of 50 in 1958) from the South and West than from the North and East.

## INSTITUTIONALIZED AND EXPRESSIVE RADICALISM: RESULTS BASED ON ECOLOGICAL ANALYSIS

A further scrutiny of the differences between the Communist support in different parts of the country yields results clearly related to the theme of the decline of ideology. The Communism in the southern and western parts of Finland is often labeled "Industrial Communism," whereas the Communism on the North and the East is known as "Backwood Communism." As the names suggest, Industrial Communism exists in regions which are industrialized and developed, whereas Backwood Communism is concentrated in less developed, rural regions. The problem here is to specify under what conditions Industrial and Backwood Communism are strong. Their background is of course different as regards the degree of industrialization in the communities in which these two forms of Communism exist, but the question is whether there are also other differences.

The social background of these two kinds of radicalism has been studied through both survey studies and ecological research. The data units in the ecological analyses have been the 550 communes in the country. The communes, both the rural and urban ones, are the smallest administrative units in Finland, and they have a certain amount of self-government. Mainly because of the long historical tradition of local self-government the communes form natural areas in the sense that they are important for people's self-identification. The communes are also the territorial units for which statistical data are easiest to obtain. In the analyses about 40 quantitative ecological variables referring to conditions in the communes in the 1950s were subjected to correlation and factor analysis.[4]

Since a single factor analysis is not always interesting—it gives just a structure or a conceptual framework—the communes were divided into five groups. For each of the groups of communes (hereafter also called communities) separate correlational and factor analyses were done. Of the five groups, three represented the more developed regions in southern and western Finland and two the more backward regions in northern and western Finland:

*Groups of developed communities*
1. Cities and towns
2. Rural communities with a Swedish-speaking population along the southern and western coast of Finland
3. Rural communities in southern and western Finland

*Groups of less developed communities*
4. Rural communes in eastern Finland
5. Rural communes in northern Finland

The intention of making separate analyses for the five different regions was to inquire whether Communist voting strength is explained by different or similar background factors in different regions.

The comparisons of the findings for the five regions reveal some quite consistent patterns. The background factors of Communist strength in the three developed regions are very similar, and so are the background factors in the two less developed regions. However, the background factors in Communist strength in the developed regions, on the one hand, and in the backward regions, on the other hand, seem to be very different.

In the developed regions the Communists are strong in communities in which:

1. Political traditions are strong. This is indicated mainly by the fact that the Communists tend to get a heavy vote in those communities in which there are stable voting patterns.

2. Economic change is comparatively slow. This is mainly indicated by the fact that communities with a strong Communist support have had a rather slow rise in per capita income during the 1950s. These communities were modernized and industrialized in an earlier period.

3. Social security is comparatively high. The communities with a heavy Communist vote are those in which there is no or very little unemployment and those in which the standard of housing is high.

4. Migration both into and out of the communities is small. The communities with a heavy Communist vote have a very stable population.

The foregoing are the conditions prevailing in those developed communities in which the Communists get a heavy vote. When focusing on the background factors of Communist strength in the less developed and more backward communities, a very different pattern is revealed. In the more backward communities the Communist vote is heavy when:

1. Traditional values, such as the religious ones, have recently declined in importance.

2. Economic change is rapid. In the backward regions the Communists are strong in those communities which have had a considerable rise in the per capita income during the 1950s and weak in those communities in which the income rise has been small.

3. Social insecurity prevails. Communities with Communist strength are those in which unemployment has been common. It

may be noted that unemployment in Finland is mainly a question of agrarian underemployment. Unemployment strikes those who are both small farmers and lumberjacks.

4. Migration is heavy. There is a heavy migration both into and out of the communities.

While Communist strength in the developed regions—the so-called Industrial Communism—seems to be associated with background factors reflecting stability, almost the contrary is true for Backwood Communism. It is strong under conditions of instability and change.[5]

Observations of particular strongholds in the developed and in the backward communities strongly support the results of the statistical analysis. The strongest Communist centers in the developed regions are towns which industrialized comparatively early. They are often towns in which one or a few shops completely dominate the community. Some of the communities voting most heavily Communist in rural Finland are located in Finland's northernmost province of Lapland. These communities are usually those in which there are many indications of a rapid modernization process.

In order to assess correctly the social background of Industrial and Backwood Communism it is important to observe also the background factors of the strength of the main competitors of the Communists. The Social Democrats are the competitors for the working-class vote in the more developed regions in southern and western Finland. In the backwoods of the North and East, however, the Agrarians are the ones who compete with the Communists for the lower-class vote. The data and the findings clearly indicate that the Social Democrats in the South and West and the Agrarians in the North and East are strong in clearly different communities than the Communists. In the developed regions the Social Democrats are strong in towns and industrial centers undergoing rapid change and having a high migration. In fact, workers who move from the countryside to the cities much more often vote Social Democratic than Communist. As has been shown, the Communists have their strength in communities with little migration. In the backward regions the Agrarians are strong in the most stable and the most traditional communities. There are strong indications that a Communist vote in the more backward regions is a symptom of modernization. A switch of the vote from the Agrarians to the Communists is also a switch from traditional, particularistic loyalties to a more universalistic form of political thinking. In northern and eastern Finland the breakdown of regional barriers and loyalties is clearly associated with a tendency to vote Communist.

All the results reported so far deal with Communist voting strength, with the 1954 Communist vote as the dependent variable. It is, however, interesting to compare these results with those we get if we focus instead on changes in the Communist vote over a period of time. The dependent variable in the analysis is now the change in the Communist vote from 1948 to 1958. During the period after World War II there has been some fluctuation in the Communist vote, although Finnish voting patterns are generally very stable. In 1948 the Communists got 20 percent of the total national vote, but in 1958 it amounted to 23.2 percent. In the overwhelming majority of the communities the Communist vote increased from 1948 to 1958. In any case, the dependent variable is a measure of the change in the Communist vote from 1948 to 1958, and it reflects mainly the amount of increase in the Communist vote.

The results indicate that the change, primarily the increase in the Communist vote from 1948 to 1958 in all regions, is explained by the same kind of factors which are also related to Backwood Communism. In all areas, including the developed ones, the Communist increase was largest in communes characterized by rapid social change, relatively high insecurity measured by the rates of unemployment and housing conditions, and a high amount of migration from one community to another. Of course, this result also means that the Communist increase from 1948 to 1958 in the developed regions most often occurred in communities in which the Communists did not earlier have a strong support. In the backward regions, by contrast, this increase most often occurs in communities in which the Communists earlier were strong.

The fact that increase in Communist strength is explained by the same background factors as Backwood Communism makes it reasonable to assume that the differences in the social background of Industrial and Backwood Communism constitute a special case of a more general pattern. The differences may be assumed to reflect differences generally found when comparing radicalism of new and old origin. If we want some more general terms than Industrial and Backwood Communism we could perhaps speak about *Traditional* and *Emerging Radicalism.*

There are additional grounds for regarding Backward Communism as being emergent in type. Before the Second World War the population in the backward communities in northern and eastern Finland had the lowest voting frequencies in the whole country. After World War II the population in the northern and eastern regions became politically conscious and mobilized. In fact, after World War II the highest voting frequencies are found among communities in the northern and eastern regions. It can be said that to a great extent this mobilization is due to Communist activity.

The two kinds of Communism here studied have been characterized by some general labels. At first the distinction between Industrial and Backwood Communism was introduced. They were considered to be special cases of two more general types, Traditional and Emerging Radicalism. The labeling could continue depending on what aspects the analysis is focused upon. The term "institutionalized and expressive radicalism" has been given as a title for this section of the paper because this term relates more or less directly to the theme of the decline of ideology. It can be shown that not only is the social background different for the two types of Communism but that they also stand for different kinds of political activity.

The relationship between the two forms of radicalism and the nature of political activity can be substantiated by at least three independent observations of the Finnish Communist movement:

1. The Communists in the developed communities in the southern and western parts of the country have an efficient organizational network. Studies of particular cities in the more developed parts of Finland reveal a network of Communist organizations which corresponds to the national network of all associations and voluntary organizations. The Communist network performs for its members the same social functions as the national network for citizens in general. There are women's clubs, sports associations, childrens' clubs, etc. The situation is on this count very different in the North and the East. It is true that the population in the northern and eastern parts of the country has become politically alert since World War II. This increase in the political consciousness is mainly displayed only during elections. It has not displayed itself as a general increase in social and intellectual participation. Communist support in the North and the East is concentrated in groups in which the opportunities for social and intellectual participation are slight. A nationwide study of youth activities shows that the young Communist voters in the North and East belong to the most passive in the country as far as general social participation is concerned.[6]

2. Many observations of the Communist centers in the developed regions of the South and West show that the Communist alternative in the elections is conventional and respectable. The Communist voters in these areas are well integrated in their communities and stable in their jobs. The population, and notably the Communist voters, in backward regions in the northern and eastern part of Finland are in an entirely different position. This is already clear from the settlement patterns in the North and East compared to the South and West. Whereas life in the latter region has been always much more village-centered, the houses and farms in the North and East have always been more isolated. Many of the Communist voters are small farmers who have to do forestry work in the winter. Unemployment in Finland has mainly the character of agrarian underemployment, and seasonal unemployment is particularly strong in those northern and eastern communities in which the Communist receive heavy support. Today work for the unemployed is provided by the

Government, but it means that the unemployed have to leave their homes and communities for long periods. In any case, whereas the Communist voters in the developed regions are strongly tied to their communities, the Communist supporters in the North and the East are much more migratory. This observation is also supported by the results from factor analysis in which much migration was characteristic of communities with a heavy Communist vote.

3. According to survey findings, the Communist voters in the more developed regions are the first to decide how to vote in elections. Among the Communist voters in the North and East, however, there is a very high proportion of voters who make their decision at the last minute. According to a national survey in 1958, as many as 82 percent of the Communist voters in the South and West have made their voting decisions at least two months before the elections, while only 56 percent of the Communist voters in the North and East made their decision at that early moment. The latter was the lowest percentage in all groups established on the basis of party and geographical area.

From these observations it can be concluded that Industrial Communism is a strongly institutionalized form of radicalism. Observers have often reported that Communism in some particular communities is a part of the cultural heritage. Sons take over the Communism of their fathers without very much debate and independent interest in ideology. In this sense the traditionalism and the institutionalized character of the Communism in the developed regions of Finland can rather clearly be taken as an indication of the decline of ideology. The expressive form of Communism existing in the northern and eastern parts of Finland is not strongly ideological in character. It is a protest movement but its protest is strongly related to actual hardships. It has been more emotional than ideological. This is confirmed by some observations according to which Backwood Communism in some areas in the North and East goes very well together with some religious, fundamentalist popular movements.

Accordingly, both the background of the Communist vote and the political activity displayed by the Communist supporters bear

witness to the same trend toward decline of ideology as has been
observed elsewhere.

## SUMMARY AND DISCUSSION

At the outset Finland was characterized as a deviant case with
many and specific qualifications. The strength of the Communist
movement in Finland can be taken as an indication of class conflict and ideological consciousness in Finnish politics. On the
other hand, it has been shown that both Finnish politics and the
Communist movement itself have displayed many of those characteristics which have been related to the decline of ideology.
Some of the most important findings can be summarized as follows:

1. Although class-based voting can be considered high in Finland, it is not higher than in the neighboring country of Sweden.

2. There are some signs that the Communists have become
more integrated into Finnish society. They are not disenfranchised. They are represented in the Cabinet and they have access
to political power. One of the most decisive factors in bringing
about this integration is a strong consensus regarding Finland's
foreign policy. In many respects this consensus represents a
clear-cut case of decline of ideology.

3. The Communist support is strongly related to regional differences. In some parts of Finland support for the Communists is
part of the cultural heritage.

4. It is indicated that there are strong traditional elements in
the Finnish Communism. Finnish Communism represents in
many respects an institutionalized form of radicalism.

On the other hand, as in other industrialized countries, the
New Left and the student activists have created a new wave of
ideological debate and interest. In 1969 the Finnish Communist
party was on the verge of becoming divided into two halves. The
opposition, which was in the minority, was the more radical and
demanded ideological revitalization in particular. The party

leadership, more liberal and committed to participation in the present coalition cabinet headed by a Social Democratic prime minister, was able to hold the majority. Student radicals who are members of the party generally support the opposition.

The new wave of ideological interest makes possible a kind of reappraisal of the hypothesis of the decline of ideology. It is apparent that to a large extent this ideological revitalization has occurred outside the institutionalized party organizations. It has influenced the general public debate in mass media, and it has produced a multitude of new publication outlets. In all political parties, not only among the Communists, youth has been on the march. They have not yet created complete new forms of party politics or brought about a breakdown of the institutionalized political life. In all parties, however, the young and their organizations have strongly irritated the older leadership. It is hard to predict how lasting this tendency is going to be. In any case, it seems reasonable to state that the hypothesis of the decline of ideology has been particularly true for party politics and party organizations. The ideological revitalization has occurred outside the institutionalized political organizations and channels. This leads at least to one specification of the theme of the decline of ideology. It has, by and large, contained a correct description of current party politics.

## NOTES

1. Ulf Himmelstrand, "A Theoretical and Empirical Approach to Depolitization and Political Involvement," special issue of *Acta Sociologica* 6 (1962) pp. 83–112, edited by Stein Rokkan.
2. S. M. Lipset, "The Changing Class Structure and Contemporary European Politics," *Daedalus,* 93:1 (Winter 1964), 271–303.
3. Status crystallization refers to the consistency with which an individual is ranked on various status criteria (such as income, education, social background). A person's status is highly crystallized if he is ranked uniformly and consistently (either high or low) on status criteria; one's status is poorly crystallized if one is ranked differently on different criteria. Thus, for example, a person with high (or low) income, high (or low) education, high (or low) social background has highly crystallized status, whereas one with high income and low education has poorly crystallized status.

4. The data are presented in E. Allardt, "Social Sources of Finnish Communism: Traditional and Emerging Radicalism," *International Journal of Comparative Sociology* V (1964), 49–72.

5. The theoretical implications of these differences have been worked out in E. Allardt, "Types of Protest and Alienation," E. Allardt and S. Rokkan (eds.), *Mass Politics: Studies in Political Sociology* (New York: Free Press, 1970), pp. 45–63.

6. Yrjö Littunen, "Aktiivisuus ja radikalismi," with an English Summary: "Activity and Radicalism," *Politiikka,* A Quarterly Published by the Finnish Political Science Association, 2:4 (1960), 182–183.

# 5 *The Netherlands: From Politics to Administration*

## A. HOOGERWERF

Is the era of political ideologies drawing to a close? In more concrete terms: are the differences in outlook of the Dutch political parties fading?

There are writers who answer these questions more or less affirmatively.[1] Their thesis is largely that, to cite P. Thoenes, while discussion on the nature and degree of the spread of prosperity still continues, it has shifted to the technical plane of the optimum choice at a given moment. "The struggle, if such there is, is no longer waged around the nature of the system, but around the application of one generally recognized system. The political and economic differences which are dusted off at election time are in practice very much a matter of technical insight and investment tables. The old opponents have become recon-

A. Hoogerwerf, "Latent Socio-Political Issues in the Netherlands," *Sociologia Neerlandica,* II (Summer 1965), 161–77.

ciled in many fields. On the strength of a jointly recognized system a policy acceptable to all can be devised."[2]

In keeping with this view is the expectation of J. Zijlstra, S. W. Couwenberg, and others that in one way or another modern socialism and modern liberalism will eventually follow the same course.[3]

Prompted by these challenging statements, we shall try here to find the answer to the following question: to what extent have the differences between the views of the political movements in the Netherlands, especially those concerning social and economic policy, diminished in the postwar period?

## THE DUTCH POLITICAL PARTIES

This article discusses views held by the four largest Dutch political parties:

1. The Catholic People's Party *(Katholieke Volkspartij;* KVP for short). In the last elections in 1963 this party won almost 32 percent of the votes and is now the strongest party both in the Cabinet and in Parliament. Its votes come from Catholics from every class of society.

2. The Labour Party *(Partij van de Arbeid;* PvdA), which is moderately socialist and receives support from every religious and social category, though its strongest support, comparatively speaking, comes from the lower income groups. It has been the largest opposition party (almost 28 percent of the votes in 1963) since 1959.

3. The Liberal Party *(Volkspartij voor Vrijheid en Democratie;* VVD). It received over 10 percent of the votes in 1963. Its supporters are most numerous among undogmatic Protestants and those affiliated to no church, especially those in the higher income brackets.

4. The Antirevolutionary Party *(Antirevolutionaire Partij;* ARP). This Protestant party owes its name to the nineteenth-century opposition to the philosophy of the French Revolution

of 1789. Its votes come above all from Calvinists of various denominations and every class of society. Since 1948 its share of the votes has gradually declined from 13.2 percent to 8.7 percent.

The Cabinet has been composed since 1959 of members of the KVP, the VVD, the ARP, and the Christian-Historical Union *(Christelijk-Historische Unie;* CHU). The last party, which won over 8.5 percent of the votes in 1963, differs little from the Antirevolutionary Party as regards its objectives, but is less dogmatic and finds its support mainly in the largest Protestant Church, the Netherlands Reformed Church.

Five smaller parties represented in Parliament but not in the Cabinet are the extremely orthodox Protestant Political Reformed Party *(Staatkundig Gereformeerde Partij;* SGP), the left-wing Pacifist Socialist Party *(Pacifistisch-Socialistische Partij;* PSP), the Communist Party *(Communistische Partij Nederland;* CPN), the Farmers Party *(Boerenpartij),* and the highly dogmatic Reformed Political League *(Gereformeerd Politiek Verbond).*

## RESEARCH TECHNIQUES

The research techniques used for this article are a systematic comparative analysis of election programs (a largely unexplored field) and an analysis of information acquired from a survey.

In the Netherlands a distinction is made between a party's election program (listing among other things its objectives for a four-year parliamentary period), its constitution (containing the main principles of the party), its general political program (its objectives for a period longer than four years), its provincial program, and its municipal program.

We shall confine ourselves here to the election programs. One reason for this restriction is that all election programs have been repeatedly renewed in the last fifteen years, while a number of constitutions have remained unchanged. A second reason is that the election program is worth analyzing, since it is important in that it requires the party concerned to reflect on its principles and on everyday political reality; it is the basis of the party's electoral campaign; it plays a part in the formation of the Cabinet; and it is the compass by which the parliamentary parties set their course.[4]

This article will deal only with the election program of 1948 and 1963. An analysis of the programs of the intervening years would require too much space.[5]

The survey data incorporated in this article are a by-product of an investigation which we carried out in Delft in April 1962. The sample that we were then required to use in connection with the object of the investigation was not one that accurately reflects the political make-up of the local population. But the relation found between adherence to specific parties and a number of social and political views is interesting enough to warrant some further account.

## EXTENT OF GOVERNMENT RESPONSIBILITY

Three points require special attention as regards views on the ideal extent of government responsibility: firstly, the relation between public and private ownership (the question of nationalization); secondly, the relation between public and private powers (a planned economy); and thirdly, the relation between public and private spending (the question of the tax burden).

For many years the differences of opinion on the ideal extent of government responsibility in the social and economic field were most marked on the question of nationalization. After 1945, however, the matter of a planned economy moved into the center of attention. In recent years the accent has shifted again, this time toward the question of the tax burden.

The election programs reveal that the parties' views have become closer as regards nationalization (on which the PvdA has taken an increasingly moderate line) and as regards a planned economy (the non-socialist parties have come to think somewhat more positively about this form of state activity). But the PvdA and the non-socialist parties still differ fundamentally in their views on taxation.

The 1948 PvdA program still called for nationalization of the coal mines, of the public utilities, and of all undertakings where such a step would be in the public interest. The 1963 manifesto goes nothing like as far; it advocates greater government influence in industry and commerce, nationalization of the insurance companies and guarantees of vigorous government influence in the energy sector being two of the measures it recommends as a means of achieving that end.

Despite this socialist moderation there is still a considerable difference between the PvdA and the other parties regarding the relation between public and private ownership. The VVD, for instance, called in its 1963 priority program for a transfer from public to private ownership of all undertakings where the need for government participation has disappeared. The KVP wants certain state property to be transferred to the private sector, provided that a sufficiently wide distribution of the latter is guaranteed by setting up, for instance, special investment funds for small savers. The ARP advocates a critical attitude toward that section of industry commerce which is in government hands and, where this is warranted, restriction of the size of that sector.

In 1948 the PvdA stressed the need for a planned economy at least as much as nationalization. Its program demanded public supervision and direction of the national economy, the drafting of both annual and long-term concrete plans and their submission to the States-General (the Dutch Parliament). In 1963 the PvdA apparently considered part of this target to have been met, and part to be no longer attractive. However, it still called for long-term economic planning, but with regard to wage policy, for instance, it now put the responsibility of social organizations first. The most recent socialist manifesto places the main emphasis on neither public powers nor public ownership, but on public expenditure. It states that the increasing production of goods and services must be directed more toward communal provisions, on which the welfare of the population is just as dependent as on the possibilities of private consumption. The term "communal provisions" proves to refer in particular to social provisions, housing, education, transport, and public health. In accordance with this emphasis on public expenditure, the socialist manifesto calls for "taxation keyed to the tasks of the future."

And what about the VVD? Its attitude to public powers in the social and economic field is obviously a more positive one now than before. In 1948 its program still reflected the strongly held conviction that government intervention in commerce and business should be drastically reduced. Nowadays it is still in favor of the further development of free wage determination and restoration of free price determination, but with the government retaining the right to intervene by means of a wage pause, a wage freeze, or the imposition of a temporary check on price increases. The expression "anticyclical policy" has a positive sound in the new liberal manifesto.

It is more reserved with regard to structural policy. According to its manifesto, the main difference between liberalism and socialism is nowadays to be found in their dissimilar views on the relation between collective and individual provisions. It is certainly not true to say that the liberals reject collective provisions. On the contrary, they are convinced that such provisions are essential if all members of the population are to be assured of a decent existence. But the liberals are opposed to "collective provisions being allowed to predominate to such an extent that insufficient scope is left for individual responsibility." The VVD is accordingly of the opinion that in making use of the opportunities created by the anticyclical policy in the present-day budget top priority should be given to the "urgently required reduction in wage and income tax for the middle categories."

The KVP and the ARP are closer to the liberals than to the socialists in their views on public powers and public expenditure. It is true that the former makes an obscurely worded plea for the adaptation of social and public provisions to changing needs, the means available, and priorities. But in the same program it states that taxation should be reduced.

The Antirevolutionary Party has also begun to think more positively about public powers, though not about public expenditure, since 1948. Its 1948 program was still in favor of "a government policy that vigorously upholds the distinction between State and Society (government and business) in order to avoid state control and state socialism, the most dangerous threat of our times." The government had to give a certain amount of guidance to economic life, but the system of a planned, fixed economy had to be rejected. In 1963 the AR program recognized "the important function of the national economy in meeting collective wants." But it is also of the opinion that policy must continue to be directed in a responsible and systematic manner toward changing the ratio between government expenditure and private spending in favor of the latter.

It is thus apparent that the PvdA and the three other parties still differ fundamentally in their respective views on the ratio between public and private expenditure. It is possible that their views on this point, as well as those on public ownership and public powers, will converge more in the future.

## SOCIAL PROVISIONS

The views of the four parties under discussion regarding social security have become much more similar over the past fifteen years. A number of what were at first controversial objectives (general provisions for the aged, the unemployed, widows and orphans, and large families) have been attained. Moreover, they show signs of agreement on various other objectives (increased old-age pensions, stable-value pensions, introduction of a disability pension, the General Assistance Act, and the introduction of national insurance against heavy medical expenses).

Fifteen years ago the struggle was fought out around national insurance as such; now it is concerned with the further development of the system. In 1948 the PvdA, for instance, was still advocating the introduction of a social security system covering the entire population, i.e. self-employed persons as well. In 1963 the party included in its platform partial financing of social security out of general revenue and revision of the incidence of social security contributions in favor of the lower income groups.

A shift of emphasis among the liberals is worthy of note in this respect. They are now more sympathetic toward social legislation. In 1948 the VVD declared itself in favor of the soundest possible guarantee of the legal position of every member of society, but "without the individual sense of responsibility being undermined." The 1963 manifesto stated that the liberals are endeavouring to "remove the social causes of inequality among the members of the population with regard to their prospects for development." This was taken more or less literally, without mention of the source, from the constitution drawn up in 1901 by the Liberal Democratic League (Vrijzinnig-Democratische Bond), in those days the organized left wing of liberalism. It stated that "efforts should be made by means of vigorous social legislation to remove the social causes or aggravations of inequality among the members of the population with regard to their prospects for development."

No concrete plans for social provisions were to be found in the 1948 liberal priority program. Its 1963 program, on the other hand, included raising the old-age pension to a socially acceptable minimum as the growing prosperity allows; introduction of a system of stable-value staff and works pension funds and government pensions; introduction of a disability pension for employed persons.

## DISTRIBUTION OF INCOME

The social provisions discussed above may be regarded as an aspect of the distribution of income. For social provisions imply that the state transfers part of the income of working persons to those who are temporarily or permanently unable to support themselves (the aged, the unemployed, widows and orphans, large families, pensioners, invalids, the sick, persons having to bear heavy medical expenses, and others).

As the system of social security approaches completion, interest grows in another aspect of the distribution of income: the differences within the very large category of persons who are able to support themselves by work. There are two issues here, firstly the permissible degree of inequality (in brief the difference between high and low incomes in general) and secondly the criteria of an unequal distribution of income (work performed, wants, sex, marital status, place of residence).

First, something about these criteria. In recent years the political parties have come to adopt the attitude that in the community today one's place of residence is no longer an acceptable criterion of the distribution of income. Abolition of the system whereby municipalities are classified in different grades with differential rates of pay for their employees, etc., is an almost universal wish. Equal pay for men and women is also generally advocated.

This cannot be said of marital status as a criterion of the distribution of income. The VVD wants a further reduction in the difference in incidence of taxation for married and single persons and the ARP also stresses the tax burden borne by unmarried persons. The KVP, on the other hand, wants a revision of the tax system which takes into account the party's views regarding large families.

There is still a fundamental difference of opinion about the general criteria of the work performed and the needs of the person concerned and, in this connection, about the permissible degree of inequality as regards incomes.

In its 1948 program the PvdA called for unremitting special attention for the groups with the lowest incomes and for maintenance of the subsidies on the necessities of life as long as necessary. In line with this was the party's desire for a systematic use of tax policy to foster a more uniform development of the national income. For instance, the PvdA advocated among other things a tax on extraordinary export profits and extension of the luxury tax.

The socialists extended this line in 1963. Groups still living at the subsistence level should, according to the manifesto, profit more from the general rise in prosperity. The available scope for improving conditions of employment should be used in part to step up the lowest wages. The rapid growth of high incomes should, on the other hand, be checked.

The 1948 liberal priority plan called for taxation in accordance with the ability to bear it and did not concern itself further with the differences in income; in other words, maintenance of the existing inequality. In 1963, on the other hand, the liberal policy was clearly directed toward further differentiation, i.e. increasing the existing inequality. The liberals stated in their manifesto that they wish to give top priority to a reduction of wage and income tax for the middle categories. In the priority program this is put into concrete terms as a reduction of the progression.

In its 1948 program the KVP still largely confined itself with regard to the income structure to taxation based on the ability to pay. In 1963 the accent was more on reducing the inequality. In the distribution of the national income it demanded special attention for the less well-off and in particular for raising the wages of the lowest-paid categories.

In the ARP, too, an increasing inclination to reduce the differences in income may be observed. In 1948 the action program did not yet include the distribtuion of income as such. The 1963 program stated that social policy should be directed among other things toward "ensuring, as far as the government is authorized to do so, that the national income accrues in an equitable manner to the various sections of the population. In particular, the minimum earned and other incomes should be increased."

To sum up, the liberals have shown an increasing tendency to enhance the differences between high and low incomes since 1948, whereas the other three parties have grown steadily more inclined to reduce those differences. The denominational parties are particularly in favor of achieving this by raising minimum incomes, while the socialists (more than the denominational parties) also aim at keeping the highest incomes in check.

We shall now consider a number of survey data.

The party support reflected in the tables was determined by the question: "For which political party do you feel the greatest sympathy?"

TABLE 1: *Party Support and Views on the Distribution of Income. "Do You Think the Differences between High and Low Incomes Should Become Greater, Smaller, or Remain as They Are?"*

| | Smaller % | Remain % | Greater % | No opinion % | Total % | Abs. |
|---|---|---|---|---|---|---|
| PvdA | 69 | 27 | 1 | 3 | 24 | 213 |
| KVP | 58 | 33 | 7 | 2 | 18 | 165 |
| VVD | 26 | 43 | 19 | 12 | 13 | 121 |
| ARP | 51 | 41 | 5 | 3 | 21 | 194 |
| CHU | 53 | 41 | 1 | 5 | 11 | 102 |
| SGP | 54 | 46 | | | 2 | 13 |
| PSP | 61 | 39 | | | 2 | 18 |
| CPN* | 33 | | | 67 | | 3 |
| No party | 51 | 35 | 7 | 7 | 8 | 71 |
| No opinion or more than one party | 42 | 25 | 25 | 8 | 1 | 12 |
| TOTAL | 53 | 36 | 6 | 5 | 100 | 912 |

* Less than 1% of the respondents.

Table 1 shows that with regard to views on the income structure there are obvious differences between the supporters of the PvdA and those of the VVD. Of the PvdA supporters questioned, 69 percent think the differences in income should be smaller, but only 26 percent of those sympathizing with the VVD favor this. On the other hand, 19 percent of the VVD supporters wish the differences in income to become *greater,* as against no more than 1 percent of the PvdA backers. In this respect the denominational parties occupy a position between the liberals and the socialists.

On this point our data display a remarkable similarity to the results of a poll held by the Netherlands Institute for Public

Opinion (the NIPO) among a random sample of Dutch families and single persons in August 1962. They were asked: "Do you consider the differences among incomes in this country too great? Or about right? Or too small?" In this survey the differences in income were adjudged too great by 66 percent of the PvdA supporters, 60 percent of the KVP supporters, 28 percent of the VVD supporters, 45 percent of the ARP supporters, and 50 percent of the CHU supporters.[6]

## THE DISTRIBUTION OF PROPERTY

What views are held on this point and, more especially, how is the difference between large private fortunes and slender purses regarded?

All political parties have been striving for more than fifteen years to reduce the inequality in private property. But on this point too there is a considerable clash of opinion. While the liberal and denominational parties choose the method of the creation of property (increasing small property), the socialists are also in favor of the diffusion of property (reducing large property or at least its growth).

In 1948 the PvdA advocated a systematic use of tax policy to further a more equitable distribution of the national wealth. It therefore desired among other things the reintroduction of progression in property tax and an increase of death duties on large fortunes. In 1963 the socialist program continued along those lines; the rapid growth of large fortunes was to be checked and the workers' share in the growth of the national wealth was to be enlarged. In this connection the party called for a system of compulsory profit-sharing among employees, introduction of a tax on private capital gains, increased death duties on large fortunes, and a tax on the increment value of land.

The liberals—whose 1948 priority program made no mention of the property structure—stated in 1963 that they were in favor of anything that might make it easier for every member of every section of the population to acquire property of his own. They find therefore that the Government will have to foster a climate conducive to the accumulation of property. The tax system will also have to be brought into line. In this context the VVD is in favor of fiscal regulations which further the payment by limited companies of share bonuses to their employees. But against this is the fact that the party rejects every form of capital gains tax, and likewise the levying of income tax on the increment value of agricultural land.

In its 1948 election program the KVP was the first to put forward a plea for "undertaking the creation of property (a home of one's own, etc.) for the mass of the Dutch people." In 1963 it argued that more people ought to be given the opportunity of accumulating personal property, especially by means of wage determination. A certain degree of unanimity between the KVP and the PvdA may be observed here. But matters change when the KVP program also proves to embrace the following: abolition of the tax on personal property and rentals and the real estate tax; a drastic reduction in death duties in the case of inheritance by lineal descendants and between husband and wife, and also the limiting of the joint sum of income and property tax to what is in the circumstances a reasonable maximum percentage. If these plans are compared with those regarding the accumulation of property, a contradiction appears: leveling on the one hand, unleveling on the other. Presumably different wings or at least different experts of the party are having their say here.

In 1948 the ARP program included furthering to an increasing extent possession by the whole people of material goods. In 1963 the party translated this into concrete terms as the continued fostering of the accumulation of private property, by among other things profit-sharing. The compulsory profit-sharing advocated by the PvdA does not, however, appear on the ARP program, any more than it does on the KVP and liberal programs.

To sum up, the socialists' wishes regarding modification of the property structure go considerably further than those of the other parties, especially those of the liberals.

This conclusion, which is based on a comparison of the election programs, is confirmed by the survey data (see Table 2).

TABLE 2: *Party Support and Views on the Distribution of Property. "Some People Own a Great Deal and Others Own Less. Do You Think This Difference Should Become Greater, Smaller, or Remain as It Is?"*

| | Smaller % | Remain % | Greater % | No opinion % | Total % | Abs. |
|---|---|---|---|---|---|---|
| PvdA | 62 | 31 | 1 | 6 | 24 | 213 |
| KVP | 55 | 38 | 3 | 4 | 18 | 165 |
| VVD | 23 | 62 | 6 | 9 | 13 | 121 |
| ARP | 37 | 52 | 1 | 10 | 21 | 194 |
| CHU | 37 | 57 | | 6 | 11 | 102 |
| SGP | 38 | 54 | | 8 | 2 | 13 |
| PSP | 67 | 33 | | | 2 | 18 |
| CPN* | 33 | 34 | | 33 | | 3 |
| No party | 38 | 51 | 4 | 7 | 8 | 71 |
| No opinion or more than one party | 50 | 25 | 17 | 8 | 1 | 12 |
| TOTAL | 45 | 46 | 2 | 7 | 100 | 912 |

* Less than 1% of the respondents.

Of the PvdA supporters, 62 percent wish the differences in property to become smaller, a desire shared by only 23 percent of the VVD supporters. On the other hand, 6 percent of the VVD supporters are in favor of an increase in the differences in property, as against 1 percent of the PvdA supporters. The denominational parties again occupy a position in between the liberals and the socialists.

## BALANCE OF POWER IN INDUSTRY

The views of the four parties under discussion may be concluded to have grown somewhat closer together in the last fifteen years as regards copartnership in industry. The liberals and the KVP, however, want much less sweeping changes than do the socialists and the ARP, to judge at least by their programs.

The 1948 PvdA program provided for copartnership by the institution of works councils. In 1963—after the Works Council Act had been in force for thirteen years, but did not function to everyone's satsifaction—the party called for increased responsibility and wider authority for the works councils. Further means of democratizing the supervision of large firms as listed by the socialists consisted of inclusion on the boards of directors of representatives from wider circles than is the case today, extension of the obligation of business concerns to publish details of their operations and the institution of a chamber of corporations.

The liberals did not include copartnership in their 1948 priority program. In 1963 they expressed a number of moderate wishes on this point. For instance, they called for more real consultation on important matters, including those of an economic nature, to take place, if possible, in the works councils. They believed that this could lead to a significant form of copartnership

TABLE 3: *Party Support and Views on Copartnership. "Do You Think the Copartnership of the Workers in Industry Should Become Greater, Remain as It Is, or Become Smaller?"*

|  | Greater % | Remain % | Smaller % | No opinion % | Total % | Abs. |
|---|---|---|---|---|---|---|
| PvdA | 68 | 24 | 2 | 6 | 24 | 213 |
| KVP | 55 | 33 | 3 | 9 | 18 | 165 |
| VVD | 21 | 49 | 18 | 12 | 13 | 121 |
| ARP | 46 | 43 | 6 | 5 | 21 | 194 |
| CHU | 47 | 42 | 3 | 8 | 11 | 102 |
| SGP | 38 | 62 |  |  | 2 | 13 |
| PSP | 78 | 22 |  |  | 2 | 18 |
| CPN* | 100 |  |  |  |  | 3 |
| No Party | 35 | 38 | 13 | 14 | 8 | 71 |
| No opinion or more than one party | 58 | 17 | 8 | 17 | 1 | 12 |
| TOTAL | 49 | 37 | 6 | 8 | 100 | 912 |

* Less than 1% of the respondents.

which would foster mutual understanding and greater cooperation between employers and employees. In other words, they
were in favor of a small step in the direction of the socialist point
of view. This also applies to another item on the liberal program: reinforcing and extending the legal requirements with
which the reports published by limited companies must comply.
It is incidentally worthy of note that measures were called for to
protect shareholders against the consequences of unsound management but that such endeavors with regard to employees were
absent.

In its 1948 program, the KVP aimed at the introduction of
copartnership in industry, as a result of which, while the employer remained in charge, labor could stand side by side with
capital instead of beneath it. In 1963 the party was more reserved on this point. It now said: "as the cultural emancipation
of the workers draws nearer to realization, their copartnership in
the various fields of social life will have to assume an active form.
Partly for this reason . . . the responsibility of the workers will
also have to be reflected in company law." In concrete terms the
KVP was now demanding extension and reinforcement of the
works councils. It also advocated a study of the desirability of
supplementing the statutory regulation of the private form of undertaking by rules for the limited company with an extended
purpose, i.e. extended to "the pursuit of profit and the welfare of
those participating in the undertaking."

The ARP, which in 1948 called for works councils with a
mainly advisory function, later adopted a more radical point of
view with regard to copartnership. It found that the possibility of
allowing the personnel to exert their influence in the undertaking's policy should be utilized via further statutory regulations.
Election of a number of the directors by the personnel was cited
as an example.

Going by the election programs, it may be stated that the
ARP's views on copartnership are now closer to those of the
PvdA than to those of the VVD and the KVP. The survey data
present a somewhat different picture on this point (see Table
3).

Of the PvdA supporters questioned, 68 percent want the co-partnership of the workers in industry to become greater, as against only 21 percent of the VVD supporters. Reduction of co-partnership is desired by 18 percent of the VVD supporters, as against 2 percent of the PvdA supporters. The denominational parties once again occupy a position between the liberals and the socialists.

## CONCLUSIONS AND SUPPOSITIONS

The data analyzed above allow of the following conclusions.

1. Comparison of the 1948 and the 1963 election programs of the KVP, the PvdA, the VVD, and ARP reveals a growing unanimity on a number of socio-political issues, viz. nationalization, a planned economy, and social [welfare] provisions.

2. As regards other socio-political issues (the differences in income, the differences in property, copartnership, and the tax burden), the socialist and liberal election programs still clash fundamentally. The programs of the KVP and the ARP are mostly half way between liberalism and socialism on these points.

3. With regard to differences in income, property, and copartnership, the views of the majority of socialist and liberal party supporters questioned in a survey also proved to differ considerably. The KVP and the ARP again occupy an intermediate position.

It is a most remarkable fact that the socio-political differences regarding the distribution of income and property and the economic balance of power, as manifested in the election programs and the views of party supporters, received relatively little attention in the controversies between the De Quay cabinet (1959–1963) and the socialist opposition, in the campaign for the last general election and in the cabinet formation.[7]

In other words, the socio-political points of dispute are reflected less clearly in the policy of the political leaders than in the election programs and in the views of party supporters. Couwenberg, Thoenes, and Zijlstra, who were to a certain extent right in pointing to a blurring of socio-political issues, have over-estimated this blurring by paying more attention to the policy of the political leaders than to the views of party supporters.

The fact that political contrasts blur more at the top than at the base is probably due largely to the technocratic nature of the present-day political élite. Among the political leaders a shift is occurring from policy decisions to administrative decisions, i.e. from the choice of ends to the choice of means.[8] A striking instance of this was the opposition policy of the PvdA against the De Quay cabinet. The opposition launched its attacks less against the objectives of the cabinet than the means chosen, less against the main lines of policy than the technical ability (or inability) of some ministers. The same holds good, *mutatis mutandis,* for the discussions in the election campaign and around the cabinet formation.

How does all this affect our interpretation of the election results?

The electors' behavior is bound up with three groups of factors. In the first place there is the changing social structure, as for instance urbanization, the increasing prosperity, the growth of the new middle classes, the extension of higher education, and the change in the birth rate. Secondly, there are the cultural changes, in which religious views are of particular importance. Finally we have the political factors, which are no whit less important than the others.

As regards those political factors which are connected with the electors' behavior, the central question is the extent to which the electorate regards a certain party as a suitable means of achieving a given end. This is the connection between the political issues and the party image. The most favorable electoral position is occupied by that party which is regarded by the greatest number of electors as the most suitable means of achieving their political objectives, in other words, the party whose image is most in harmony with the issues.

A few examples follow by way of illustration.[9] Part of the reason why the denominational parties did well in 1948 is because in that year issues such as the struggle against communism, the policy toward Indonesia, the planned economy, and fear of a third world war played a major part. The decline of the denominational parties since 1948 is linked up with the increasing interest in such matters as wages and prices, full employment and social [welfare] provisions.

Though nothing has been proved on this point, we surmise that a relatively larger number of electors regarded the controversy around commercial television, atomic armament, and the Agricultural Board as the main issues of the 1963 general election. The proponents of unilateral disarmament will have been inclined to consider the PSP a suitable means. Opponents of unilateral disarmament will have been drawn to the denominational parties or the VVD. The image of the PvdA, which passed a majority vote against unilateral disarmament but at the same time tolerated the supporters of this policy in its midst, was not clear on this point. Similar assumptions can also be made with regard to commercial television and the Agricultural Board.

It is not unlikely that the election results would have been quite different if the distribution of income and of property and copartnership had been the central issues. Would this have been possible? To qualify as an issue in an election campaign, a political question must satisfy two requirements: the electors must have alternative objectives and the parties must be capable of being regarded as alternative means of achieving those objectives. As regards the socio-political differences on the distribution of income and property and copartnership, the first requirement was probably met more fully than the second one in the last elections. The policy of the political leaders was less obviously in conflict on these matters than were the election programs and the views of the party supporters.

The socio-political fire smolders underground like a peat moor fire which can unexpectedly burst out into the open.[10] It is all connected in some way with the social distance between leaders and followers or, in other words, with "political alienation." A number of investigators have demonstrated that political alienation is conducive to movement such as McCarthyism and Poujadism, which operate outside or against our democratic institutions.[11]

NOTES

1. Foreign literature: R. Aron, 'Fin de l'Age ideologique?' (The End of the Ideological Era?), in *Sociologica* (Frankfurt, 1955); D. Bell, *The End of Ideology: On the Exhaustion of Political Ideas in the Fifties* (Glencoe, 1960); O. Brunner, 'Das Zaitalter der Ideologien' (The Age of Ideologies), in *Neue Wegeder Sozialgeschichte* (Göttingen, 1956); S. M. Lipset, "The End of Ideology?" in *Political Man* (London, 1960); G. Vedel *et al.*, *La Dépolitisation: mythe ou réalité* (Depolitization: Myth or Reality; Paris, 1962). Dutch literature: S. W. Couwenberg, *Het Nederlandse partijstelsel in toekomstperspectief* (The Dutch Party System: Prospects for the Future; The Hague, 1960); P. Thoenes, *De elite in de verzorgingsstaat* (The Elite in the Welfare State; Leiden, 1962); J. Zijlstra, *Economische orde en economische politiek* (Economic Order and Economic Policy; Leiden, 1956); cf. also by the present author: *Ontwikkelingen in de Nederlandse politieke partijen* (Developments in the Dutch Political Parties; The Hague, 1961).
2. P. Thoenes, *op. cit.*, pp. 143, 144
3. S. W. Couwenberg, *op. cit.*, pp. 40 and 132.
4. E. Meester in the foreword to the PvdA's 1963 election manifesto.
5. The 1948 election programs may be found in the *Parlement en Kiezer* (Parliament and Elector) year books, XXXII and XXXIII.
6. See H. Daudt and H. Lange, '63% van de gezinnen in Nederland meent: er heerst welvaart in het eigen gezin' (63 percent of Dutch Families Consider Themselves Well-off), *Ariadne* XVIII (1963) No. 7, pp. 359–366.
7. This article was written before the cabinet was formed.
8. P. Thoenes, *op. cit.*, pp. 153–159.
9. J. J. de Jong, *Overheid en Onderdaan* (The State and its Subjects; Wageningen, 1956), pp. 207–212.
10. Cf. S. M. Lipset's remark: "The democratic class struggle will continue, but it will be a fight without ideologies, without red flags, without May Day parades" *(Political Man)*, pp. 407–408.
11. W. Kornhauser, *The Politics of Mass Society* (London, 1960), pp. 7, 228, 237.

# 6 *The United States: Politics of Affluence*

## ROBERT E. LANE

Marx is surely right when he says that the way men earn their living shapes their relations to each other and to the state; but this is, of course, only the beginning. Aside from all the other noneconomic factors which also have these effects, there is the matter of the *source* of income, the *level* of income, and, especially, the *security* of income. Moreover, each of these factors has both an individual effect, a set of influences apparent in the study of individual enrichment or immiseration, and a social effect, the influences which appear when whole societies become richer or more secure economically. So I am led to inquire into what is happening to men's political interests, behavior, and attitudes toward politics and government in an Age of Affluence, a period when men's economic security and income have increased and when, for the first time in history, it appears likely

Robert E. Lane, "The Politics of Consensus in an Age of Affluence," *American Political Science Review,* 59:4 (December 1965), 874–895.

that the business cycle can now be controlled. Like Marx's, my interest is in change over time.

Quite candidly, this is a descriptive account of attitudinal change in recent years, portrayed against a background of economic change. Only argument supports the inference that it is the economic change—implied in the term "Age of Affluence" shortly to be explicated—that is accountable for much of the attitudinal change. It would take another paper with closer attention to subsections of the population and specific economic conditions to establish this argument on a firmer footing. In the meantime, perhaps these findings can help illuminate the more general problem of the relationship between economic development and stable and effective politics, as well as to help us to see where American politics is heading.

The elements of the economy which are most relevant to such an investigation are fivefold, and the term "affluent society"[1] or "Age of Affluence" refers here to more than higher per capita national income, though it includes that. The term embraces: (1) a relatively high per capita national income; (2) a relatively equalitarian distribution of income; (3) a "favorable" rate of growth of per capita Gross National Product (GNP); (4) provisions against the hazards of life—that is, against sickness, penury, unemployment, dependence in old age, squalor—the features now associated with the term "welfare state"; and (5) a "managed economy" in the sense of conscious and more or less successful governmental use of fiscal and monetary powers to smooth out the business cycle and avoid depressions, as well as to provide for the economic growth mentioned in (3) above. These five points include both economic conditions and governmental policies.

The appropriateness of the term "affluent society" or "Age of Affluence" rests upon intercultural and chronological comparisons; but in making these comparisons it is important to remember that an affluent society may still include a large number of very poor people: the average income of the poorest fifth of the families (consumer units) in the United States in 1962 was $1,662 and this had to provide for a little over three people, on the average.[2] The term "affluence," however, is clearly relative both to other societies and previous periods. On the first point, comparison with other societies:

1. The United States ranked second (out of 122 countries) in GNP per capita (Kuwait was the first) in 1957, with no other country even a close competitor.[3]

2. According to one measure of "inequality of income distribution before taxes," the United States ranks about 7th in equality of income distribution. (Four British Commonwealth countries and India, for different reasons, are somewhat more equalitarian.)[4]

3. Although until the last few years the annual increase of GNP was lower in the United States than in most developed and many developing countries (in Russett's volume, the United States is about 45th out of 68 countries), recently this has changed and the rate in the United States 1962–65 is about the same as in the Common Market countries.[5]

4. Although relatively less extensive than in most European countries, the American welfare programs, now that medicare has been enacted, compare favorably in coverage and especially in absolute level of support with contemporary European programs.

5. With the possible exception of Italy, no European or developed Commonwealth country has suffered a recession (after the postwar reconstruction period) with anything like the depth or duration of the depressions of the twenties and thirties. This is also true of the United States, as we shall see below.

But our main interest here lies, not in comparative economics and politics, but in changing patterns in the United States. Were we not always an *Affluent Society, a People of Plenty,*[6] bothered by the question *"Abundance for What?"*[7] Relative to other nations, perhaps! But the modern era is different from previous eras in several important and relevant ways. It will be convenient to designate four economic time periods in the United States, of which only the last three are of current interest to us (and only the latter part of the earliest of these). The periods are: Agricultural State of Nature (1789–1869), Industrial State of Nature (1870–1929), Period of Economic Crisis (1930–1941), and Age of Affluence (marked by a preliminary uncertain period, 1946–1950, and beginning to take on its central characteristics in 1951 and then continuing through the present). Inevitably, since we are dealing with more or less continuous change, the margins of the periods blur into each other. Each leaves its historical "deposit" in the milieu of the next, so that—as with countries still struggling with the remnants of the feudal order in the modern period—we have with us today substantial economic characteristics of the Agricultural State of Nature (not to mention the political and cultural residues of that period).

But since periods must have boundaries, let us mention our reasons for selecting these. The Industrial State of Nature began in 1870 when the society became more than half industrial and commercial, as indicated by the decline below the 50 percent mark in value added to the national product by agriculture. During this industrial period, and prior to the great economic crisis of the 1930s, we find a decelerating rate of development, as indicated by the number of years required for the GNP to double (in constant prices): 13 years, then 18 years, then 21 years—taking us up to the mid-twenties. But we are concerned with more than economic performances; we are interested in government policy as well. "Reform" during this period focused upon the regulation of "natural monopolies," such as railroads, grain elevators, and the like; pure food and drugs laws; and policing certain trade practices. There was no concept of a welfare state, and the nearest thing to an argument over a "managed economy" was the chronic debate over "easy" versus "hard" money.

The period of Economic Crisis (1930–1941) was, of course, marked by economic depression, the most extended and severe in our history. In this period GNP (in constant dollars) remained below the 1929 figure until 1939; investment fell off drastically, and widespread unemployment and suffering ensued. The period defines itself by these facts of economic life *plus* two things: first, the advent of welfare state policies (especially social security, unemployment insurance, extended home and work relief, and a variety of agricultural policies designed to relieve the insecurities and penury of farm life); and second, the early beginnings of a fiscal and monetary policy (pump priming, inflationary monetary policies) designed to eliminate the troughs of the business cycle. These policies, of course, were extremely controversial, but—if we omit the war years—one might say that the passage of the Employment Act of 1946 represented a turning point in governmental (but not business) acceptance of responsibility for a "managed economy" in this special moderate sense. Specific policies to implement this concept remained controversial in many circles for a long time thereafter.

The 1940s represent an anomalous period, partly because of the war, and partly because per capita GNP (hovering around $2,000 in constant 1954 dollars) scarcely changed during the reconversion period, with its widespread shortages and rapidly rising prices, from 1946 into 1950. People were much better off than in the 1930s, but civilians generally were not much better off (economically) than they had been in the first half of the decade. Although there were no recessions as serious as the 1920–21 recession, yet both 1947 and 1949 were difficult years. As a consequence the annual rate of growth of GNP was low (1.8 percent from 1946 to 1950), and, moreover, this period, like all postwar periods, was marked by high industrial strife. Yet there was an important difference, compared to 1929, and also compared to 1935–1936; the share of income going to the very rich, the top 5 percent, declined substantially (1929 = 1930 percent, 1935–1936 = 26.5 percent, 1946–1950 = about .21 percent). From 1950 on, this proportion going to the richest 5 percent scarcely changed, drifting down a percentage point or two, for the next fifteen years. Aside from this last feature, however, the period of the forties seems to have been characterized by some of the economic elements of earlier periods; but at the same time, the basic welfare state measures provided assistance for the very poor, the economically insecure, and for the unemployed —rapidly increasing in 1949 and 1950.

The Age of Affluence, after its poor beginning in the 1940s, may be said (for analytical purposes) to commence in the 1950s, especially after the Korean fighting had stopped. From that time on, although three recessions have occurred, only the one in 1957–1958 involved any decline at all in per capita GNP in real terms. The rate of growth improved substantially: from 1950 to 1961 the annual rate of growth was 3.1 percent in constant dollars. Industrial strife declined; prices were more stable, and in this decade available spending money rose dramatically (50 percent increase in disposable income—current dollars) with goods to spend it on.

While the 1950s began to resemble a period appropriately termed an "Age of Affluence" (except for the unemployment), the 1960s look even better. From early 1961 into 1966 there have been *no* recessions, the longest continuous period of prosperity in our history. The annual rate of increase of GNP in constant dollars is about 4.2 percent in real terms. Unemployment has declined somewhat, though it remains a "spot" on the affluent portrait. Equally important, the Kennedy and Johnson administrations make an explicit point of their use of fiscal policies, especially tax policies, to reduce or eliminate depressions and to encourage growth. Finally, in 1964 certain antipoverty programs were instituted to attack unemployment, poverty, and squalor with more precise instruments; and in 1965, for the first time in 20 years, major new advances were scored toward the realization of the welfare state, especially medicare, extension of social security coverage; and a "break-through" was made on federal aid to education.

This long (but too brief) review of the economic and policy characteristics of recent times shows, then, a profile of increasing per capita income but decreasing economic effectiveness in the period of Industrial State of Nature (1870–1929); a period of Economic Crisis (1930–1941) with low income and no growth; an anomalous decade in the forties; and then an accelerating economy in the Age of Affluence. No doubt the implications as drawn seem overly optimistic, but I see no reason to anticipate a reversal of any of the major trends (unless there is a war), though a slowing down of growth may take place. The question, then, is how these changes relate to political behavior and attitudes, especially in the contemporary period.

## POLITICS AND CIVICS IN AN AGE OF AFFLUENCE

The relationships between individual affluence and political attitudes are comparatively well known, but the relationships between communal affluence and political behavior are somewhat obscure. Even more obscure are the relationships between *change* in affluence and *change* in politics. Consider the following plausible hypotheses:

One might expect an increased conservatism in the Age of Affluence, on the ground that as people become more prosperous they take on the known attitudes of prosperous individuals in an earlier period. Or, to the contrary, one might expect increasing support for the kinds of measures which have worked successfully in the past in helping to bring about the Age of Affluence, i.e., support for an extension of the welfare state.

One might expect a declining urgency of political concern, on the ground that when men are more satisfied with their lot in life they become less desperate for political help. Or, one might expect increased political interest and concern because these attitudes are generally related to higher income and an improved capacity to take an interest in matters other than immediate day-to-day breadwinning problems.

One might expect a shift in political cleavage from social class to religious and ethnic bases on the ground that economic issues would become less important, thereby releasing men's attention for other submerged conflicts. Or, one might argue that because religious and ethnic cleavages are nourished by economic insecurity and poverty, growing affluence and security would weaken the intensity of these conflicts too.

Finally, one might expect a decline in political partisanship, i.e., the extent and intensity of identification with a political party, on the ground that both parties are likely to accept the policies of the welfare state and the managed economy, thus depriving party differences of much of their meaning. Or, one might argue that since social class is likely to lose its cuing function in elections, parties will remain important, or even become stronger, as intellectual and emotional "props" in electoral decisions.

The fact is that, as usual, both "theory" and common sense lead in diverse incompatible directions, and only evidence will help. The evidence to be presented here suggests a lessening of hostility between parties and religious groups, and a *rapprochement* between men and their government—a combination of changes which I cover in the term "politics of consensus." This does not imply that there are no sharp, intensely felt, hostile cleavages in society, but rather that these have (1) lost most of their political and emotional impact for most people (but not for civil rights workers), and (2) changed from cleavages in which the public was more or less evenly divided, to cleavages where the division is between a main body of opinion and a small and dwindling group. Specifically, the thesis has six themes. In the Age of Affluence:

(a) people will come increasingly to trust each other, to feel less at the mercy of chance and more in control of their lives, and so to be more optimistic regarding the future. These changes, in turn will help to promote others:

(b) people will slowly lose their sense of high national, personal, and group stakes in elections; political partisanship, while not changing on the surface, will change its meaning.

(c) people will slowly change their class awareness and consciousness, so that the relationship between ideology and class status will change; but occupation and class will continue to influence electoral choice—even as the electoral "pivot" shifts.

(d) religious institutions and dogmas will slowly lose their influence over men's secular thought, interfaith hostility will decline, but religious community identification may retain a constant political "cuing" function.

(e) the struggle for racial equality will be facilitated by affluence and its associated attitudes, but the sense of crisis and strife in this arena will continue or grow for an indefinite period.

(f) there will be a *rapprochement* between men and their government and a decline of political alienation.

We cannot explore (for want of time and survey data) these changes in the earlier periods, so we will focus upon recent changes. The reader will understand the difficulties of relying on survey materials, with their different questions, eclectic timing, and, hence, ambiguous inference. He will, I hope, further understand that the nature of the changes we are considering are glacial in their slow movements, interrupted by dramatic events abroad and influenced by changing leadership appeals at home. One can, moreover, write interpretative historical essays without data, or more closely controlled and specific studies well documented by data, and both seem equally immune from criticism. This paper lies in between; it is a speculative historical study making use of such data as come to hand.[8]

## TRUST, OPTIMISM, AND ALIENATION

(a) *In an Age of Affluence, people will come increasingly to trust each other more, to feel more in control of their lives, and to be more hopeful regarding the future. Social alienation will decline.*

Greater economic security and protection against life's hazards should, one would imagine, increase people's sense of well-being or happiness, and occasion a decline in various kinds of anxiety. In some ways, this seems to be the case, while in other respects it is not. Over the years, both in the United States and abroad, survey organizations have asked people "In general, how happy would you say you are—very happy, fairly happy, or not very happy?" (AIPO). The question, in spite of its superficial naiveté, has been found to be related to many concrete symptoms of adjustment and happiness and thus to have a promise of some validity.[9] Comparatively speaking, by this test, the United States was in 1949 the third happiest nation (this statement sometimes amuses one's friends), with Australia by far the happiest and France the unhappiest.[10] But over time, it would be impossible to conclude that the evidence suggests that Americans have become "happier" in the Age of Affluence. In the three-year period 1946 to 1949 there seemed to be a drift in this direction (from 39 percent "very happy" to 43 percent), but, when in 1957 the Survey Research Center asked an almost identical question of a national sample ("Taking all things together, how would you say things are these days—would you say you're *very happy, pretty happy,* or *not too happy* these days?"), only 35 percent reported themselves to be "very happy."[11] Since happiness, as the reader might suspect, is strongly related to education and income and since both education and income have been increasing, the findings are puzzling and suggest further inquiry.

But there is other evidence to suggest the kind of basic changes in orientation predicted in the Age of Affluence. One of the fundamental attitudinal ingredients of successful democracies is a relatively widespread sense of interpersonal trust.[12] It is a correlate of several important democratic attitudes[13] and, I believe, an ingredient in economic development itself, since this requires cooperation, responsibility, and integrity to facilitate the working out of informal agreements.[14] Comparatively, the United States is a "trusting" nation, perhaps the most trusting; but we may not always have been that way. In Table 1(a) there is some suggestion that interpersonal trust has increased since the war and the immediate postwar period. If this is true it would provide the strongest attitudinal foundation for some of the political changes we shall examine shortly.

While the sense of current happiness does not seem to have grown in the Age of Affluence, nevertheless an important change has occurred in attitudes about the past, present, and future

TABLE 1: *Trust in Others; Perceptions of Life Now, Earlier, and Later; Control over One's Own Life and Share of Good Luck*

(a) "Do you think most people can be trusted?" (OPOR, March 26, 1942; NORC, Aug. 1, 1948; Jan. 1964)[a]

|  | 1942 (%) | 1948 (%) | 1964 (%) |
|---|---|---|---|
| Yes | 66 | 66 | 77 |
| No | 25 | 30 | 21 |
| No opinion | 9[b] | 4 | 2 |

(b) "Do you think Americans were happier and more contented thirty years ago than they are now?" (AIPO, Mar. 8, 1939).[a] "Do you think the average man gets more satisfaction out of life these days or do you think he got more out of life 50 years ago?" (SRC, Nov. 1964)[c]

|  | 1939 (%) | 1964 (%) |
|---|---|---|
| In earlier period people were happier; got more satisfaction out of life | 61 | 34 |
| Not happier in earlier period; get more satisfaction out of life these days | 23 | 59 |
| Other, it depends, no opinion | 16 | 7 |

(c) "Ten years from now, do you believe Americans will generally be happier than they are today? (AIPO, May 18, 1939). "As you look to the future, do you think life for people generally will get better—or will it get worse?" (AIPO, March 15, 1952; Aug. 29, 1962)[a]

|  | 1939 (%) | 1952 (%) | 1962 (%) |
|---|---|---|---|
| Better (happier) | 42 | 42 | 55 |
| Worse (not happier) | 35 | 34 | 23 |
| No difference |  | 13 | 12 |
| No opinion | 23 | 11 | 10 |

(d) "When you make plans ahead, do you usually get to carry out things the way you expected, or do things usually come up to make you change your plans?" (SRC, Nov. 1958; Nov. 1964)[c]

|  | 1958 (%) | 1964 (%) |
|---|---|---|
| Things work out as expected | 52 | 59 |
| Depends, other | 1 | 4 |
| Have to change plans | 42 | 36 |
| Don't know and NA | 4 | 1 |
| No. of cases | (1822) | (1450) |

(e) "Do you feel that you are the kind of person that gets his share of bad luck, or do you feel that you have mostly good luck?" (SRC, Nov. 1958, Nov. 1964)[c]

|                      | 1958 (%) | 1964 (%) |
|----------------------|----------|----------|
| Mostly good luck     | 63       | 75       |
| Pro-con; it depends  | 5        | 10       |
| Bad luck             | 29       | 14       |
| Don't know and NA    | 4        | 1        |
| No. of cases         | (1822)   | (1450)   |

[a] Erskine, *Public Opinion Quarterly*, pp. 517, 523, 525 [see n. 10 below]. AIPO refers to American Institute of Public Opinion; OPOR to Office of Public Opinion Research; and NORC to National Opinion Research Corp.
[b] Includes 5% qualified answers.
[c] Interuniversity Consortium for Political Research. Codebook for 1964 Survey Research Center Election Study. These sources will hereafter be abbreviated as "Consortium Codebook" and the initials SRC will be used for the Survey Research Center (University of Michigan).

chances for happiness or life satisfaction. In Table 1(b) we see a very strong suggestion that, compared to people in the later phases of the Period of Economic Crisis, people today believe that their lives provide greater satisfaction than their parents or grandparents had. The nostalgia of the thirties for an earlier, possibly "village" America, seems to have declined, in spite of the resurgence of these attitudes said to be characteristic of the Goldwater campaign. If this is a measure of an emotional traditionalism, this change, too, is important.

Looking toward the future as a period offering greater promise of a happier life could imply some dissatisfaction with the current state of things; but, on the contrary, it seems to me to imply exactly the opposite view, namely, that the present is full of hope, carrying within it the seeds of fruitful change. In any event, the increase in the past ten years of faith in the future compared to a plateau of relatively lower hope during the previous 13 years (Table 1[c]) seems to me to reflect exactly that sense of security in the future which one might expect from the protective arm of the welfare state and newly acquired control over the ravages of the business cycle.[15]

This theme is further reflected and more directly stated in a question on the carrying out of plans, shown in Table 1(d).

Here, unfortunately, the time span between measures is short (1958 to 1964), and the change in attitudes relatively small. Moreover, the first measure is taken in a period of recovery from the only important recession in the Age of Affluence. Nevertheless it is suggestive that a growing sense of mastery over fate emerges—the very antithesis of the traditionalist orientation suggesting that one is the helpless object of forces beyond human control.

Finally, we must note in Table 1(e) a somewhat larger increase in the belief that one is, in some sense, the child of fortune, blessed with better than the average share of good luck. Again we are dealing with "late" (for us) changes in the Age of Affluence, but the halving of the proportion of those who think of themselves as dogged by bad luck is surely significant. The implication is twofold: men feel more in control of their lives, as we said before, and "nature" or "the fates" or even "society" is less malevolent—perhaps even benign.

In review, in spite of the findings on "happiness," one can only conclude that during this period the direction of changing personal orientation has been toward a sense that life is better than it was, and will get still better; that people are more trustworthy; that events are more under control and fate is kinder. There is a group of intellectuals who have, in one sense, inherited the place once held by the proponents of Marx's immiseration theory of capitalism. With tongue in cheek, we may refer to them as "alienists," for their apostle is a psychoanalyst, Erich Fromm, and their theme is the increasing alienation of men from work, society, and government. I have long suspected that they reflected their own discontent with society rather more than any mass discontent—some, like C. Wright Mills, have said as much.[16] Partly too, I think, their views reflect their own alienation from the field of endeavor where there is a true *élan,* the field of science. Whatever the reason, and somewhat apart from the main argument of this piece, I suggest that the above data cast doubt upon the principal themes of these alienist thinkers.

## POLITICAL PARTISANSHIP

(b) *In an Age of Affluence, the sense of crisis and of high
national, personal, and group stakes in national elections declines; political partisanship takes on a new meaning.*

This change in "sense of crisis" is, perhaps, the most important attitudinal change from the Period of Economic Crisis to the
Age of Affluence, and it is the most difficult to substantiate with
really good evidence. The argument, however, is straightforward.

In an Age of Affluence an increasing proportion of the working class achieve sufficient income and security to adopt middle
class social and political patterns—but they nevertheless are
likely to remain Democrats. At the same time, the middle class
will associate its own increasing welfare and security with the
policies of the welfare state, including flexible fiscal policies, and
will be in no mood for change. Many will become Democrats;
others will be liberal Republicans. Many industrialists and businessmen will come increasingly to perceive that the fight against
a limited management of the economy is not in their interests because these "liberal" policies provide the basis for the prosperity
and growth in which they share. It is certainly not true that the
more prosperous a person becomes, the less likely he is to be
alarmed about political events. But, generally, I think it is true
that the more secure he is about his income, and the more it appears to him that the government will not jeopardize that income, the less intense he is likely to feel about political decisions
in the realm of economic affairs.

Before turning to time comparisons in the United States,
something may be learned from cross-cultural comparisons of attitudes toward victory by opposition parties. From the data in
Table 2, one learns that the sense of electoral crisis is lower in
the United States than elsewhere. This is enormously significant
for the smooth functioning of democratic institutions, not only
because it makes transition easier from one administration to another but also because it reduces antagonism and hostility in

TABLE 2: *Sense of Alarm over the Victory of an Opposition Party, in Five Nations*

"The Republican Party now controls the administration in Washington. Do you think that its policies and activities would ever seriously endanger the country's welfare? Do you think that this *probably* would happen, that it *might* happen, or that it *probably wouldn't* happen?"*

"If the Democratic Party were to take control of the government, how likely is it that it would seriously endanger the country's welfare? Do you think that this would *probably* happen, that it *might* happen, or that it *probably wouldn't* happen?"

| Country/ Response | Percent "probably would happen," of total sample |
|---|---|
| **United States** | |
| Republicans probably endanger welfare | 5 |
| Democrats probably endanger welfare | 3 |
| **Great Britain** | |
| Conservatives probably endanger welfare | 7 |
| Labour probably endangers welfare | 17 |
| **Germany** | |
| Christian Democrats probably endanger welfare | 7 |
| Socialists (SPD) probably endanger welfare | 12 |
| Right wing (DRP) probably endangers welfare | 35 |
| **Italy** | |
| Christian Democrats probably endanger welfare | 10 |
| Communists (PCI) probably endanger welfare | 60 |
| Socialists (PSI) probably endanger welfare | 43 |
| Socialists (PSDI) probably endanger welfare | 23 |
| Right Wing party like MSI probably endangers welfare | 41 |
| **Mexico** | |
| Party of Revolutionary Institutions (PRI) probably endangers welfare | 13 |
| PAN (minor party) probably endangers welfare | 18 |
| PP (minor party) probably endangers welfare | 37 |

* Appropriate changes in wording, of course, for each nation.
Source: Almond-Verba five-nation study; *Consortium codebooks*. The major report on these surveys is made in Gabriel A. Almond and Sidney Verba, *The Civic Culture, op. cit.* [see n. 12 below]. The number of cases for each country is about a thousand; U.S. survey was made in March 1960, others in June and July 1959.

TABLE 3: *Does It Make Much Difference to the Country Which Party Wins?*

(a) "Do you think it makes much difference or only a little difference which party wins the elections for Congress this fall?" (AIPO, Sept. 1946)[a]

"Do you think it makes a great deal of difference or just a iittle difference which political party runs the country?" (AIPO, May 1965)[b]

|  | 1946 (%) | 1965 (%) |
|---|---|---|
| Great deal of difference | 49 | 39 |
| Little difference | 31 | 40 |
| No difference | 11 | 14 |
| Don't know | 9 | 6 |

(b) "Which one of these ideas comes closest to the way you feel about this election: It is very important to the country that Roosevelt be elected; the country will be better off if Roosevelt is elected; the country will be better off if Dewey is elected; it is very important to the country that Dewey be elected?" (NORC, Oct. 2, 1944)[a]

"Do you think it will make a good deal of difference to the country whether the Democrats or the Republicans win the election this November or that it won't make much difference which side wins?" (SRC, Oct. 1952)[c]

"Do you think it will make a good deal of difference to the country that Eisenhower won instead of Stevenson, or don't you think it will make much difference?" (SRC, Nov. 1952)[c]

|  | 1944 | 1952 October | 1952 November |
|---|---|---|---|
| Very important to the country: (%) | (%) | (%) | |
| good deal of difference | 54 | 21 | 20 |
| Country will be better off; some difference; it depends | 34 | 40 | 42 |
| Won't make much difference; no difference | 9 | 32 | 31 |

[a] Hadley Cantril and Mildred Strunk, *Public Opinion, 1936–1945* (Princeton University Press, 1951).
[b] AIPO release, May 1965.
[c] *Consortium Codebook.*

electoral campaigns. The data also show a sensitivity in these foreign nations to real dangers, but for our purposes, let us note only one other point. In every country except Mexico the more conservative party is in power, but only in the United States— and there only in a minor way—is a larger proportion fearful of the conservative party policies than of the more liberal party. So much has the welfare state been accepted here that its mild opponents, even when in power, were considered more threatening than its apostles. This was true in 1960—perhaps the 1964 election may be interpreted as further confirmation of this point.

Not infrequently the American experience is taken by (American) scholars to represent a kind of prototype for modernizing societies, a model of what is to become of them. If that interpretation is true, it implies that we have passed through some of the phases of economics and politics which these other nations are now experiencing—a hypothesis which runs counter to the notion of American uniqueness, and runs counter to much common sense as well. Nevertheless, the implication of Table 2 is in line with our major theme: the decline of a sense of high stakes involved in national electoral decisions.

These stakes might be national stakes, where the welfare of the *country* is somehow "risked," as implied by the question eliciting the Almond-Verba data; or the stakes might be more personal, turning on one's *own economic condition;* or they might refer to the welfare of the *group* to which one belongs. Changing attitudes toward these three kinds of stakes are reflected in Tables 3 and 4.

The argument for a declining sense of national urgency in electoral outcomes must rest on two comparisons over time, the only comparable ones I could find (Tables 3 [a] and [b]). One of them compares the responses to two similar questions: how much difference it makes which party wins, in 1946, and how much difference it makes which party runs the country, nineteen years later in May 1965. Note that the latter time follows by only several months an election in which the candidates were thought to have sharply different views on domestic and foreign policy. The decline in those believing partisan victory or partisan government of one kind or another makes "a great deal of difference" is suggestive of the process of consensus revealed in Table 2 and anticipated in our argument. The other comparison is between attitudes directly mentioning "difference to the country" or "important to the country" in 1944 and in 1952—the beginning of the politics of consensus. Fortunately, in 1952 the question was asked twice, once before the election—mentioning only parties—and again after the election, mentioning the candidates' names. The lack of difference between these two times and wordings gives us a sense of the reliability of the attitudes involved. And the magnitude of the apparent change in attitude over this 8-year period suggests that chance or sampling error or minor differences in wording could not account for the change. But perhaps it is the difference between a war election and a peacetime election, rather than any between an election colored by the politics of the Period of Economic Crisis compared to the politics of consensus in the Age of Affluence? This would be a more plausible construct were it not for a previous (AIPO) poll in (August) 1942 asking people whether they thought the outcome of the election would "make *any* difference in the war effort"; only 30 percent thought—correctly, as the election consequences for domestic mobilization programs showed—that it would make any difference in this particular respect, compared to 88 percent seeing some unspecified difference in 1944. The implication is clear: people were carrying into the 1944 election —when postwar reconversion anxieties loomed—their sense of partisan alarm learned in the 1930s. In 1952, with a war in the Far East still unresolved, and the cold war in full swing, the sense that the country's welfare hinged on the election nevertheless dwindled drastically and the conditions were prepared for the very low sense of partisan alarmism seen in the 1960 Almond-Verba data presented above.

Part of the political style of the period of transition to the welfare state—and, we must add, its brief resurgence in 1964—is the hostile posture of each partisan toward his opponents, something which follows naturally from the view that a great deal is at stake in the political contest. Not infrequently, in such a

TABLE 4: *Does It Make Much Difference to a Person's or a Group's Welfare Which Party Wins?*

(a) "Do you think it will make any important difference in how you and your family get along financially whether the Democrats or the Republicans win? How is that?" (SRC, Oct. or Nov. of years indicated)[a]

Percent saying "no difference" or unable to think of any difference (don't know)

| | 1952 (%) | 1954 (%) | 1956 (%) | 1958 (%) | 1960 (%) | 1964 (%) |
|---|---|---|---|---|---|---|
| Presidential elections | 53 | | 66 | | 66 | 66 |
| Congressional ("off year") elections | | 65 | | 72 | | |
| No. of cases | (1799) | (1139) | (1762) | (1822) | (1954) | (1571) |

(b) "As of today, which political party—the Democratic or the Republican—do you think serves the interests of the following groups best: Business and professional people? White collar workers? Farmers? Skilled workers? Unskilled workers?" (AIPO, months uncertain, years as indicated)[b]

Percent saying "no difference"

| | 1952 (%) | 1960 (%) | 1964 (%) |
|---|---|---|---|
| Responses referring to own group (business and professional people referring to the interests of business and professional people, etc.) | | | |
| Middle groups (less class conscious) | | | |
| White collar | 12 | 15 | 17 |
| Skilled workers | 13 | 14 | 16 |
| Farmers | 10 | 16 | 17 |
| Extreme groups (more class conscious) | | | |
| Business and professional | 11 | 15 | 12 |
| Unskilled workers | 11 | 13 | 12 |

[a] *Consortium Codebooks* for election studies of years indicated.
[b] AIPO release, Feb. 28, 1965.

strained atmosphere, the election seems more of an effort to keep the other man out rather than to elect one's own candidate. The evidence (not presented here) suggests that the intensity of opposition—except on the extreme fringes—is greater among the *defenders* of the liberal established order; the threat of deprivation of the welfare state is apparently felt more intensely than the threat which the welfare state, once established, implies to its opponents. In any event, it is our thesis that the politics of consensus is also the politics of support, rather than the politics of opposition. There is some evidence for this in the responses of three national samples to questions almost identically worded asking "would you say you are voting mostly to get one man into office (for 'R's candidate'), or mostly to keep the other man out (against 'opposing candidate')?" In 1944 the oppositional vote was 25 percent, and in 1964, with the return of antiwelfare state politics, it was 21 percent. By contrast, in the 1960 election— marked by some anti-Catholic voting, but not by threats to the welfare state and a managed economy, and basically in the consensual style—oppositional voting was only 10 percent, less than half as large.[17]

These findings and arguments deal essentially with the question of national stakes and concerns, but one might well argue that political life more directly reflects a person's own perceived self interest—at least Campbell, Converse, Miller, and Stokes do seem to take this position.[18] This is a fundamental question, for the heart of my argument rests on the view that the Age of Affluence produces, with occasional regression, political contests which do not jeopardize a person's income or economic security. Unfortunately, here, the time series only goes back to 1952 and hence the comparison must rely upon trends within the later era. My thesis, as it turns out, is only partially supported by the evidence, as may be seen in Table 4(a). Where, according to the argument, a slowly growing number of persons should emerge who do not believe that their own income will be greatly affected by the outcome of an election, we find instead, for the presidential years, a marked increase in this sense of "indifference" only between 1952 and 1956—followed by no change at all, a plateau. For the congressional years, a crucial datum is missing for 1962, but the change from 1954 to 1958 is in the expected direction. There are, of course, natural limits to the rise of this "indifference curve" and a counter tendency in the increased level of education in the population, for the more educated are more likely to see the links between their economic well-being and governmental policy. Nevertheless, if one might project these figures backward into time, one would infer, albeit somewhat hesitantly, a lower sense of indifference in the politics of the Period of Economic Crisis to correspond to the greater sense of national stakes we discovered in the earlier data.

Finally, there is the question of perceived group or class stakes in a national election. As has often been said, politics is a group process, men often take their cue for party identification by some simple phrase such as "party of the business man" or "party of the working man." Where issues are obscure, categoric group tradition and alignment, mediated through primary groups, is central. The measure for this perception of group stakes in politics, as seen in Table 4(b), is the response to a question on the party which best serves the interests of each of five groups, classified by the group membership of the respondent. Here I have omitted some data on 1962 since congressional years are different in most series from presidential years (these data suggest an acceleration of the indifference effect prior to the 1964 election) and I have grouped the socioeconomic classes in two divisions: the more flexible middle group and the more extreme and usually more class conscious group. The evidence, again rather tenuous, suggests that within the middle groups whose class identifications are likely to be less clear, there is a slowly growing sense that neither party will jeopardize the interests of one's own particular class. Even among the unskilled workers who have been the most partisan of any of these groups, this sense of indifference seemed waxing in 1962 (when the "no difference" responses were 19 percent, a gain of 6 points in two years), only to be sharply cut back in 1964. Since the 1964 election was, as I have mentioned, a return to welfare state issues, the fact that the sense of "no difference" continued to grow at all, compared to 1956, for these three middle groups is a tribute to the strength of this attitude.

The importance of this measure of sense of indifference is, I think, much greater than is indicated by the small size of the groups involved. For if, at this extreme, the group is slowly growing which claims that there are no important group stakes in an election, then, for a much larger group, there must be doubts, inarticulate mood changes, and declining intensity of conviction.

Before closing this section on the declining sense of crisis, declining perception of threatened policies that might endanger the country, and declining belief that personal or group welfare is involved in an electoral decision, let us note two implied consequences which do *not,* in fact, take place. One implication is that people are becoming less interested in politics. Two extensive series of questions have been asked over time, inquiring into people's interest in the elections, and neither of them shows any decline; indeed, the SRC series catching every national election from 1952 to 1964 (except 1954) shows, with some variation over the years, a peak interest in 1964 (41 percent "very much interested") and a marked increase from 1958 to 1962 (from 26 percent to 36 percent "very much interested")—suggesting, if anything, an increased interest in this time period.

Moreover, rather paradoxically, no decline has been reported in the strength of party identification. That is, the proportion reporting that they are "strong Democrats" and "strong Republicans" has remained remarkably constant (with a slight increase in "strong Democrats" in 1964). Furthermore, although the proportion of people reporting themselves "independent" has increased slightly—from around 20 percent in the 1930s and 1940s, to between 21 and 24 percent in the 1950s and 1960s—the change is very moderate indeed.[19]

The consequent pattern emerging, therefore, is of the interested, party-identified citizen, following politics at least as closely as he did in the days of the great intense clashes when the welfare state was first launched and when men were harassed by insecurity and poverty; voting more regularly, and, indeed "per-

TABLE 5: *Political Partisanship and Approval of the President's Course*

"Do you approve or disapprove of the way (name of President) is handling his job as President?" (AIPO)

| Time | President | % Support by Pres. own party | % Support by opposition party | Partisanship of support: Pres. party less opp. party | Average partisanship difference |
|------|-----------|------------------------------|-------------------------------|------------------------------------------------------|----------------------------------|
| *A. Presidents Associated with Conflict over Welfare State* (%) | | | | | |
| Feb. 1941 | Roosevelt | 90 | 40 | 50 | |
| Feb. 1947 | Truman | 59 | 41 | 18 | 36.3 |
| Oct. 1952 | Truman | 50 | 9 | 41 | |
| *B. Presidents in the Age of Affluence (post-transition)* (%) | | | | | |
| Jan. 1953 | Eisenhower | 90 | 70 | 20 | |
| Jan. 1957 | Eisenhower | 95 | 66 | 29 | |
| Feb. 1960 | Kennedy | 84 | 55 | 29 | 27.5 |
| Jan. 1964 | Johnson | 85 | 74 | 11 | |
| May 1965 | Johnson | 77 | 51 | 26 | |

sonally caring" about the outcome as before; but believing that
the national and personal stakes involved were not so great. People need their party identification as cues for voting decisions.
For most voters, these identifications are the most significant
means of orientation in politics. Hence, people will not give them
up easily, and if they did, they would have to find others, such as
race, or class, or religion, or charismatic leadership. But people
are changing the meanings assigned to their party membership,
and increasingly believe that the opposition is not so dangerous
after all.

We can apply one test to this theory of the politics of consensus. If partisanship has lost some of its "bite" and acrimony, one
would expect the views of partisans of both parties on the way in
which the president is conducting his business to vary more or
less together. Approval of the way the president is "handling his
job as president" has usually been higher than the partisan vote
for the president, in any case. But if we could show that the difference between the approval of members of his own and of the
opposition party (Republicans for Roosevelt, Truman, Kennedy,
and Johnson; Democrats for Eisenhower) was less in the Age of
Affluence than in the Period of Economic Crisis (including the
ambiguous 1940s), our case for historical change would be that
much stronger. Since approval and disapproval fluctuate within
presidential terms, an ideal measure would take each president
at the beginning of his term; but we are forced here to employ
the time periods in which the data are given by party breakdown
as shown in Table 5. By subtracting the percent of the opposition party approving the president's handling of his job from the
percent of his own party so approving, we have a measure of
partisanship.

As may be observed (Table 5) from the average figures for
the two periods, a substantial decline occurred in the partisanship of judgment, the degree to which the judgments reflect partisan divisions. Moreover, except for the special tragic circumstances bringing Johnson into power—circumstances which
produced a burst of sympathetic good will toward the new incum-

bent—the variation in partisanship in this period is rather slight. It seems to have stabilized (to the extent that any set of attitudes at the mercy of historical events may be so described) in a modest 20 to 29 percent range. In short, our expectations of the consequences of a consensual politics are generally confirmed.

## SOCIAL CLASS

(c) *In an Age of Affluence, (1) people slowly lose (or relax) their class awareness, (2) the link between social class and ideology changes; but, (3) in spite of their security and prosperity, people do not increasingly think of themselves as middle class, and (4) social class does not (after a transition period) lose its link to partisan political choice, although the changing political "pivot" diminishes the importance of class voting in many electoral districts.*

The absence, in American history, of a feudal structure or a landed class—and therefore of a peasant class—has given it a unique lack of class consciousness, as so many observers have noted. Yet American society has always been stratified and important differences in life chances, honor, and distribution of rewards inevitably enter into the experience of Americans, like others, and have been historically associated with political choice as well as many other attitudes toward society. Different social strata have always been the vehicles or milieux for different social movements, social ideas, and political parties. In the Age of Affluence, we would expect a continuation of past behavior and opinion modified very slowly by new feelings of security, life styles, and perspectives. I stress the slowness because social class, unlike political party, refers to the basic pattern of life experiences, learned early, reinforced daily, and inevitably loaded with emotion.

First, one wants to know both the nature of objective social change and the nature of subjective responses. Briefly, the proportion of white-collar workers has increased by an average of a little less than five percentage points in every decade for fifty years, with a much smaller increase during the Period of Economic Crisis and a larger increase in subsequent years (1940 to 1960). In 1960 43.2 percent of the employed persons were in white-collar occupations (professional, technical, managerial, clerical, and sales).

But, of course, there is a great deal of slippage between objective and subjective class identifications (some estimates indicate that self-misclassification is as large as 25 percent), and, hence the objective occupational change is not a very good immediate indication of how people will see themselves over time. Measures on this go back to 1945[20] and 1946[21] and, after 1952 continue in rather orderly fashion to 1964.[22] Any expectation that the increasing proportion of workers engaged in white-collar jobs, and the general leveling up of economic security and income, would produce an increased middle class identification, would turn out to have been wrong; about 40 percent thought of themselves as middle or upper in 1946, and about 40 percent again in 1964. In between, the decline in middle class identification noted by Converse in his comparison of 1945 data with 1952 and 1956 data has subsequently been reversed[23] and, without finer examination of special groups, one can only conclude in 1965 that this aspect of "bourgeoisification" of society has not taken place. Men appear to be as willing today as they were about twenty years ago to see themselves as members of "the working class." As a nation we are certainly not "putting on airs."

But, as with party identification, it may be that class identification is slowly assuming a new meaning, a lack of intensity, a different reference. Here the SRC series shown in Table 6(a) gives us some clues, though rather slight ones. We would not—particularly just before the 1964 election—have expected much change, in any event; but we would expect a drifting decline in class awareness or consciousness in the sense of "thinking of oneself as belonging to a social class," partly because of the erosion of the intense feelings evoked by the experience of the 1930s, and partly through a change in age cohorts (in 1956 people in their fifties were the most class conscious age group).[24] The time period is short, one of the figures is anomalous and is

TABLE 6: *Changing Patterns of Class Consciousness and Class Ideology*

(a) "There's quite a bit of talk these days about different social classes. Most people say they belong either to the middle class or the working class. Do you ever think of yourself as being in one of these classes?" (SRC, Oct., Nov. years indicated)[a]

|  | The late 1950s (average for 1956 and 1958) | | The early 1960s (average for 1962 and 1964) | |
| --- | --- | --- | --- | --- |
|  | Percent | (N) | Percent | (N) |
| No, never thinks of self as being in a social class | 34.6 | (1241) | 37.6 | (1078) |
| Yes, thinks of self as being in a social class | 64.2 | (2302) | 60.8 | (1744) |
| Don't know and other | 1.1 | (41) | 1.6 | (46) |
| Total | 99.9 | (3584) | 100.0 | (2868) |

(b) "Are you in favor of labor unions?" (AIPO, Oct. 26, 1941). "In general do you approve or disapprove of labor unions?" (AIPO, Feb. 19, 1959; Nov. 11, 1953; Feb. 8, May 1, 1957; Feb. 8, 1959; Feb. 15, May 26, 1961; Jan. 30, 1963)[b]

|  | Percent Approve | | | Index of Unlikeness | |
| --- | --- | --- | --- | --- | --- |
|  | Manual workers | Business & prof. | White collar | Manual wkrs. minus bus. & prof. | Manual wkrs. minus white collar |
| 1941 (October) | 73 |  | 69 |  | 4 |
| 1949 (February) | 67 | 65 | 63 | 2 | 4 |
| 1953 (November) | 81 | 70 | 75 | 11 | 6 |
| 1957 (February) | 83 | 73 | 77 | 10 | 6 |
| 1961 (February) | 77 | 64 | 65 | 13 | 12 |
| 1963 (January) | 75 | 61 | 67 | 14 | 8 |

(c) "As things stand today, do you think the laws governing labor unions are too strict, or not strict enough?" (AIPO, Jan. 15, 1960). "Do you think the laws regulating labor unions are too strict, or not strict enough?" (AIPO, Oct. 22, 1961)[b]

| | Percent "not strict enough" | |
| --- | --- | --- |
| | 1950 | 1961 |
| Business and Professional | 54 | 60 |
| White collar | 43 | 48 |
| Manual workers | 34 | 35 |

ᵃ *Consortium codebooks.*
ᵇ Erskine, *Public Opinion Quarterly,* Vol. 26 (1962), pp. 284, 288 (and AIPO release, Jan. 30, 1963).

omitted from the table (in 1960 the comparable figure was 25 percent), but after grouping contiguous years and thus doubling the sample sizes, a slow increase does appear in the proportion of people for whom social class is not a conscious reference. And if this is overtly true of this third of the population or so, one suspects that the meaning of class is *changing* for the other two-thirds, as well.

Converse, in neat analysis, has already given a strong indication that this is probably the case. He relates, for each of the two periods, class identification and certain social opinions dealing with the government's responsibility for employment, medical care, and housing and electricity; and finds that the correlations between class and opinions decline markedly in each case. Moreover, this is true of both objective status and subjective class identification.[25] This is strong evidence for a changed meaning of class identification so far as government policy is concerned. After all, government is increasingly seen as the agent for improving *everyone's* prosperity.

But would this also be true of attitudes toward unions, organizations which do not have this trans-class role and which, indeed, are often seen as (and are) the agents of class conflict? From 1936 to 1963 the Gallup polls have asked national samples about their attitudes toward unions: "Are you in favor of labor unions?" and "In general do you approve or disapprove of labor unions?" (Responses in contiguous years to these different questions indicate no difference in response patterns.) Three things are most notable about these responses. First, in this 26-

year period, some fluctuation has occurred (from 58 percent approve in 1938 to 76 percent in February 1957), with increased disapproval following severe strikes or critical investigations (like McCellan's in 1957), but no long term decline or increase in public criticism or support. Second, at no time has a majority of any group, including the business and professional group, failed to approve of unions. And third, and most important for our purposes, the discrepancy between working class and middle class support of unions seems to be growing, as may be seen in Table 6(b). Moreover, in the eleven years between 1950 and 1961, a modest increase has occurred in the proportion of business and professional and of white collar workers—but *not* of manual workers—who believe that the laws regulating labor unions are "not strict enough" (Table 6[c]). Such evidence, running contrary to my main thesis (the weakening effect of socioeconomic status upon "ideology") suggests that there may be two themes here instead of one. Social class (objective and subjective) may have a weakening relationship to opinions about welfare state policies but not to opinions about labor unions. Perhaps, in a period when attention turns to questions of productivity and growth, rather than social justice and equality, and when the government, rather than unions, is the main agent of economic protection—especially for the underdog—unions will seem somewhat different to middle class and working class people. If this were the case, it would give us a better understanding of why it is that just at the time when the relationship between class and opinion on the welfare state is (in Converse's measure) weakening, the relationship between class and attitudes toward unions is growing stronger.

But political choices, as we know, are only loosely related to ideology. The facts seem to be as follows: the relationship between social status or class membership and political choice ("status polarization" or "class voting") tended to become closer, as one might expect in presidential elections during the Period of Economic Crisis, at least from 1936 to 1940; then, after a depressed relationship in 1944 due to attention to war issues, the correlation reached a peak in 1948, whereupon it declined in 1952 and again in 1956. At this point it reached a plateau and remained at about the 1956 level in 1960 and, surprisingly, in 1964.[26] By Alford's measure (a variation of Rice's "index of likeness")[27] this 1956–1964 plateau is at about the same level as the starting point of the series in 1936, suggesting that class voting has a kind of "natural level" for a given country in a given period, altered only occasionally by certain "critical elections."

But, while the measure of likeness (or, actually, "unlikeness") which Alford uses and which I have employed elsewhere in this paper, is useful in indicating some elements of similarity, it does not take into account, the *level* at which these similarities and discrepancies occur. For example, a situation where 60 percent of the manual workers and 40 percent of the non-manual workers vote Democratic (index $= 20$), and another situation where 80 percent of the manual workers and 60 percent of the non-manual workers vote Democratic, (index $= 20$) are scored alike. Yet in the first instance, a majority of the manual workers is on one side of the political division, and a majority of the white collar and business and professional workers is on the other, whereas in the second case, a majority of both groups is on the same side.

Let us suppose that the party responsible for innovative institution of welfare state measures, and fiscal and monetary measures designed to level out the business cycle and promote growth, gradually extends its following in the Age of Affluence so that it becomes overwhelmingly the dominant party. This is done partly by a gradual shift in the middle "white collar" groups so that they see the more liberal party as appropriately "their own," and by some defection of business and professional groups, especially among Catholic and Jewish communicants. Our measure of political likeness does not change, but the pivot changes and we have a situation where class voting differences, with their winner-take-all payoff, become less important.

The evidence that this is the case is strong. A majority of the skilled and unskilled workers have been Democrats at least since 1928 and probably before,[28] with a variable minority occasionally voting outside the party (especially in 1952 and 1956). Even these defectors, however, tended to identify with the Democratic party throughout. On the other hand, historically the business and professional groups, the white collar groups, and usually the farmers, have identified with the Republican party, occasionally voting for Democratic candidates, but then returning to the fold—though returning in decreasing numbers. The consequence was that in terms of party identification at the end of the Period of Economic Crisis both parties started about even: in 1940 some 42 percent of the population said they were Democrats, 38 percent Republicans, and 20 percent claimed to be Independents. By July 1964, just prior to the nomination of Barry Goldwater, the count was 53 percent Democrats, 25 percent Republicans, and 22 percent Independents. And the shift seemed to be accelerating: between 1960 and 1964 all major groups became more Democratic, with the business and professional group moving a little faster than average (7 percent shift compared to an average of 6 percent) and thus becoming more Democratic than Republican for the first time.[29] Thus, as far as party identification goes, all groups have Democratic pluralities, and although proportions differ between social classes, majorities tend to agree.

The difference between the kind of situation where majorities of all major social groups (business and professional, farmers, manual workers, etc.) agree, compared to a situation where the majority of one group is for one party and the majority of an opposing group is for another, is illustrated by the 1964 election. In such an election business and union spokesmen (like Henry Ford and Walter Reuther), support the same candidate; the candidate of the dominant coalition assumes a moderating "national unity" tone and his opponent sounds "shrill"; references to class-linked slogans such as "union bosses," and "economic royalists" are muted in the dominant party. In short, the shifting "pivot" of class allegiance implies a very different kind of "democratic class conflict"—even though the index of unlikeness or of "class voting" may remain constant. Within the dominant party, the politics of consensus takes over, while the minority party occasionally reverts to the older politics of economic crisis.

# RELIGION

(d) *In the Age of Affluence, religious institutions slowly lose their influence over men's thought and behavior; religious prejudices and hostilities decline; but the influence of religious identification upon partisan political choice is among the slowest influences to change.*

It may be argued that class divisions in politics, and the influence of status upon social and political opinion, are "healthier" for a society than are religious divisions and influences. They are less likely to be "moralized," therefore less likely to be intransigent; conflicts are more easily solved by economic growth and economic change; compromise is easier because the stakes are often divisible and allocable by small units; the controversies are increasingly subject to empirical proof, referring, as they do, to cause and effect in *this* world. Therefore, whatever one's feelings about religion in its own sphere, a declining influence of dogmatic religion (as contrasted to some Judeo-Christian ethics) on social thought, and of religious affiliation on political choice, might be seen as a step toward a more healthy polity.

Since the space is brief, let us, for the record, summarize some evidence pointing generally, with some exceptions, in this direction. The basic facts on religious affiliation and church attendance are these: the proportion of the population with some kind of religious affiliation increased in the 1920s, remained constant in the 1930s, increased substantially in the 1940s, increased very moderately in the 1950s, and from 1959 to 1962 (the latest date on which I have figures) increased not at all. Church attendance (as contrasted to affiliation) increased in the late 1940s and early 1950s to a peak average attendance of 49 percent in 1958, and from that time decreased slowly but steadily to 45 percent in 1964, with Protestants and Catholics moving in the same direction.[30] Since affiliation and church attendance have been higher among while collar than blue collar, and among better educated than less well educated groups, this leveling off and decline are, so to speak, "bucking" the educational and occupational trend. Some perception of this tendency seems to have entered the public consciousness. Asked whether religion is "in-

creasing or losing its influence on American life," the proportion
seeing religion losing its influence has recently grown: 1957:
14 percent; 1962: 31 percent; 1965: 45 percent.[31] These changes
are late in the Age of Affluence; their political and ideological
effects would not be expected to appear for some time.

Such observations refer to the theological or institutional aspects of religion, but the community effect, the identification
with coreligionists, is something else.[32] This can take a variety
of forms, but, briefly, identification with coreligionists in recent
years seems to include a declining element of suspicion and declining ideological component. The evidence for this is partly in
the changes among Catholics (but not so much among Protestants) indicating greater hope for *rapprochement* of the Christian religions—ecumenicism.[33] Among Protestants, on the other
hand, there is increasing support for federal aid to religious
schools, thus almost eliminating one of the major bones of contention between communicants of the two religions. National resistance to voting for "a well qualified man who happened to be
a Catholic," decreasing over the years, collapsed with Kennedy's
term in office (Table 7[a]). Attitudes toward Jews, as measured
by the same question, willingness to vote for a "well qualified
person who happens to be Jewish," have continuously been more
accepting (Table 7[b]). And Jews themselves, a declining proportion of the population, indicate, in a brief series (1956, 1958,
1960) a modestly declining sense of greater "feelings of closeness" to other Jews, compared to closeness to non-Jews.[34] The
evidence is strong that ideological divisions, suspicion, prejudice,
and sense of difference, especially as these relate to political
matters, are declining.

But not, apparently, the influence of religious identification on
political choice. Employing, once again, the "index of unlikeness" (percent of Catholics voting Democratic, less the percent
of all Protestants so voting), the series is as follows: 1948: 19;
1952: 19; 1956: 14; 1960: 40; 1964: 21.[35] The decline of the
relationship between religion and vote, predicted by Berelson on
the basis of age-group differences in 1948, has not materialized,
at least at this gross level.[36] But, as the above attitudinal evi-

dence indicates, the meaning has changed; and as the above trends in affiliation and attendance portend, the institutional reinforcement is likely to decline.

## RACE

(e) *In an Age of Affluence, the struggle for equality by a deprived racial group will be facilitated by the expanding economy, the availability of governmental resources for special assistance, and the relative security of otherwise challenged and more hostile "opposition" groups. These conflicts will be expressed by the increased militance of the deprived minority group, and the vacillating, often reluctant, sometimes idealistic acceptance of these claims by the more affluent majority.*

Racial cleavage, strife, and politics are different from class politics in the United States, and, indeed, everywhere. Mobility ("passing"), intermarriage, ecological scattering, and intergroup communication are much more difficult across race (caste) lines than across class lines; the middle groups identifying now with one side, now with the other are smaller; the role of property and relations of the different groups to the means of production are different; visibility and, hence, treatment by the dominant group are different. Changing group proportions are not induced by technology and the demand for new and different services; rather they are a matter of birth and mortality rates. And, most important, in the United States there are only 22 million Negroes, about half of them still in the South. As a consequence, there cannot be a Negro party and a white party, except in some Southern communities; but for a national or a state contest, current trends suggest a division between one party regarded as more friendly to the Negro, made up of Negroes *and whites* pitted against a predominantly all-white party. These trends rest in large measure on the wholesale northward migration of Negroes, stemming initially from wartime conditions of extreme manpower shortages and consequent job opportunities, and the repercussions of the migration in the South as well as the North.

TABLE 7: *Indications of Declining Religious Hostility in Politics*

(a) "If your party nominated a generally well-qualified man for President, and he happened to be a Catholic, would you vote for him?" (AIPO, Oct. 4, 1963)

| Year | Yes (%) | No (%) | Undecided (%) |
|------|---------|--------|---------------|
| 1940 | 62 | 31 | 7 |
| 1958 | 68 | 25 | 7 |
| 1959 | 69 | 20 | 11 |
| 1960 | 71 | 20 | 9 |
| 1961 | 82 | 13 | 5 |
| 1963 | 84 | 13 | 3 |

(b) "Would you vote for a Jew for President?" (AIPO), Feb. 8, 1937). "If your party nominated a generally well-qualified man for President, and he happened to be a Jew, would you vote for him?" (AIPO, Oct. 23, 1963)

| Year | Yes (%) | No (%) | No Opinion (%) |
|------|---------|--------|----------------|
| 1937* | 49 | 51 | (excluded) |
| 1958 | 62 | 28 | 10 |
| 1960 | 72 | 22 | 6 |
| 1963 | 77 | 17 | 6 |

* Data for this year are from Cantril and Strunk, *Public Opinion*.

Under these circumstances, how have the Age of Affluence and the politics of consensus affected the situation?

In the first place, one needs to know whether or not the non-white population has shared in the affluent society. The answer, of course, is that they are still faring very badly, economically, educationally, and socially:

The median income of the nonwhite population is about half the median income of the white population (1962).

The median school years completed for nonwhites is 8.2; for whites it is 10.9 (1960). This understates the difference, for the caliber of education in most nonwhite schools is notoriously poorer.

The proportion of nonwhites in white collar jobs is 17.7 percent; for whites it is 46.9 percent (1963).

When, however, we turn to recent rates of change, the picture is a little better, for the Negro rate of increase in median income is about half again as high as for whites in recent years (1959–1962) and also in the war period. Similarly, in the past decade and a half, the proportion of workers in white collar jobs has increased about three and a half times as fast among Negroes as among whites. But in terms of education, there is little difference in rate of change; indeed, most recently it seems the white rate of increase has been greater than the Negro rate. On balance, the Negro has participated increasingly in some of the rewarding aspects of affluence, but for him the term "affluence," comparatively speaking, is anomalous: aspirations are running much beyond achievement, and the current *level* seems to belie the hopes for full equality.

I know of no available series of questions asked of Negroes over time to indicate whether or not they experience a greater or lesser sense of deprivation today compared to some previous time; whether their anger at the white community is greater or less; whether the frustration expressed in recent riots is greater or less than it was when anger and frustration may have been differently expressed; whether a sense of special community among Negroes is growing or declining; and whether or not whites are more easily embraced in this community than they once were.[37] But, perhaps these are straws in the wind:

1. Electoral participation in the South has been increasing for the past 15 years and will now (1965 and 1966) increase dramatically in certain places with federal voting registrars. It has always been high (education and income held constant) in the Northern cities. Where nonvoting indicates coercion, the lifting of this coercive force may remove some sources of hostility; where it indicates apathy and withdrawal, the change may mean a decline of these symptoms.

2. In 1960 a set of extended interviews (by a Negro) of working class Negroes in New Haven revealed, in the midst of hostility and frustration, a kind of nonalienated faith in "Washington" as a reliable (indeed, almost omnipotent) source of help.

3. Two AIPO surveys in August 1963 and May 1965 revealed in the South (but not in the North) an increase of about 20 percentage points in the Negro group believing that Negroes were treated "the same as whites."[38]

I put little stock in these indicators. I suspect the fact that about the same proportion of Negroes in 1946 and 1965 (roughly 70 percent) believed that the Negro was "unfairly treated" or "treated less well than whites" in his community is a better meas-

TABLE 8: *Changing Attitudes Toward Integration*

(a) "Would you, yourself, have any objection to sending your children to a school where a few of the children are colored? Where half of the children are colored?" (AIPO)

|  | Percent "Yes" | | | |
|  | Where a few children are colored | | Where half of children are colored | |
|  | Outside South | South | Outside South | South |
|---|---|---|---|---|
| 1958 | 13 | 72 | 39 | 81 |
| 1959 | 7 | 72 | 34 | 83 |
| 1963 (June) | 10 | 61 | 33 | 78 |
| 1965 (May) | 7 | 37 | 28 | 68 |

(b) "Do you think the day will ever come in the South when whites and Negroes will be going to the same schools, eating in the same restaurants, and generally sharing the same public accomodations?" (AIPO)

|  | South only | | |
|  | Yes (%) | No (%) | Uncertain (%) |
|---|---|---|---|
| 1957 (August) | 45 | 33 | 22 |
| 1958 (October) | 53 | 31 | 16 |
| 1961 (January) | 76 | 19 | 5 |
| 1963 (July) | 83 | 13 | 4 |

Sources: Erskine, *Public Opinion Quarterly* 26 (1962), 138, 141; AIPO releases, July 19, 1963 and May 23, 1965.

ure of resentment.[39] At the same time, I would expect a substantial change in the quality of this resentment: fear, apathy, self-hatred, and latent hostility in the 1940s and earlier; disappointment, frustration, manifest hostility, ambivalence, and qualified hope, in the later period. One indication of this last quality, hope, lies in the growing support among Southern Negroes for integrated schools, and the high proportion (70 percent in 1956) of Southern Negroes who believe that "the day will come in the South when whites and Negroes will be going to the same schools, eating in the same restaurants, and generally sharing the same public accommodations."[40]

The survey evidence is substantial that for the white community, nationally, there is a growing sense that integration in schools (without bussing), residential neighborhoods, and in public accommodations is inevitable, socially desirable, and, with many reservations, personally acceptable. These data are presented in Table 8. The rate of change is slow, and there are setbacks, now and then; but the series reveals a growing willingness to accommodate to the demands for change of a deprived group. At the same time, variable tensions emerge over the actual implementation of these demands by governmental action (or, probably, over any action by any agency). Thus, when asked "Do you think the Kennedy (Johnson) administration is pushing integration too fast, or not fast enough?" from 36 to 50 percent have said "too fast." This is a measure of resistance to change, a measure of the lack of strength or salience of the ideal and of the discrepancy between verbal and behavioral support. Perhaps, too, it indicates a response to style or manner of "pushing"— consensual or argumentative and coercive; Johnson has fared better than Kennedy in this respect. In any event, this apparent ambivalence and reluctant acceptance indicates exactly those attitudes which, in an insecure, depression-ridden, stagnant society might easily become violent hostility and implacable opposition. The lower income and less well-educated people are more resistant than others to integration. What would their responses be if they were fearful of unemployment, less hopeful of the future, more suspicious of people generally, and feeling victimized by fate; if, in short, they had the attitudes which we saw had changed with growing affluence in recent years?

How then has the Age of Affluence, shaped for the Negro by a partially sympathetic dominant white majority, affected his politics? In one sense "consensus" describes two aspects of the situation. First, Negroes have, ever since the New Deal, become partisan advocates of welfare state policies. Ideologically, in this sense, they are in tune with the dominant political theme of the times. Second, their partisan party preference has gradually, and with some reversals of direction in the 1950s, shifted toward the Democratic camp so that they are now more partisan than any other major group. In 1964, only 6 percent voted Republican; nine months later only 9 percent identified with the Republican party.[41] Since there are about twice as many Democrats as Republicans in the United States, again, it seems, the Negro community has adopted the "in" party; in this respect they are in agreement with majorities in almost all other major demographic groups.

On the other hand, this dramatic increase (and it might be viewed with caution since, in the past, the Negro vote has been more volatile than others—more volatile than the manual worker vote, for example) has meant, according to the index of unlikeness, an increase in racial voting and partisanship, at least in 1964 and 1965. In one sense, this *is* a measure of hostile cleavage, since it reflects the partisan politics and policies of recent years. Moreover, the Republican party, having lost almost all of its Negro following, may come to believe that it is in its interest to stress "states rights," "law and order in the streets," "voluntarism in school assignments," and other themes with barely disguised white racial appeal; in which case there will be a re-sorting, not of the Negroes, but of some village traditionalists, many Southerners, and some alienated and marginal Northern and Western urban dwellers. The Goldwater trial run for these themes was not encouraging in the North, but feelings on such matters run deep for an uncertain number of people, and the search for a winning theme may lead the Republican leadership in this direction. Then, racial voting, unlike class voting, will take on a new intensity and move away from the politics of consensus.

But, probably, for most white people, neither the Negro's problem nor the "threat" of integration in their own communities (and certainly not elsewhere), is sufficiently important to determine partisan choice. The politics of consensus can go on around this "American dilemma," within sound of the battle but relatively undisturbed by it.

## POLITICAL ALIENATION

(f) *In the Age of Affluence, there will be a rapprochement between men and their government and a decline in political alienation.*

It is easier to make the argument that political alienation should decline than to find the evidence to support this view. The argument, again, is simple: the declining intensity of partisanship implies a decline in hostility toward government on the part of the "out" group—with, perhaps, a reverse effect and embitterment on the "far out" right. Politics, then, deals less with moral absolutes and becomes more a discussion of means than ends—its ideological component declines. Since everyone is "doing better" year by year, though with different rates of improvement, the stakes are not so much in terms of gain or loss, but in terms of size of gain—giving government more clearly the image of a rewarding rather than a punishing instrument. Taxes, while primarily the instrument for financing government, now also may be seen as instruments for maintaining prosperity and financing benefits for all rather than for redistributing income.

The difficulty with the use of some evidence supporting this is that I seem to have adopted a "heads I win, tails you lose" strategy with respect to the main source of recent data, the 1964 surveys. If these data show a decline in symptoms of alienation, they seem to support the argument that historical trends are thus revealing themselves. If they show an increase in alienation symptoms, they support the argument that the 1964 election was a regression to the politics of crisis. If we had a long enough time series, this dilemma of ambivalence could be avoided by showing a decline in alienation symptoms up to 1964, with a rise at that time.

In one series we do have exactly this pattern. Figure 1 shows a decline from 1952 to 1960 and then a rise in the proportion of (1) people who feel that public officials are indifferent to what "people like me think," and (2) those who believe "people like me don't have any say about what the government does," and (3) those for whom politics and government are "too complicated" to understand. The trouble is that I can see no very plausible reason why the themes or personalities of the 1964 election

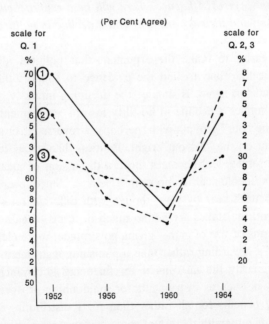

Figure 1. Decline and Rise of Political Alienation. Q. 1. "Sometimes politics and government seem so complicated that a person like me can't really understand what's going on." Q. 2. "I don't think public officials care what people like me think." Q. 3. "People like me don't have any say about what the government does." Source: SRC questions in election studies of years indicated, reported in *Consortium codebooks*.

should occasion these particular changes. That particular election might well have increased the crisis atmosphere; it might (and apparently did) increase the salience of "corruption in politics" themes;[42] it might have created new cleavages in society and thus have disrupted the politics of consensus. But why this campaign, at least compared to 1956 and 1960, should encourage a sense of ineffectiveness and lack of responsiveness in government, is obscure. Therefore, in spite of the appearance of a confirming pattern, we must leave this evidence as anomalous.

Nevertheless, as may be seen in Table 9, some evidence exists for believing that in certain ways there has been a *rapprochement* between men and their government and a decline in political alienation. In the first place, the increase in the proportion of the public who would like to see their sons (if they had any) enter politics as a career, is, I think symptomatic of a growing attitude that political life is both rewarding and honorable. One reason for interpreting this series in this way is the sharp decline in the proportion of arguments against such a career which refer to corruption: from 30 percent in 1946 to 17 percent in 1965.[43]

On the other side of politics, the voter side, note the marked increase in the sense that one "ought" to vote under various more or less discouraging circumstances. These items, taken together, have been called a "citizen duty" scale and one may interpret these data as indicating a reinforced or growing belief that good citizenship means a politically more active citizen. From 1952 to 1960, in the eight possible comparisons over time in Table 9(b), each shows a growth of the sense of citizen duty.

In the argument set forth above, I suggested that attitudes toward taxation should change. The AIPO question, "Do you consider the amount of income tax which you (your husband) (had, have) to pay as too high, too low, or about right?" has been asked many times since 1947. The earlier years are noncomparable for several reasons, and show great variability, but we have data from 1952 to 1962 not only by national totals, but also by major occupational groups (Table 9[c] ). The data reveal two things, especially: first, the lack of any substantial association between occupational status and attitudes toward taxation. We have

TABLE 9: *Rapprochement Between Men and Politics: Politics as a Career, Elections as a Duty, and Taxes as a Burden*

(a) "If you had a son just getting out of school would you like to see him go into politics as a life-work?" (NORC, Nov. 1943, Nov. 1945). "If you had a son would you like to see him go into politics as a life's work when he gets out of school" (AIPO, Dec. 28, 1944). "If you had a son would you like to see him go into politics as a life's work?" (AIPO, July 20, 1953; March 5, 1955; March 3, 1965)[a]

|  | Yes (%) | No (%) | No Opinion (%) |
|---|---|---|---|
| 1943 (Nov.) | 18 | 69 | 13 |
| 1944 (Dec.) | 21 | 68 | 11 |
| 1945 (Nov.) | 24 | 65 | 11 |
| 1953 (July) | 20 | 70 | 10 |
| 1955 (March) | 27 | 60 | 13 |
| 1965 (March) | 36 | 54 | 10 |

(b) The duty to vote in elections: 1952, 1956, 1960.[b]

|  | Percent Agree | | |
|---|---|---|---|
|  | 1952 | 1956 | 1960 |
| "If a person doesn't care how an election comes out he shouldn't vote in it." | 53 | 45 | 43 |
| "A good many local elections aren't important enough to bother with." | 17 | 13 | 12 |
| "It isn't so important to vote when you know your party doesn't have any chance to win." | 11 | 9 | 7 |
| "So many other people vote in the national elections that it doesn't matter to me whether I vote or not." | 12 | 10 | 8 |
| No. of cases | (1799) | (1762) | (1954) |

(c) "Do you consider the amount of income tax which you (your husband) (had, have) to pay as too high, too low, or about right?" (AIPO)[c]

Percent Saying "Too High"

| Year | Prof. and bus. | White collar | Farmers | Manual workers |
|---|---|---|---|---|
| 1952 (March 12) | 74 | 73 | 63 | 72 |
| 1953 (March 8) | 61 | 61 | 55 | 59 |
| 1957 (April 24) | 63 | 69 | 51 | 62[d] |
| 1959 (April 15) | 50 | 51 | 51 | 51[d] |
| 1961 (March 8) | 42 | 50 | 47 | 49 |
| 1962 (March 11) | 50 | 49 | 36 | 51 |

[a] Cantril and Strunk, *Public Opinion,* p. 534; AIPO releases as indicated for 1953, 1955, 1965.
[b] *Consortium Codebooks;* SRC election studies, October or November of years indicated. These questions were not asked in 1964.
[c] Erskine, *Public Opinion Quarterly,* 28 (1964), 161.
[d] Skilled workers only; in 1957 unskilled workers were 65%, in 1959, 58% saying "too high."

known for some time that working class attitudes toward taxation did not fit into conventional concepts of "liberalism" (high taxes and high welfare payments); this is only further illumination of that point. And second—the point to be made here—is the general decline in a sense of taxation as too burdensome. (These findings, it will be observed, do not include the period of great discussion and final legislative action on tax reduction to improve the state of the economy.) Since opposition to "tax-eaters" and the burdens of taxation have traditionally been symptomatic of alienation from government, I think we may quite appropriately see this set of changing attitudes as a part of the *rapprochement* between men and their governments.

In spite of certain anomalies associated with 1964 data, including a constant state of "trust in government" from 1958 to 1964,[44] I am persuaded that there has been a growing state of confidence between men and government, perhaps especially men and politics, during the Age of Affluence. This argument takes on weight when it is placed against the increased life satisfactions and self-confidence examined earlier, the decline in sense of crisis in elections, the changed meaning of class cleavages, the slow drift toward religious harmony, and even the reluctant yielding to the demands for racial equality. The headlines will not show this consensus, nor will the demonstrations at city hall or on the campus, but the ordinary man in the Age of Affluence is beginning to find some greater sense of hope and peace and self-assurance expressed in a less acrimonious political style.

## NOTES

1. John K. Galbraith, *The Affluent Society* (Boston, 1958).
2. These data and the economic and social statistics to follow are taken (or derived) from three main sources all by the U.S. Bureau of the Census: *Historical Statistics of the United States, Colonial Times to 1957* (Washington, D.C., 1960), and its *Continuation to 1962 and Revisions* (1965); *Statistical Abstract of the United States, 1964* (85th ed., Washington, D.C., 1964).
3. Bruce M. Russett and associates, *World Handbook of Political and Social Indicators* (New Haven and London, Yale University Press, 1964), p. 155.
4. *Ibid.*, p. 245.
5. *Ibid.*, pp. 160–161; also First National City Bank, *Monthly Economic Letter*, August 1965, p. 89.
6. David M. Potter (Chicago, University of Chicago Press, 1954).
7. David Riesman (Garden City, N. Y., 1964).
8. The difficulties of showing change through survey data are substantial. Sampling error may often account for the differences (though it should be recalled that most comparisons are between a proportion in one survey, with a sample usually around 1600, and a proportion in another; not, as is more familiar, proportions of subgroups in only one survey). Great differences such as one hopes for in correlational analysis, would here imply some rather unstable attitudes and hence indicate the influence of transient events rather than historical change. The most solid evidence is provided, rather rarely, by many observed changes in the same direction over a long period. Unfortunately, the data for this paper often come from sources which do not give the size of the sample, eliminating the possibility of significance tests or correlational tests. Wherever possible [Tables 1(d), 1(e), 4(a), 6(a), and 9(b)], I have tested the significance of the distributions by the method of difference of proportions ($Z$). The dichotomized differences are all significant beyond the .01 level. I wish to thank Mary Frase for these computations.
9. See Norman M. Bradburn and David Caplovitz, *Reports of Happiness* (Chicago, Aldine, 1965).
10. See compilation of survey material by Hazel Gaudet Erskine in *Public Opinion Quarterly*, 28 (1964), 519. Future reference to these compilations will be as follows: Erskine, *POQ*.
11. Gerald Gurin, Joseph Veroff, and Sheila Feld, *Americans View Their Mental Health* (New York: Basic Books, 1960), p. 22.

12. See Gabriel A. Almond and Sidney Verba, *The Civic Culture* (Princeton: Princeton University Press, 1963), pp. 266–268.
13. Morris Rosenberg, "Misanthropy and Political Ideology," *American Sociological Review*, 21 (1956), 690–695.
14. This is the implication in David McClelland's discussion of other-directedness. See his *The Achieving Society* (New York, 1961), pp. 190–203.
15. Candor compels me to note here that between 1937 and 1964 there was virtually no change in the belief that we will never do away with poverty in this country: in both 1937 and 1964 some 83 percent said "no," we will never do it. Erskine, *POQ*, p. 526.
16. See Erich Fromm, *The Sane Society* (New York, 1955); C. Wright Mills, *The Sociological Imagination* (New York, Oxford University Press, 1959), especially pp. 165–176.
17. *Consortium Codebooks*, NORC 1944 election study and SRC 1960 and 1964 studies.
18. Angus Campbell, Philip E. Converse, Warren E. Miller, Donald E. Stokes, *The American Voter* (New York, 1960), pp. 205–207.
19. These findings on "interest," "personal caring," and partisanship are from the *Consortium Codebooks* of the relevant years.
20. Richard Centers, *The Psychology of Social Classes* (Princeton, Princeton University Press, 1949).
21. Hadley Cantril and Mildred Strunk, *op. cit.*, p. 116 (AIPO).
22. *Consortium Codebooks* (SRC).
23. Philip Converse, "The Shifting Role of Class in Political Attitudes and Behavior," in E. E. Maccoby, T. M. Newcomb, and E. Hartley, *Readings in Social Psychology* (New York, 1958), pp. 388–399. The consortium codebooks show the following proportions of national samples reporting themselves as "middle class": 1952: 37 percent; 1956: 36 percent; 1960: 31 percent; 1964: 40 percent. The 1952 figure includes "upper class."
24. Campbell and associates, *The American Voter*, p. 357.
25. P. Converse, "The Shifting Role of Class," *op. cit.*, pp. 391–393.
26. The 1944–1956 changes are documented in Converse, *ibid.;* these, and the 1936, 1940 and 1960 data are reported in the most extensive available study of "class voting," Robert R. Alford's *Party and Society* (Chicago: Rand McNally, 1963), pp. 103, 352–353. The 1964 figures are based upon AIPO release, December 13, 1964.
27. See Stuart A. Rice, *Quantitative Methods in Politics* (New York, 1928), pp. 210–211.
28. See Alford, *Party and Society,* pp. 225–231.
29. AIPO releases, Feb. 21, 1960, and July 5, 1964.
30. The U.S. Bureau of the Census, *Historical Statistics,* gives the basic data on affiliation; The American Institute of Public Opinion conducts surveys every year on church attendance. The percentages given above are averages based on several surveys a year. Erskine, *POQ*, 28 (1964), 671–675.
31. AIPO release, April 18, 1965.
32. See, for example, Gerhard Lenski, *The Religious Factor* (Garden City, 1963).
33. AIPO release, April 21, 1965.

34. *Consortium Codebooks;* SRC data from election studies for years indicated.
35. The 1948 data are computed from Angus Campbell, Gerald Gurin, and Warren Miller, *The Voter Decides* (Evanston, Ill., Row, Peterson, 1954), p. 71; the data for the other dates are based on AIPO release, Dec. 13, 1964.
36. See Bernard R. Berelson, Paul F. Lazarsfeld, and William N. McPhee, *Voting* (Chicago, University of Chicago Press, 1954), p. 70. On the cognate matter of ethnic influences, see Raymond E. Wolfinger and Joan Heifetz, "The Development and Persistence of Ethnic Voting," *American Political Science Review,* 59 (1965), 896–908.
37. Some of these data are available and are increasingly accessible both at the Roper Center, Williamstown, Mass., and Interuniversity Consortium for Political Research, University of Michigan, Ann Arbor. Further exploration of these data is needed.
38. AIPO release, May 5, 1965.
39. NORC, May 1946, reported in Erskine, *POQ,* 26 (1962), 139; AIPO release, May 5, 1965.
40. AIPO release, March 1, 1956.
41. AIPO releases, Dec. 13, 1964 and Aug. 15, 1965.
42. This evidence, based on a comparison between SRC 1958 and 1964 findings, runs contrary to my main argument regarding the increasingly favorable view of men toward government in the Age of Affluence, but supports the minor theme: 1964 as a return to the politics of crisis and alienation. Actually, I think it is a more or less ephemeral response to discussion about corruption in the Bobby Baker case and the Johnson administration more generally. Compare reasons for not wanting one's son to enter politics, reported below.
43. AIPO release, March 3, 1965.
44. The SRC 1958 and 1964 election studies asked, "How much of the time do you think you can trust the government in Washington to do what is right—just about always, most of the time, or only some of the time." Proportions in each category are nearly constant. I interpret this as a long run increase in trust equalized by an election which stirred up (short term) doubts on the matter. But perhaps it is better to leave it uninterpreted for now.

# 7 Japan: The Erosion of Ideology

## MASAAKI TAKANE

Since the middle 1950's, research in the social sciences has focused upon increasing depoliticization, or the "end of ideology." For the contemporary radical intelligentsia, the old ideologies have lost their power to persuade. At the same time "classical" liberals no longer insist that the State should play no role in the economy, and even many conservatives, at least in England and on the Continent, decline to argue that the welfare state is "the road to serfdom." According to Daniel Bell, "there is today a rough consensus" in the West.[1] That is, in many Western nations there is basic agreement on the goals to be attained; debate now focuses on the means, or administrative technologies, to be employed in achieving these goals.

Masaaki Takane, "Economic Growth and the 'End of Ideology' in Japan," *Asian Survey,* V (June 1965), 295–304. *Author's note:* This paper is a summary of the author's Master's Project in Communication and Journalism, Stanford University. He appreciates the thoughtful advice of Professor Richard R. Fagen and Mrs. Ann Waswo of Stanford and Professor Wolfram Eberhard of University of California, Berkeley.

In this paper I shall seek to determine whether the "end of ideology" phenomenon has yet appeared in Japan. If we compare Japan with the United States or some European countries—England or Sweden, for example—Japan is still an arena of ideological tension. Nevertheless, there is some evidence of an "end of ideology" tendency in Japan, since the end of the Pacific War.

To analyze this trend I shall survey the contents of two Japanese magazines—*Chuo Koron* (The Central Review) and *Sekai* (The World)—both monthly magazines which have a strong influence on Japanese intellectuals, comparable to *The New Republic* or *Harper's* in the United States. These magazines contain articles on social, political, economic, and philosophical subjects, reports, novels, and photographs. There are, of course, other influential magazines and other forms of mass media as well, but the two selected will provide a useful measure of the changes in ideological tension in Japan.

Furthermore, I shall be interested in discovering if there is any correlation between the "end of ideology" tendency and Japan's economic growth since 1945. As Herbert Passin has suggested, there appears to be a close relationship between the political and economic modernization of a country and what he calls the professionalization of its journalism. In the earlier and more intense phase of the nationalist movement, the close union of literature, politics, and journalism is very striking. The journalist is not a mere reporter but a commentator, essayist, propagandist as well—a "writer." Most of the journals in the early stages of modernization of various countries have been committed to modernization and reform and have been against the government even if it was not colonial in character. However, the professionalization of journalism seems to accompany even a moderate measure of economic growth, thus separating the close union between journalism and politics. In the process, the journalist becomes an objective reporter.

According to Passin, however, this is not yet the case in Japan, where journalism and literature still enjoy a close relationship:

Today the ideal of journalistic objectivity remains in Japan, but it is a highly qualified one. Journalists share the same political passions that stir the intellectual classes in general, and the highly polarized politics reflects itself in a very political journalism.[2]

Passin refers to *Chuo Koron,* one of the magazines surveyed here, as "one of the leading journals of comment," treating it as typical of journals in Japan. As will be demonstrated below, his view of journalism in Japan is not wholly accurate, but his concept of the professionalization of journalism and its implied connection with the "end of ideology" is a valid and useful one.

To supplement Passin's descriptive approach, I shall offer some quantitative proof of the correlation between economic growth and the "end of ideology" in Japan. First let us examine Japan's economic growth from 1945 to 1964, using the stage theory employed by W. W. Rostow. With real national income per capita and the number of private automobiles, as shown in Table 1, we can divide Japan's growth in these years into the following three periods:

*Period I (Post-War Recovery):* Rostow judged that the Japanese economy had reached a maturity stage by the end of the fourth decade of the 20th century. Data for 1940 provides the real national income per capita at the time of maturity in Japan. Table 1 shows that in 1946 and 1950 indices did not recover to

TABLE 1

| Period | Year[3] | Private auto-mobiles per million population | Real national income per capita |
|--------|------|------|------|
| | 1934–36 | 850 | 210 yen |
| | 1940 | | 220 |
| I | 1946 | 350 | 98 |
| | 1950 | 520 | 171 |
| II | 1954 | 1,560 | 211 |
| | 1958 | 2,770 | 278 |
| III | 1962 | 7,000 | 428 |
| | 1964 | | |

the level of 1940 or even the pre-war level, i.e., 1934–36. Thus, the sample years 1946 and 1950 cover the immediate post-war period of recovery and rebuilding.

*Period II (Transfer to Mass-Consumption):* Rostow concluded that Japan entered the high mass-consumption period in the 1950's. In 1954 national income per capita was still below the level of 1934–36, but the number of private automobiles surpassed the level of 1934–35, and in 1958 it was three times that of 1934–36. There is ample reason, therefore, to argue that the sample years of 1954 and 1958 represent the period of transfer to a high mass-consumption stage.

*Period III (High Mass-Consumption):* From 1958 to 1962 the number of private automobiles rose about 250%. Data concerning 1964 is not available at present, but it is certain that the number has again increased substantially. The sample years of 1962 and 1964 thus constitute a high mass-consumption period in Japan.

Now let us consider trends in Japanese journalism during these same years, 1945–64. First let me describe briefly the two magazines with which we are concerned. *Chuo Koron* was first published under that name in February 1899, as a continuation of *Hanseikai Zasshi* which had been published between 1887 and 1899. During the second and third decades of this century, the magazine was an active supporter of the movement for democracy in Japan. Because of their opposition to militarism, its editors were arrested in May 1944, and publication of the magazine was prohibited for the duration of World War II.

After World War II, publication of the *Chuo Koron* was renewed. At the same time, Iwanami Shoten, one of the biggest and most respected publishing houses in Japan, began to publish a new magazine, *Sekai* (The World). This was a period of liberation and enlightenment in Japan, and people thirsted after knowledge and thought. Along with *Chuo Koron* and *Sekai,* many other intellectual magazines were published. However, from 1950 to 1952 most of them went out of business and finally in 1956 one of the most important in this field, *Kaizo* (the Reform), which had been started in 1919, ceased publication.

Today *Chuo Koron* and *Sekai* remain as the big two and, indeed, virtually the only two journals of this type in Japan.

According to *Nihon Shuppan Nenkan* (The Japan Publishing Yearbook) the monthly circulation of these two magazines for the period 1952 to 1960 varied from 110,000 to 130,000 for the *Chuo Koron,* and from 100,000 to 140,000 for the *Sekai.* One of the chief characteristics of these two magazines is that they are respected and trusted by many Japanese intellectuals who are otherwise critical and distrustful of mass media in Japan.

To analyze the contents of these magazines, items, or lead articles and second articles appearing in *Chuo Koron* and *Sekai* between January 1946 and 1964 have been used. In Japan, lead articles usually are most important and represent the policy of the editor of the magazine. Second articles occupy a supplementary place and in many cases treat the subject matter of lead articles from another viewpoint by another author.

I shall use lead and second articles, appearing each fourth year from 1946 to the present: that is, 1946, 1950, 1954, 1958, 1962, and 1964. For each of these years, I have analyzed 48 articles, making a total of 288 articles for the period under consideration. In addition, I have analyzed 48 articles appearing in 1960, a year of widespread demonstrations against the U.S.-Japanese Security Treaty. In all then, 366 articles were surveyed.

Both the authors and the contents of the articles concerned have been investigated in the following terms: (1) profession of author, (2) political sympathies of author, (3) subject matter of article, (4) degree of consensus, and (5) domestic issues and foreign issues. For the reader's convenience I have combined discussion of hypothesis and results under each of the above headings.

## PROFESSION OF AUTHOR

Our basic hypothesis is that there has been a tendency toward professionalization among contributors to intellectual journals. In the past a large portion of the articles in intellectual magazines have been written by professors, especially the professors of Tokyo University (the former Tokyo Imperial University). A decline in the number of professors writing articles, and an increase in authors drawn from professions involving special techniques, i.e., journalism, business, or administration, would indicate that professionalism is increasing.

The *categories* for analyzing the professions of authors are as follows: (1) university professors, (2) persons in professions involving special techniques (such as journalists, businessmen, and bureaucrats), (3) members of political parties, and (4) others. The relevant data for the three periods under discussion are presented in Table 2:

TABLE 2

| Period | Professors | Profession special | Party member | Other | Total |
|--------|-----------|--------------------|--------------|-------|-------|
| I | 60 | 3 | 3 | 30 | 96 |
| II | 56 | 8 | 5 | 27 | 96 |
| III | 56 | 13 | 1 | 26 | 96 |

Contributions from university professors decrease from 60 to 56. While this is only a slight change, it may suggest a gradual tendency toward a decline in the role of professors in Japanese intellectual magazines. It is an interesting note that Tokyo University professors decrease from 29 to 20 in number, while professors from other universities increase from 31 to 36. This may reflect a relative decline in the status of the former Tokyo Imperial University.

In contrast, those in professions involving special techniques, i.e., journalists, businessmen, and bureaucrats, increase from 3 to 13. Journalists provided most of this increase; the number of bureaucrats totalled only 3 and no businessmen were represented in these periods. The figures for articles authored by political party leaders is also suggestive. In period I there were 3 Communists and no Socialists; period II has no Communists and 5 Socialists; in period III political parties are represented by only one Socialist contributor.

## POLITICAL SYMPATHIES OF AUTHOR

The hypothesis here is that there will be a decline in the number of authors who are outspoken partisans of Communism, Marxism, or Socialism. If this prediction is confirmed, it will mean in the Japanese context that depoliticization among the authors in these magazines has occurred.

The *categories* of analysis are (1) Communist or Marxist—overt members of the Communist party, overt Marxists, and authors who use Marxist theory to support their fundamental ideas; (2) Socialist—members of the Socialist party, Social Democratic party, active members of the leftist movement other than overt members of the Communist party; (3) Neutral—even though they are not active in the movement, most of them probably vote for the Socialist party; and (4) Right—authors who support conservative parties, or are members of the cabinets formed by conservative parties.

TABLE 3

| Period | Communist or Marxist | Socialist | Neutral | Right | Total |
|--------|------|------|------|------|------|
| I   | 19 | 24 | 49 | 4 | 96 |
| II  | 10 | 36 | 50 | 0 | 96 |
| III | 5  | 18 | 70 | 3 | 96 |

From periods I to III, Communists or Marxists decrease from 19 to 5, while the number of Socialists reaches a peak in period II. From periods II to III, the depoliticization tendency is clear. A movement of leftist intellectuals away from the far left is also suggested.

## SUBJECT MATTER OF ARTICLE

A decrease in the number of articles on politics, and an increase in articles on other subjects would suggest a depoliticization of the contents of the magazines. The *categories* of analysis are: (1) politics—including international politics, law, testing of nuclear weapons, labor movement, the student movement, the problems of education as a political issue; (2) economics; and (3) others.

TABLE 4

| Period | Politics | Economics | Others | Total |
|--------|----------|-----------|--------|-------|
| I | 47 | 21 | 28 | 96 |
| II | 63 | 13 | 20 | 96 |
| III | 66 | 11 | 19 | 96 |

Thus, from periods I to III articles on politics increased from 63 to 66. This suggests that even though a depoliticizing tendency has been observed among the authors of articles in these two journals, politics is still the favored subject matter. The reason for this phenomenon will be discussed later.

## DEGREE OF CONSENSUS

In this section we shall analyze the degree of consensus among authors by measuring the attitude of the articles toward the government which has, with one brief exception, been controlled by the conservatives since the end of World War II. The hypothesis is that there will be a decline in the number of attacks on the government and an increase in the number of neutral positions, i.e., a tendency toward consensus.

The *categories* of analysis are: (1) concrete and severe attack on the government, including attacks on the imperial system, the conservative party, the policy of the conservative party, and the support of anti-governmental movements; (2) abstract and theoretical criticism of the government—and articles which describe facts or views which are contrary to the policy or the views of the government; (3) neutrals; and (4) abstract and theoretical support of government.

TABLE 5

| Period | Attack and Criticism | Neutrals | Support Government | Total |
|---|---|---|---|---|
| I | 24 | 69 | 3 | 96 |
| II | 63 | 32 | 1 | 96 |
| III | 53 | 41 | 2 | 96 |

Contrary to what might have been expected, severe attacks upon and theoretical criticism of the government reached a peak in period II, and even in period III anti-governmental articles were more than double those of period I. Moreover, the number of neutrals is lowest in period II, and even in period III the number of neutral articles is substantially less than in period I. This demonstrates that the greatest degree of political discontent, as expressed in intellectual magazines, occurred in period II. Period III is lower than period II, but is still at a very high level (56% of all sample articles of the period).

## DOMESTIC ISSUES AND FOREIGN ISSUES

Articles which attack or criticize the government focus on both domestic issues and foreign affairs. It can be argued that with the approaching "end of ideology," controversy over domestic issues should decline. Therefore, articles which have attacked or criticized the government (categories 1 and 2 under *degree of consensus* section above) have been investigated to determine whether they dealt with domestic or foreign issues. When an author has discussed both, I have determined which of the issues the authors have emphasized.

TABLE 6

| Period | Foreign | Domestic | Total |
|---|---|---|---|
| I | 11 | 12 | 23 |
| II | 32 | 31 | 63 |
| III | 30 | 23 | 53 |

The ratio of domestic problems to foreign issues changed from 12 domestic to 11 foreign in period I, to 22 domestic to 30 foreign in period III. The hypothesis that the ratio changes from the preponderance of domestic issues to the preponderance of foreign issues in accord with economic growth was confirmed, but it should be noted that the ratio in period I is only 12 to 11, and that both issues reached their peak in period II.

To summarize, between periods I and II, data concerning the professions of authors clearly supported the hypothesis that depoliticization was occurring. The data concerning neutrals in political sympathies and the data concerning domestic issues and foreign issues also support the hypothesis, but in this period only to a very slight degree. The other three hypotheses were not supported here, and the data shows an increase of ideological tension from period I to II. The data for period II to III supported the hypotheses, with the exception of a slight increase in the number of articles on politics.

In order to find out why the data showed an increase of ideological tension from period I to period II, it is necessary to analyze the character of period I. The sample year 1946, the first sample year for period I, was the year just following the surrender of Japan. At this time the Japanese Communist Party officially defined the Occupation as "the liberation army." The people who were in official positions during the war had been purged by the Allied Forces. This was a period of intensive social and political reform in Japan, and thus many Japanese intellectuals may not have been moved to criticize the government strongly. Also, editors and authors had become accustomed to extensive censorship before and during the Second World War, and still were often reluctant to touch contemporary political problems.

The sample year 1950, the second sample year for period I, was the year of the outbreak of the Korean War. In that year the Central Committee of the Japanese Communist party and the editorial staff of the party's central newspaper, *Akahata* (The Red Flag), were purged, and publication of the paper itself was prohibited by General MacArthur. Also, the so-called "red purge" was implemented in almost all industries, and the press —where 2.3% of the personnel were purged—was the hardest hit of all commercial undertakings.

Also, until the early 1950's both the major newspapers and the intellectual journals were in basic agreement on most crucial issues. But then a split occurred. One of the most important examples of this split was the debate over the San Francisco Peace Treaty. For instance, the *Asahi,* one of the "big three" Japanese newspapers, first supported the inclusion of the USSR and Communist China in the prospective peace treaty negotiations. In its editorial of November 8, 1949, the paper said that "the prospective peace treaty should be agreed to by all countries involved in the Pacific War." However, at the time of the San Francisco Treaty Conference in September 1951, the *Asahi* agreed to a treaty which did not include the USSR and Mainland China, and also accepted the U.S.-Japanese Security Treaty. Many authors in the intellectual magazines who wanted "a complete peace treaty" called this treaty "the one-sided peace treaty" and opposed it. This was the point at which the editorial policies of the big newspapers and the intellectual magazines collided. The magazines made their opposition to the treaty clear especially after the end of the Occupation in April 1952.

Thus, I would suggest that issues of ideological conflict were created only toward the end of period I and were not reflected well in the intellectual magazines until early in period II. For this reason, presumably, the data contradicted the hypothesis and showed an increase in ideological tension between period I and period II.

Another aspect of the data presented in this paper that requires explanation is the fact that from period II to period III the number of articles on politics increased from 64 to 66, thus appearing to contradict the depoliticization hypothesis. If, however, we re-examine these same articles in terms of their attitude toward the government, a different picture emerges. The number of articles which attacked or criticized the government decreased from 47 out of 63 to 42 out of 66. This would seem to support the hypothesis that there was a trend toward the "end of ideology" despite an increase of interest in political questions themselves.

Finally, the year 1960 must be considered. This was the year of the movement against the newly revised U.S.-Japan Security Treaty. The movement had its peak in May and June, forcing the resignation of the Kishi Cabinet and the cancellation of President Eisenhower's trip to Japan. The events of this year seem to present strong evidence against the "end of ideology" tendency in Japan. But what does an analysis of articles in *Chuo Koron* and *Sekai* reveal?

In 1960, in terms of the categories of analysis previously described, the number of professors authoring articles did not change. From the viewpoint of political sympathies, the number of "leftist" (Communist party members, Marxists and Socialists) authors declined from 23 in 1958 to 19 in 1960. The number of "Neutrals" increased from 25 in 1958 to 28 in 1960. Articles on politics increased slightly.

However, attacks on and criticism of the government reached a high level in 1960, particularly with respect to foreign policy questions. On the other hand, articles critical of the government upon domestic issues showed a tendency to decline between 1958 and 1964. These figures suggest that political tension in Japan is decreasing with regard to domestic issues but still remains high for foreign policy issues.

## INTELLECTUALS AND MARXISM

In 1963 Yasumasa Kuroda argued that:

A majority of political scientists, sociologists, economists, and historians in Japan are Marxian-oriented. Academic journals and *Sogo Zasshi* (Japanese magazines written by and for the intellectuals) are often dominated by Marxists' ideas.[4]

As far as the intellectual magazines are concerned, however, my study yields different results. These data reveal a trend toward an "end of ideology." In this section, I shall discuss some additional facts which are relevant to this phenomenon but which cannot be readily determined by content analysis.

The first is the decline in the prestige of the Japanese Communist party, especially among intellectuals. From 1960 to the present, because of the authoritarian and bureaucratic attitude of the Communist party, most of the intellectuals who were once in the party have defected or have been purged from it.

Another important factor is the impact of the nuclear explosion by Communist China in October 1964. Almost all the articles which appeared in *Chuo Koron* and *Sekai* just after the explosion were strongly critical of Peking on this issue, the first time that most of the authors in these journals had opposed the policy of the government of Communist China. There is a possibility that this explosion will accelerate the trend toward the destruction of the myth of the "sanctity" of the Chinese Communist party which was once an article of faith with many Japanese intellectuals.

And finally, the idea that Marxist theory is obsolete in the 20th century is spreading among intellectuals. Ikutaro Shimizu, one of the most frequent contributors to intellectual magazines and a leading figure in the Japanese peace movement, for example, recently said that Marxism is useless for the interpretation of Japanese history. In place of Marxism, Japanese intellectuals are becoming more interested in the problems of modernization and economic growth as analyzed by Rostow and other Western economists. These intellectuals feel that since Japan was the first Asian nation to become industrialized, a closer study of Japan's experience is especially important today.

Herbert Passin once said about the future of Japanese journalism:

> There are signs of change, but it would be over optimistic to look for immediate results. What can be expected is a gradual penetration of journalism by the long-range political and social development now in progress.[5]

Yet as the data presented in this paper have shown, such changes —at least among the intellectual magazines and their authors— are already under way. So far, no drastic results can be seen, but a trend toward the "end of ideology" has been established. Presumably, if economic growth continues, and if there is no serious increase in tension in other parts of Asia, this trend will become stronger and more widespread.

## N O T E S

1. Daniel Bell, *The End of Ideology* (New York: Collier Books, 1962), p. 402.
2. Herbert Passin, "Writer and Journalist in the Traditional Society," in Lucian Pye, ed., *Communication and Political Development* (Princeton, N.J.: Princeton Univ. Press, 1963), p. 121.
3. Data for 1958 and 1962 were calculated from the data of *Nihon Tokei Nenkan*.
4. Yasumasa Kuroda, "Recent Japanese Advances in Human Science," *The American Behavioral Scientist,* VII (February 1964), 5.
5. Passin, *op. cit.,* p. 122.

# 8

# The Soviet Union: Ideology in Retreat

## DANIEL BELL

The word *ideology*—it has so many ambiguous meanings and emotional colorations. What is not an ideology today—ideas, ideals, beliefs, passions, values, *Weltanschauungen*, religions, political philosophies, moral justifications, and so on, and so forth?[1] One hears about "communism and capitalism as competing ideologies," about the "ideology of the small businessman," about the "failure of the United States to develop an ideology," and, *pace,* "the end of ideology." In an essay in *Partisan Review* on pornography, ideology is defined as "fantasy cast in the form of opinion or assertion," a loose and associative form of thought "sharing qualities in common with pornography itself." A front-page essay in the *Times Literary Supplement* on pre-Christian religious tracts discusses the effects of trafficking in "hostile ideologies" (early Epicureanism) on Christian apolo-

Daniel Bell, "Ideology and Soviet Politics," *Slavic Review,* 24:4 (December 1965), 591–603.

gists. A sociology colleague sends me an essay entitled "Change, Ferment, and Ideology in the Social Services."

Surely by now some specific meaning should have developed out of common usage. And yet it has not. The word remains both descriptive and pejorative, both analytical and normative. The word does not remain neutral. Neither do people who are influenced by ideology. (In talking about the "end of ideology," one is accused of calling for an end to ideals!) Ideologies, because they somehow catch up one's passions, move people to action. This is the source of their initial power, for in a world committed to change, often quite violent change, ideologies become prime agencies of movements. But this is also the seed of their decay, for when passions are spent or betrayed, or when harsher realities confound initial promises, ideologies also can wane or, if used coercively, induce cynicism.

And yet, although the meaning of the word has shifted so much over time, there is need for some working definition which will allow us to pin down this elusive term. Let me begin by distinguishing, historically, four usages of the term "ideology" in order to see how the concept has functioned in different ways and to see if by this sorting some further clarity can be achieved.

A first meaning of ideology, as, for example, Marx used it in *The German Ideology,* is to deride the proposition that ideas are autonomous or the belief in the power of ideas to shape or determine reality. In this sense ideology is a "false consciousness," and the "end of ideology," as Engels used the phrase in his essay on *Ludwig Feuerbach and the End of Classical German Philosophy,* meant the time when men would achieve "true consciousness," or the awareness of the direction of history and the material basis of society. But that would also be the "end of history," for then men would no longer be subject to causal laws (that is, necessity) and consciousness would be free to change social circumstance. But "during history" ideology can only be a masquerade, and the critique of ideology, *an evaluative critique,* is therefore to denounce the claims of autonomous ideas.

A second use of the concept is the argument that all ideas are conditioned—class-conditioned, *zeitgebunden,* language-bound;

thus, all ideas are socially determined. Though Marxism, in one important sense, is a source of this idea, as it was developed scholastically, the chief stimulus was the idealist school of historical relativism, in particular, Wilhelm Dilthey. From this point of view all knowledge is a function of the concepts selected to organize the meaning of events; but if in human actions these a priori concepts are not absolute (as space and time were thought to be) but change over time, if all ideas, thus, are time-bound or conditioned in some other fashion, how does one know about a previous period of history, or objectively know the truth about the present? Such questions led, in the work of Scheler, Durkheim, Sorokin, Mannheim, and others to the sociology of knowledge. When Mannheim, for example, speaks of thought as *ideological* or *utopian,* he is distinguishing two modes or styles of thinking in relation to time perspectives. Lukacs, when he distinguishes types of consciousness, does so from a class perspective. But the effort in all these instances, whether by invoking science, or contrast perspectives, or history, is *to transcend* the partialities of conditioned ideas.

A third, by now quite common usage, is to see ideologies as justifications which represent some specific set of interests. Thus, ideas are looked at not to see whether they are true or false but in terms of their function. The analytical intention is not to uncover the origin of ideas or to test their validity but to assess their consequences. In this respect, elements of the positivist, pragmatic, Freudian, and Marxist traditions all converge in regarding the concept of ideology in these terms. The intention here is not to debase ideas; yet the effect, in many instances, is to assert that ideas really have no influence in social action and to challenge the notion that ideology carries much weight in the affairs of politics. In the crudest version politics is seen largely as *qui gagne,* or *kto-kogo,* or who gets what when and how. Ideas are not regarded as instrumental but as epiphenomenal.

Finally, there is the viewpoint which sees ideologies as social formulas, as belief systems which can be used to mobilize people for action. Here the instrumental and functional aspects are fused. Now all social movements to some extent use ideas in an instrumental sense: to reorganize old habit patterns and to provide new means of comprehending experience. But in revolutionary politics ideology becomes completely instrumental, becomes, in fact, a way of life. And the prize example of this is Leninism. In Lenin's terms, ideologies are belief systems fashioned by intellectuals or professors for use in organizing the masses. In *What Is to Be Done?* it is clear that Lenin uses the term "ideology" to mean the combat of ideas. (Ideology, in fact, becomes simply another term for "consciousness.")

"All those who talk about 'overrating the importance of ideology,' " he wrote, "about exaggerating the role of the conscious element, etc., imagine that the pure working-class movement can work out, and will work out, an independent ideology for itself, if only the workers 'wrest their fate from the hands of their leaders.' But this is a profound mistake."[2]

And, continued Lenin:

> Since there can be no talk of an independent ideology being developed by the masses of the workers themselves in the process of their movement, the *only* choice is: either the bourgeois or the socialist ideology. There is no middle course (for humanity has not created a "third" ideology, and, moreover, in a society torn by class antagonisms there can never be a non-class or above-class ideology). Hence, to belittle the socialist ideology *in any way,* to *turn away from it in the slightest degree* means to strengthen bourgeois ideology.[3]

While it is doubtful whether Marx ever would have accepted the designation of his set of ideas as an ideology (after all, he believed it was science), Lenin, by concentrating on the mobilization of ideas, talked a language of conflicting belief systems in the same temper as the previous wars of religion. He spoke of the Zubatovs who were dragging the working class "along the line of clerical and gendarme 'ideology.' " He described the German working class as "broken up among a number of ideologies." The bourgeois ideology had prevailed, he wrote, because "it possesses *immeasurably* more opportunities for being spread."[4]

By casting ideology in these "either-or" terms Lenin, more than any other thinker or leader, gave politics its *totalistic* framework and made ideology synonomous with total belief.

But one does not have to accept the concept in these terms. If ideology is an aspect of behavior, a sociologist has to fit it into some social framework which shows how it is linked to other aspects as well, and which allows one to understand the limits of ideology as well as its functions. And an analytical framework has to specify the level of generality as well as the range of application of a conceptual term. The sociological analysis of ideology gains coherence only in relation to the value system of a society, and it is by understanding the complicated interplay of the operation of the value system with ideology that one can identify some specific social processes and see how they shape social action.

## IDEOLOGY AND THE VALUE SYSTEM [5]

Every modern society has to justify itself in one way or another to its members. Even the most coercive of societies has to establish some justification of the coercion; it has to transform *Macht* into legitimacy in order to govern without turning an entire society into a concentration camp. As Rousseau wrote in the third chapter of *The Social Contract*, "The strongest is never strong enough always to be the master unless he transforms strength into right and obedience into duty." In that sense, perhaps, one understands the meaning of Emile Durkheim's statement that "every society is a moral order." In more formal terms, as Talcott Parsons has put it: "All human societies embody references to a normative cultural order which places teleological 'demands' upon men," an allegiance to something beyond themselves. And this normative order is expressed in the central value system of a society.

The value system of the society is the implicit creed subscribed to, or unquestioningly accepted by, the members of the society which defines for them the good society and which shapes the evaluative judgments on actions taken by members of the society. The values are formulated in "sacred" pronouncements (for example, the French Declaration of the Rights of Man, the United States Constitution, the Communist Party Program), become exemplified in history, are presented as tradition, and act to facilitate or inhibit change to the extent that the innovation can be reconciled with established doctrine. The values define what it means to be a member of the society (what it means, for example, to say, "I am a Bolshevik" or "I am an American"), just as a religious creed defines what it means to be, say, a Catholic or a Moslem, and a professional credo defines what it means to be a physician or a scientist. The value system legitimates the distribution of authority and the performance of roles in a society.

Now it is true that a creed, broadly defined, can be compatible with a large number of different political policies, that one cannot deduce one, and only one, course of action from necessarily abstract formulations. Societies guided by a belief in natural law or divine justice have as much difficulty defining the moral correlate of an act as secular societies encounter in rationalizing political actions. So one cannot take ideational formulations as concrete guides to political policy.

But neither can one ignore them. For each society needs some creed, intellectually coherent and rationally defensible, both to justify itself and to meet the challenges of—or to challenge—other creeds. The value system, like the rule of law, provides a set of standards to evaluate actions, but, being the most abstract level of the normative order, these standards arc directions of actions, not directives. In societies (or social movements) that seek to mobilize people for the attainment of goals, some sharper specification of doctrine is necessary. The function of an ideology, in its broadest context, is to concretize the values, the normative judgments of the society. And in some instances, as in the Soviet Union, ideology indicates the direction of the future, and the realization of some further values in that future.

In sum, within every operative society there must be some creed—a set of beliefs and values, traditions and purposes—

which links both the institutional networks and the emotional affinities of the members into some transcendental whole. And there have to be some mechanisms whereby those values can be not only "internalized" by individuals (through norms) but also made explicit for the society—especially one which seeks consciously to shape social change; and this explicating task is the function of ideology.[6]

An *official* ideology is both a principle of inclusion and a principle of exclusion. It defines the official creed, and it identifies the enemy or heretic against whom sentiments must be mobilized. By its very formulation of a public creed it requires an overt statement of allegiance from those who occupy responsible positions in the society.

Thus, ideologies also are forms of legitimation, a link between the generalized values of the society and the institutionalized action of the collectivities (for example, government) in order to set the limits of action. And, if authority is defined as the regulative pattern which is relevant, too, to the normative control of political functions, then ideology can be seen as an aspect of authority, and part of the control system of the society.

## IDEOLOGY AND REALITY

We have accepted the proposition, advanced by Talcott Parsons, that "a system of value-orientations held in common by members of the social system can serve as the main point of reference for analyzing structure and processes" of that system. To this we have added the function of ideology as the mobilization of these values through a codified system of beliefs and, thus, the explication of the goals of the society.[7]

With this in mind, the value system of the Soviet Union might be characterized as one of "ideological activism," that is, a self-conscious set of directives to change the society in accordance with a generalized theoretical doctrine.[8] This involves a constant scrutiny of canonical texts, a testing of achievements by the double standard of practical results and concordance with doctrine, and a constant specification of goals in order to spur the people to the ends set by the regime. Such a society has a high, built-in drive toward social change and a great flexibility in the choice of means. But the stress on ideological conformity also creates a rigid submission to authority and evasions of responsibility, both of which serve to inhibit change and create great tensions in the society.

For the individual, values are grounded in the existential beliefs about the world, his own motivational needs as a personality, and his relation to others in a society. Ideology serves to organize the cognitive validity of the ideas and to demand a practical commitment—putting one's interests at the service of the beliefs. But an ideology, to be effective, must be "congruent" with reality. Official actions must conform to the ideological tenets or be rationalized in some acceptable way. When elements of the doctrine are "utopian"—that is, promise performance in the future rather than the present—the present actions must be justified as moving in the expected direction. When the doctrine conflicts with performance, some "textual answer" must be found to justify a change. Thus ideology is in constant revision in the society. The discrepancy between ideology and reality becomes a continuing source of strain.

For the elites, the very possession of authority forces them to maintain a conscious relationship to the official creed. No society, however, is so completely homogeneous, nor a creed so monolithic, that the different segments of the elite must maintain an allegiance to the creed with the same degree of intensity. Clearly the different social strata within the elite display variable sensitivities to the vicissitudes of ideology. For the hierophants, the interpreters of ideology, the strains are masked, for one of the chief tasks of these pulpiteers is to provide a seemingly unbroken line of continuity in the validity of the doctrine. For the scientific and intellectual members of the elite, however, who, as members of the wider international scientific and intellectual community, are subject to counterdoctrines or independent interpretations, the vicissitudes of ideology become an important source of support for their efforts to make the ideology more consonant with the common standards of professional belief. The differential degrees of attachment, or alienation, on the part of the scientific and intellectual elites to the creed thus become significant indicators of the cohesion of the society and its ability to mobilize support for its stated goals.

The major ideological problem for a regime, then, is to maintain the central core of the creed, or to be able to redefine it successfully when it is challenged, so as to achieve a continuity with the past and a realistic orientation to the present. In the Soviet Union the core doctrines have come under increasing attack from within the system, and the crucial questions are whether it will be able to maintain the given doctrine, modify significant sections successfully (that is, control the consequences for the existing elite's power as well as rationalize it with other elements of the creed), or face an erosion of doctrine that would result in the alienation of a substantial segment of the scientific and intellectual elites from the system as a whole.

To put the questions in more substantive form: Do the current debates in science, philosophy, economics, sociology, and literature portend a revision of Marxist-Leninist dogma to bring it in line with the mainstream of Western rationalist thought (as so much of Marxism actually was, in its pre-Stalinist phase)? Will there be a more open forum of intellectual discussion and literary and philosophical "experimentation" so that some new doctrinal commitments will emerge? Or is the current ferment simply an "accommodation" on the part of the regime to momentary pressures, an accommodation that might be revoked by the ruling elite when it feels that the changes have gone too far? In short, is the process of ideological change irreversible, or can it be halted? If the evolution continues, will it be toward the creation of a doctrine sharing a common intellectual foundation with Western thought and values, or will it be toward some new doctrinal formulations of Marxism-Leninism? No complete answer can be given on the ideological plane alone; a "surrender" of the Russians to the Chinese line might result in new controls and the effort to reassert particular dogmas, or intensified conflict between Russia and China might result in more rapid changes moving toward newer ideological formulations. One can deal here only with "immanent" tendencies, rather than with the total political context in which the major changes will be played out.

## ACCOMMODATION OR CHANGE?

The fact that a doctrine or an ideology is changing does not necessarily mean the disintegration of faith, a loss of the power to hold or move believers, or inability to sustain an intellectual argument against outside challenges. The history of the great faith-systems of the past—Catholicism, Islam, Buddhism, and others—illustrates their remarkable ability to reorder their doctrines, assimilate diverse intellectual currents (Platonism and Aristotelianism, for example, in the case of Catholicism), and maintain a following among the faithful—though it is a moot question whether the survival of a faith can be attributed to the intellectual flexibility of its doctrines or to the fact that these religions were embedded within powerful economic and social systems that allowed them to wield temporal as well as spiritual influence.

A number of people, Professor Joseph Bochenski, for one, argue that the present changes in Soviet doctrine do not portend the disintegration of a powerful faith or the loss of allegiance among the elite but represent simply a complex process of accommodation that is the feature of every doctrine-centered system. In the paper he presented to the 1964 Hoover Institution conference, Bochenski sought to demonstrate the process of change. The Communist countries, he admitted, face a dilemma in that every Marxist-Leninist "must hold that everything in science, art, morals, and so on" has to conform to the "absolutistic standards of the totalitarian state doctrine," while at the same time "he must face the developing realms of thought, and more generally of spiritual life."

The regime, he argues, seeks to overcome the dilemma by a tactic, so to speak, of "three truths." First, there is the basic dogma that is stated in simplified terms for public consumption.

Second, there is a "speculative superstructure," consisting of statements in a technical, Marxist terminology that must be acknowledged by everybody but which can be interpreted freely. And, finally, there is a third kind of statement ("on the borderline between ideology and pure science"), "declassified doctrines" (such as the legitimacy of mathematical logic), about which there can be "practically unlimited freedom of discussion."

By this balancing act the regime seeks to accommodate the different elements in Russian society. But Dr. Bochenski is dubious about the prospects of the revision of "basic faiths." "A generation of truly Marxist-Leninist thinkers has been formed," he argues, "and its control is strong enough to assure that no radical breach with the past will occur. . . . Changes may be slow, all the slower in that this doctrine has now become a unifying ideology of a great and proud nation."

Dr. Bochenski, as a philosopher and a scholastic, assumes that a system of faith containing an intellectually coherent creed has to be articulated in all its parts so as to embrace every aspect of intellectual activity. Like Father Wetter, a good Thomist, he assumes that dialectical materialism, despite its intellectual primitiveness, is a sufficiently articulated, comprehensive system (and for that reason more dangerous, intellectually, than Western thought, with its eclectic hodgepodge of idealism, Kantianism, empiric-criticism, positivism, naturalism, and the like) which, in scholastic fashion, can and does serve as a unifying feature of Soviet thought.[9]

My principal objection to Dr. Bochenski's argument is that the picture he draws is too static. Even the image of "three truths" (one more than Plato's) is cast in the mold of a settled system that has discovered how to make harmless accommodations and now exercises this device as a subtle means of social control. My own feeling is that Marxism-Leninism as a unified doctrine is becoming disjointed and losing its *élan;* where significant philosophical changes are in the offing, they point in the direction of rejoining the diverse traditions (naturalism, positivism, philosophy of science) of Western thought.

There are four broad factors, intellectual and sociological, that put Marxism-Leninism increasingly on the defensive these days: (1) the inherent contradictions that appear in the logic of the doctrine (particularly the "dialectic" and its conflict with science); (2) the incompatibility of the doctrinal structure with the complex differentiation of Communist society—expressed, on the one hand, in the inadequacy of Marxian economic theory and, on the other, in the idea of the "laws of socialist development" as they apply to different countries; (3) the influence of Western thought, partly through the emergence of a world community of science, partly through the interchange of literature and ideas; and (4) the crumbling of the "walls of faith," as a result of Khrushchev's 1956 speech and the bewildering reversal of his own fortunes. The sense of betrayal about the past and the uncertainty about how far present leaders can be trusted undermine the certitudes of the faith. Marxist-Leninism is no longer an all-embracing, aggressive ideological doctrine. As in the breakup of Islam, perhaps, different elements of the doctrine may now become of differential importance for different groups in various Communist countries.

Within the Soviet Union there are three currents of change that work to modify, reshape, or erode Soviet doctrine: first, the role of science as a new legitimating agency in challenging older orthodoxies; second, the disillusionment of the young intellectuals, particularly the literary, with the old doctrines, and the adoption of a negative attitude toward all ideology; third, the need of the new intellectual elites, no longer believing in "historical reason," to confront the existential questions—the meaning of death, suffering, anguish, and the "ultimate" questions about life.

## THE "END OF IDEOLOGY"?

In the face of all these changes in doctrine, what is the central core of Soviet ideology? It should be clear here (as in my more extensive review) that no single element of doctrine is a keystone whose removal would cause the collapse of Soviet ideology. In his book *Soviet Politics* (subtitled "The Role of Ideas in Social Change") Barrington Moore sought to compare the prerevolutionary expectations and ideology of the Communist Party with the Soviet reality and concluded that, among all the aspects of Bolshevik doctrine, the transfer of the means of production to the state represented one of the few instances of congruity between anticipation and fact.[10] In the expectations concerning the organization of industry, social and economic equality, the school, the family, the power of the state—basic themes of the socialist vision—reality has turned out to be far different. Equality of wages and workers' management of industry have turned into sharp differentials and managerial authority. The 1919 Party Program demand for the organization of the army as a people's militia faded long ago before the stratified organization, ranks, and epaulets, no different from those in any other army. The schools, once organized along the lines of progressive education, have become authoritarian institutions (in the jargon of sociological pedagogy, "teacher-centered" rather than "child-centered"). The themes of equality and sacrifice, nobly sounded during the Revolution, turned into class distinctions so severe that when drastic food rationing was introduced in 1941, in the months after the Germans invaded Russia, the population was "split up into favored, semi-favored and unfavored categories, the rations of the latter being already extremely meager."[11] Could the abandonment of revolutionary ideology be more dramatic? By 1941 such conditions were accepted as "normal."

But does this mean, as Robert Daniels has maintained, that ideology, or any description of the Soviet system in terms of direction or purpose, is meaningless? In reviewing the trends of Soviet thought, Daniels argued in 1956: "The pattern of changes within the core of official ideology, the official-purpose system, cannot convincingly be written off as a series of mere tactical ruses or strategic zigzags. The Soviet regime has no higher conception of society or social purpose or of the objectives of its own existence than the ideology which has been under discussion here—which ideology has been reduced to an instrument for rationalization after the fact. It has apparently lost all long-run directing power, no matter what the direction. There is no fixed star for the Soviets to steer by; they have no ultimate pattern which has not thus been subject to reshaping over the years."[12]

Thus the question is polarized: Is Soviet doctrine a "unifying ideology," or is it only a "rationalization after the fact"? Neither answer is suitable, not because each represents an extreme and the truth is always the happy middle but because each misunderstands the nature and function of ideology.

Every society, as I have argued earlier, has some value system, implicit or explicit, reflecting the underlying moral core that is the "irreducible" source of legitimacy and emotional affinity. To the extent that the society has to mobilize its people (for war, for economic development, and the like), it has to create an official ideology—some creed, intellectually coherent and rationally defensible, to justify that set of actions and to meet the challenges of other creeds. To the extent that a society does not mobilize its people and becomes pluralistic and diverse, the ideology becomes more diffuse. The question of legitimacy remains then on the more general and abstract level of the value system (for example, in the American system, the belief in equality, achievement, and so forth), which is compatible with a wide range of practices and even attenuated loyalties. But some ideological base always remains. The meaningful question, therefore, in view of all the changes that have taken place in the content of Soviet doctrines, is this: What is the persistent or underlying thread of Soviet ideology, and under what conditions might one expect that element to change, if at all?

I think the underlying thread is fairly simple: the claim to a "historic mission" (to realize "communism") and the legitimacy of "the chosen instrument" (the "leading role" of the Party). To this extent the vicissitudes of ideology in the short forty-eight-year history of the Soviet regime have not been different, in sociological principle, from the vicissitudes of dogma in the history of the Catholic Church. (In comparing the two, of course, the change of time scale must be kept in mind. Because of the na-

DANIEL BELL : 235

ture of communication and feedback the Soviet time period has been vastly compressed.)

While dogmas such as dialectical materialism, historical materialism, the superiority of collective property, and the nature of scientific communism remain on a formal level, the doctrinal core, the central fact is not any specific theoretical formulation *but the basic demand for belief in the Party itself.* Any movement based on a creed but hierarchically organized encounters this blunt necessity when it is forced, through the pressure of experience or doctrinal challenge, to surrender one or another contradictory element in the creed: it is not the creed but the insistence on the infallibility of the interpreters that becomes the necessary mechanism of social control. Thus, the crucial feature of Soviet ideology is not any formal doctrine but the idea of *partiinost'* itself—that Party direction is essential in all fields of work. Only in this way can the Party rationalize the abandonment of once-hallowed doctrines and adopt new doctrines that may have little justification in the old dogma.

In the Soviet Union the legitimacy of Communist rule derives in great measure from the claim of the Party to know the truth and direction of history. But, as Zbigniew Brzezinski has asked, what is the role of the Party in a technical-managerial society; more specifically, what is the role of the pure Party functionary —the *apparatchik?* He has no functional role in such a society, whether technically competent in industry or as an administrator in government.

In the formative years of Soviet society the role of the Party was solidary (through "Bolshevik man" to provide a coherent social identity), ideological (to formulate goals for the future and to rationalize changes in doctrine), instructional (to train elites and supply the cadres to replace the bourgeois elements), and regulative (to set up a "control apparatus" to push and prod functionaries in other sectors). In the army, for example, Party men long served as "political commissars." But the system of "dual power" was inherently unworkable, and the purely political officer has been withdrawn; the Party "trusts" the higher army officer, as a Party member, but his primary role is that of the army man. In factories today few successful managers listen to the *obkom* Party secretary as a guide or controller. At the top of the Party, in fact, more and more of the Party leaders are drawn from among the engineers and technicians rather than, like Khrushchev, from the *apparatchik* cadres. But the question is not just one of social composition, but of structural relations.[13] What role remains for the Party when technical functions begin to predominate, and these are located in technical and governmental institutions?

None of this is meant to suggest that the Party will disappear. Since the society lacks any other mechanism, the Party remains, crucially, as the arena where factions can coalesce to put forward one policy rather than another as decisive for the society. But a role as a decision-*making* center is already different from one as a decision-*administering* center; and in all this the role of the Party—and with it perhaps, the role of mobilizing ideology —may diminish.

All of these are tendencies; in a complex society their consequences take many years to unfold. But the direction is clear— the breakup, on all levels, of a monolithic society and the consequent fact that different groups will have, as in any diverse society, a differential degree of attachment to and alienation from the society. This does not mean that ideology, in the sense of a formulated creed or an articulated belief system, will disappear. But in the abatement of the *dynamism* of a creed, and the reduction of the role of ideology as a "weapon" against external and internal enemies, it may signify the "end of ideology" in the sense that this polemical idea has been postulated.[14]

### NOTES

1. And under such conditions the word surely has its observe. Thus in a recent *Times Literary Supplement* one read: "Alexandre Marc, director of the Centre International de Formation Européene, has been preaching the federalist faith for well-nigh forty years, and he, if

anyone, may claim to be an exponent of the pure gospel. . . . It is a spiritual concept. What is needed (for Europe, first of all), he assures us, is not a federal *state,* which is only a new, more extended version of *'le statonational,'* but a federalist *society.* And that consists of personalist, realist, dialectical, and revolutionary elements: *it is in the modern parlance an 'anti-ideology'* " (last italics added).

2. V. I. Lenin, "What Is to Be Done?" in *Selected Works,* I, Part One (Moscow, 1950), p. 242.

3. *Ibid.,* pp. 243–244.

4. *Ibid.,* pp. 245–246.

5. In this and succeeding sections I have drawn freely from a longer paper entitled "Marxism-Leninism: A Doctrine on the Defensive" which was prepared for the 1964 Hoover Institution conference on "A Hundred Years of Revolutionary Internationals."

6. More formally, then, ideology may be defined as an interpretative system of political ideas embodying and concretizing the more abstract values of a polity (or social movement) which, because of its claim to justification by some transcendent morality (for example, history), demands a legitimacy for its belief system and a commitment to action in the effort to realize those beliefs.

7. For Parsons, in looking at the integrative mechanisms of a social system, values stand at the apex of a hierarchy which includes, in descending order, *differentiated norms, collectivities,* and *roles* as the analytical units in the institutionalization of social action. But Parsons begins from the viewpoint of *society.* If one starts from the problems of politics, one is aware of the need to identify more conscious mechanisms of action. For the analysis of *mobilized* societies, certainly, one gains considerably by seeing the role of ideology as an intervening mechanism of social control. For an elaboration of Parsons' argument see his essay "Authority, Legitimation, and Political Action," in *Structure and Process in Modern Society* (Glencoe, Illinois, 1960).

8. The phrase is chosen self-consciously as a parallel to the characterization by Parsons of the American value system as one of "instrumental activism," an attitude to active mastery over nature, a commitment to generalized progress, and a pragmatic attitude toward organization and authority. See Parsons, pp. 172–173.

9. The discussion of parallels, formally in method and substantively in categories, between Soviet philosophy and Catholic scholasticism, while relevant to our problem, is far beyond the scope of this paper. For an outline of these parallels see Gustav Wetter, *Dialetical Materialism: A Historical and Systematic Survey of Philosophy in the Soviet Union* (New York, 1958), pp. 555–556. For a critique see Franz Borkenau, "A Thomist on Leninism," *The Twelfth Century* (London), February 1954.

10. *Soviet Politics—The Dilemma of Power* (Cambridge, Mass., 1950), especially Chaps. 7 and 8. For an illuminating discussion of this problem, see also Alex Inkeles, "Social Changes in Soviet Russia," in Morroe Berger, Theodore Abel, and Charles Page, eds., *Freedom and Control in Modern Society* (New York, 1954).

11. Alexander Werth, *Russia at War 1941–1945* (New York, 1964), p. 183.

12. Robert V. Daniels, "Soviet Thought in the Nineteen-Thirties," in *Indiana Slavic Studies,* Vol. I, ed. Michael Ginsburg and Joseph T. Shaw (photolithoprinted by Cushing-Malloy, Inc., Ann Arbor, Mich., 1956).

13. As Talcott Parsons has observed: "In the U.S.S.R. the primary problem concerns the long-run status of the Communist Party—can this quasi-religious structure remain differentiated from the 'State' and still maintain a tight control over it? This question involves both the status of religion (in the more analytical sense) and the possibilities of relaxing control in the direction of political democratization. The major problem is closely linked to the latter—it is a question of genuine autonomy, relative to both party and state, of non-political spheres of organization; notably both of the economy, and of the professions and the services in which they are involved. At present, the most acute focus of tendencies to seek this type of autonomy is the 'intellectuals'—in what sense may science and the arts be treated as the simple handmaidens of the Party?" Talcott Parsons, "Differentiation and Variation in Social Structures," in Parsons *et al., Theories of Society* (New York, 1961), p. 263.

14. For a discussion of the theme of the "end of ideology" as it relates to the Communist world, see the essay by Michael Polanyi, *Beyond Nihilism,* the Eddington Memorial Lecture (Cambridge, Eng., 1960). For a general discussion of the theme, see this writer's *The End of Ideology* (rev. ed.; New York, 1965), especially the epilogue.

# III Critique

# Introductory Note

The decline of ideology controversy revolves around a number of issues, of which two are the most important: the meaning of "ideology" and the meaning of "decline." Both issues have been discussed in detail in the opening chapter.

The range of the controversy surrounding the decline hypothesis has also been elaborated above (pp. 16–25). The five papers that comprise this section bring into sharp focus some principal issues of the debate.

In the first article reprinted below Joseph LaPalombara sets out to debunk the decline hypothesis as itself ideological and nonscientific. He wishes to show in particular that the situation in Italy represents an "upswing" in ideology, not a decline.

The article by Rejai, Mason, and Beller is a critique of LaPalombara and others set in a broad context. The authors attribute the confusion among the antidecline writers to two sources: (1) a failure to appreciate the substance of the decline thesis in terms of a relative attenuation of ideological politics; and (2) a failure to appreciate the significance of the decline thesis as an empirical proposition, not an ideological one.

241

In the succeeding paper, Roy Pierce undertakes a wide-ranging appraisal of the decline of ideology hypothesis with particular reference to the situation in France. Of the French contributors, he draws special attention to the work of Albert Camus and Raymond Aron.

The student movement to which Pierce refers in the closing paragraphs of his article becomes the focus of the essay by Michael Novak. Novak considers the students' denunciation of the ideological biases inherent in academic life and their attack upon the ties between the university on the one hand and industry, technology, government, and the military on the other. He contrasts the New Left with the Old Left, stressing the relative intellectual poverty of the latter, its inability to come to grips with new needs and conditions, and its collusion with the established order. He is sharply critical of the "pragmatism" of the Old Left and characterizes its emphasis on "consensus" and "equilibrium" as a self-serving ideology of the status quo.

In the final article Kenneth Keniston shares much of Novak's criticism of the Old Left. Keniston discusses the fragmentation of the New Left and faults the movement as a whole for its failure to provide a new ideology capable of uniting the various factions. He then reviews three new books that he thinks set the stage for a radical critique of American society and a radical ideology addressing itself to the contemporary situation.

# 9 *A Dissenting View*

## JOSEPH LA PALOMBARA

### INTRODUCTION

With increasing frequency and self-assurance, the scientific objectivity of American social science is proclaimed by some of its prominent practitioners. Various explanations are offered for the onset of social science's Golden Age, but central to most of them is the claim that modern social science has managed to resolve Mannheim's Paradox,[1] namely, that in the pursuit of the truth the social scientist himself is handicapped by the narrow focus and distortions implicit in ideological thought. Presumably, the social scientist can now probe any aspect of human organization and behavior as dispassionately as physical scientists observe the

Joseph LaPalombara, "Decline of Ideology: A Dissent and an Interpretation," *American Political Science Review*, 60:1 (March 1966), 5–16. *Author's note:* Research for this paper was made possible in part by assistance from the Office of International Programs of Michigan State University, and in part by support from the Stimson Fund of Yale University. In gathering information on the Italian situation, I had highly valuable assistance from Gloria Pirzio Ammassari, of Rome.

243

structure of the atom or chemical reactions. For this reason, it is claimed by some that the ideologically liberated social scientists —at least in the United States—can expect to be co-opted into the Scientific Culture, or that segment of society that is presumably aloof from and disdainful toward the moralistic speculations and the tender-heartedness of the literary intellectuals.

The behaviorial "revolution" in political science may have run its course, but it has left in its wake both obscurantist criticisms of empiricism, on the one hand, and, on the other hand, an unquestioning belief in "science." Quite often the latter belief is not merely anti-historical and anti-philosophical but also uncritical about the extent to which empirical observations can be colored by the very orientation to values that one seeks to control in rigorous empirical research.

The claims of modern social scientists are greatly buttressed by the views of Talcott Parsons.[2] In response to criticisms of his work offered by a group of scholars at Cornell University, Parsons asserts that the "break-through" in the behavioral sciences occurred in the United States in part because of that country's intellectual openness and receptivity. A critical cause of this latter quality, according to Parsons, is the American intellectual's " . . . relative immunity to the pressure to put problems in an ideological context," and thus his refusal to worry too much about "global" problems.[3] For Parsons, science and ideology are simply incompatible concepts.

This is not the place to explore the ideological underpinnings of Parsons' formulations, particularly since the reader can turn for this to Andrew Hacker's somewhat polemical but nevertheless extremely cogent analysis (which Parsons chooses essentially to evade).[4] It is worthwhile noting, however, that Parsons' refusal to be concerned with the "global" questions, and his claims for the scientific objectivity of his emerging general theory, underpin the claims of other social scientists who extol the "scientific" qualities of their disciplines.

One interesting extrapolation from these assumptions about social science objectivity, and of the essential incompatibility of social science and normative orientations, is found in the so-called "decline of ideology" literature. Presumably, social-scientific generalizations have been made about the waning of ideology. The irony attaching to arguments in and against these "findings" is that they have themselves taken on many of the undeniable earmarks of *ideological* conflict. Thus, I wish to acknowledge that my own effort in this paper may be in part—and quite properly—identified as ideological. Indeed, the underlying theme of my argument here is that we have not, in fact, resolved the Mannheim Paradox and that perhaps the future of social science will be better served if we acknowledge this fact and face up to its intellectual and theoretical implications.

More particularly, however, I wish to deal in this paper with these topics: 1) what it is that is meant when social scientists write about the "decline of ideology"; 2) an examination of some empirical evidence from the West that strongly challenges some of the "findings" of these writers; and 3) a somewhat tentative ideological-social scientific interpretation of what these writings may represent in contemporary American society.

## THE MEANING OF IDEOLOGY

It is abundantly clear that those who write about ideology's decline, with few exceptions,[5] intend a pejorative denotation and connotation of the term. Taking their lead from Mannheim, these writers contend that ideological thought means at least that such ideas are "distorted," in the sense that they lack "congruence" with reality. Beyond this, however, they seem to support the Mannheim view that the lack of congruence may be either emotionally determined, and therefore the result of subconscious forces, or "conscious deception, where ideology is to be interpreted as a purposeful lie."[6]

It can be argued, of course, that one is free to define ideology as it happens to suit one's mood or purpose, and we have a vast literature demonstrating the considerable range of meaning that can be assigned to the concept.[7] But if one elects a definition that is based too heavily on the notion of wilful or unintended deception or distortion, much of what social scientists generally identify as ideological would simply have to be ignored, or called something else. Moreover, if the central purpose of the analysis is to demonstrate something as significant as ideology's decline, it seems to me to be the essence of intellectual legerdemain, or downright slovenliness, to leave the definition of ideology vague, or to confuse the demonstrable decline of something one finds objectionable with presumably empirical generalizations about the gradual disappearance of something which is much broader in meaning.

My usage of ideology is quite close to the definition suggested by L. H. Garstin, in that it involves a philosophy of history, a view of man's present place in it, some estimate of probable lines of future development, and a set of prescriptions regarding how to hasten, retard, and/or modify that developmental direction.[8] While the concept, ideology, is certainly one of the most elusive in our vocabulary, we can say about it that, beyond the above, it tends to specify a set of values that are more or less coherent and that it seeks to link given patterns of action to the achievement or maintenance of a future, or existing, state of affairs. What makes such formulations of particular interest to political scientists is that ideologies frequently insist that in order to achieve or maintain desired ends, deemed to be morally superior and therefore desirable for the entire collectivity, public authority is expected to intervene.

It is in this broad sense, then, that I am using the concept in this paper. This being the case, several caveats are in order. For example, an ideology may or may not be dogmatic; a relative lack of dogmatism does not necessarily make a given set of cognitions, preferences, expectations, and prescriptions any the less ideological. An ideology may or may not be utopian. I assume that conservative movements of the last century or two, as well as the so-called Radical Right in the United States at present, have strong ideological dimensions, notwithstanding their vociferous denials of utopias. Similarly, Catholicism is no less ideological in many of its political dimensions by reason of its rejection of the Enlightenment's assumptions concerning man's perfectability. An ideology may or may not be attuned to the claimed rationality of modern science; the place of scientific thought in ideological formulations is an empirical question that should not be begged by the assumption that science and ideology are incompatible. Technocrats and others who enshrine the Managerial Society certainly engage in the most fundamental kind of ideological reasoning. Ideology may or may not emphasize rhetoric or flamboyant verbal formulations. The language of ideology is also an empirical question; it will surely be strongly influenced by the socio-historical context in which it evolves, and a decline or, better, change in rhetoric should not be confused with a decline in ideology itself.[9] Finally, an ideology may or may not be believed by those who articulate it. Whether an ideology is cynically used as a weapon or instrument of control; whether it emanates from subconscious needs or drives or is rationally formulated and incorporated into one's belief system; indeed, whether it is narrowly or widely, publicly or privately, shared with third persons are also legitimate and fascinating questions that require careful investigation rather than a *priori* answers.

It seems to me that the "decline of ideology" writers[10] commit one or more of all of the errors implied above. For example, ideology is said to apply to passionately articulated prescriptions, evidently not to those which manifest calm rationality. As Daniel Bell puts it, "ideology is the conversion of ideas into social levers. . . . What gives ideology its force is its passion."[11] Lipset, in his personal postscript on ideology's passing, tells us that "Democracy in the Western world has been undergoing some important changes as serious intellectual conflicts among groups representing different values have declined sharply."[12] In the case of Aron, his passionate and intemperate attacks on the ideas of certain French intellectuals are so extreme as to represent not so much social science analysis as they do a fascinating example of the rhetoric aspect of ideological exchange.[13]

It seems equally apparent that what these writers mean by ideology is not any given set of values, beliefs, preferences, expectations, and prescriptions regarding society but that *particular* set that we may variously associate with Orthodox Marxism, "Scientific Socialism," Bolshevism, Maoism, or in any case with strongly held and dogmatically articulated ideas regarding class conflict and revolution. Thus, "the exhaustion of political ideas in the West" refers to that particular case involving the disillusionment experienced by Marxist intellectuals when it became apparent that many of Marx's predictions were simply not borne out, and when the outrages of the Stalinist regime were publicly revealed. We need not document the evidence for the widespread disillusionment, or for the agonizing ideological reappraisals to which it has led. But, as I shall briefly document below, to limit the meaning of ideology to absolute utopias, to concentrate one's analytical attention upon what some Marxian socialists may be up to, and to equate certain changes in rhetoric with ideological decline is to narrow the meaning of the central concept to the point where it has very limited utility for the social scientist.

The writers I have in mind also seem to see ideology as a dependent phenomenon, whose rise and fall is conditioned by a number of ecological factors, most of them economic. This curious determinism suggests that if there are marked differences in poverty and wealth—or in life styles—ideology emerges; if these differences are reduced, ideology (i.e., class-conflict ideology) declines. Thus, Lipset tells us that "Ideological passion may no longer be necessary to sustain the class struggle within stable and affluent democracies."[14] At another place he says, "As differences in style of life are reduced, so are the tensions of stratification. And increased education enhances the propensity of different groups to 'tolerate' each other, to accept the complex idea that truth and error are not necessarily on one side."[15]

These writers are far too sophisticated to suggest that there is a simple correlation between increases in economic productivity or distribution and decline of ideology. They recognize, for example, that religious and other cleavages may cut against tendencies toward ideological quiescence. Nevertheless, I came away from this literature with the uncomfortable impression that these writers claim that moral imperatives, differences of opinion re-

garding the "good life," and opposing formulations regarding
public policy must necessarily give way before the avalanche of
popular education, the mass media, and greater and greater
numbers of washing machines, automobiles, and television sets.
How else judge the assertion—as clearly debatable as it is
subjective and ideological—that ideology is in decline because
"the fundamental problems of the Industrial Revolution have
been solved."[16]

There are certainly thousands of European intellectuals, as
well as tens of millions of other Europeans, who would react to
the last quoted statement sardonically, or in sheer disbelief.

Since the generalizations about ideology's alleged decline
apply to the West, and therefore to Europe as well as the North
American continent, it may be instructive to look at one of these
countries, Italy, to see exactly how accurate these generalizations
are. It should be noted that the time span I will consider are the
years since World War II; my point will be that since generalizations for such a short period are so manifestly inaccurate, it is
useless to lend any kind of serious attention to prognostications
about where we will be a century or two from now. Keynes, I
believe, authored the most appropriate aphorism about the "long
run."

## IDEOLOGY IN ITALY

The points I wish to stress about Italy can be briefly stated, although their detailed documentation would require more space
than is available here. First, notwithstanding the existence within
the Italian Communist party of both a "crisis of intellectuals"
and a "crisis of ideology," there has recently occurred within
that party a new ferment of ideas which in a certain sense has
actually enriched rather than diminished attention to ideology.
Second, if one bothers to look away from the Communist party
(P.C.I.) and toward Christian Democracy (D.C.), it is possible
to conclude that ideology in the latter is actually on the upswing.
Third, and following from these two observations, the so-called
decline-of-ideology theory is simply not valid for the Italian case.[17]

## The Italian Communist Party

The most frequent—and most wishful—interpretation of P.C.I. is that it is moving in a reformist direction that will eventuate in its accepting the existing system and limiting its demands to social, political, and economic manipulations designed to effect needed, but not revolutionary, reforms from time to time. This view of the party is superficial in the sense that "reformism" dates back to 1944 when Palmiro Togliatti returned from Moscow articulating a moderate line which was an unnerving as it was unexpected. This line was carefully followed in the Constituent Assembly, which drafted the Italian Constitution, and in this broad sense the party has been "reformist" throughout the post-war years.

What has changed in recent years is neither the party's will to power nor its commitment to a basically socialist ideology. Rather, I would say that the changes include: 1) the party's use of extreme rhetoric; 2) its now openly expressed polycentrist view regarding the nature of the international socialist or Communist movement; and 3) the party's notions regarding how the class struggle should be conducted in contemporary Italy. The debates and agonizing reappraisals that the party has experienced in recent years must be construed not as a sign of ideological decay but, rather, as a sign of ideological vigor which is largely responsible for the party's steady and increasing attraction at the polls.

The list of P.C.I. errors in prognosticating about Italian society is long and impressive; it led observers at Bologna not long ago to comment on what a "grotesque assumption" was the party's belief that only it possessed a scientifically infallible method for analyzing reality.[18] The errors included such things as predictions about the comparative rate of economic growth in Communist and free countries, expectations regarding the European Common Market, impending economic crises in capitalistic countries, etc. One observer of this pattern of inaccurate prognosticating notes that it was not until the middle of 1961 that the "Communists awoke from their dogmatic dream and almost in a flash learned that their judgments did not correspond to reality."[19]

The truth is that the alarm had sounded for P.C.I. several years before, and precisely at the VII Party Congress of 1956. It was here that the party's activities in the underdeveloped South first received a public airing. The critics of the party's *"Movimento di Rinascita"* in southern Italy openly noted that the movement was in crisis and that the crisis grew out of the party's failure to adapt ideology and consequently policy to the concrete conditions of Southern Italy. Members of the party itself scored it for its "sterile and negative" approach to national problems, for its rigid and doctrinaire adherence to fixed schemes, for its permitting the movement to lose whatever dynamism it may have had in earlier years.[20]

Both Togliatti and Giorgio Amendola (the latter considered the leader of the P.C.I.'s "reformist" wing) urged that the party must be flexible and overcome the inertia of pat formulations. They admitted that both the party and its trade union wing seemed to be unprepared to confront the great changes in local conditions that had occurred in the years since 1945.[21] It is possible that, within the party's secret confines, this kind of self-appraisal had begun before 1956, but in those earlier days one would not have expected Togliatti to say publicly that the party was not keeping up with basic social and economic transformations in Italy or that it was necessary for that organization to engage in the kind of total re-examination that will finally sweep away "ancient and recent moldiness that impede the action of P.C.I."[22]

To be sure, removing ideological mold is not easy for Communists, who tend to be ultra-intellectual in a society where intellectual elegance is highly prized. One can therefore note in the party's literature the care—and the web-like logic—with which recent changes are reconciled with Marx and Lenin, and particularly with the writings of Antonio Gramsci, the intellectual fountainhead of Italian Communism, and a formidable dialectician whose work is too little known in the English-speaking world.[23] Nevertheless, the party's public posture has changed radically.

The most recent and important indication of this change is the party's decision to seek alliances with elements of the middle class—peasants, small land-owners, artisans, small and medium industrialists, and even with entrepreneurs who are not involved with industrial monopolies.[24] The importance of this change should be strongly emphasized; the P.C.I. has managed in one stroke to shift largely to monopoly capitalism all of the attacks that had previously been leveled against an allegedly retrograde, decadent bourgeoisie. The party's open strategy is to attract to its ranks the mushrooming members of the middle and tertiary strata that large-scale industrial development tends to proliferate. The fire of opposition is no longer directed against proprietors in general but against the monopolists who allegedly exploit all others in society, who are oppressive, and who increase the degree of imbalance or disequilibrium in the social system.

This, then, is not the party of the Stalin Era. Not many who followed the antics of P.C.I. up to the Hungarian Rebellion would have predicted changes in orientation such as the ones so briefly summarized. The fascinating question to pose here, however, is whether what has happened represents a *decline* in P.C.I. ideology, or something else. If by decline is meant the abandonment of some of the rhetoric, the verbal symbols, the predictions and expectations voiced until the late fifties, there seems little doubt about the validity of such a judgment, although the more appropriate word would be *change*. However, if by decline is meant that P.C.I. is becoming bourgeois or "social-democratized," or that it is abandoning any commitment to ideological formulations, I believe one should hesitate before leaping to such a conclusion. As Palmiro Togliatti significantly put it, "There is no experience regarding the way in which the battle for socialism can or must be waged in a regime of advanced monopolistic state capitalism. . . . There do not even exist explicit prescriptions in the classics of our doctrine."[25]

Communist leaders who spearhead this reappraisal are not calling for ideological retreat but, rather, for a concerted search for new ideological underpinnings for party policies and actions. In noting that Marxism offers, at best, vague guides to party behavior in modern Italian society, these leaders seem to me to be a long way from abandoning such key concepts as class, dialectical conflict, the exploitative nature of monopoly capitalism, and the fundamental need for effecting structural—not mild, reformist—changes in the social system. They, and the millions of Italians who support them at the polls, are far from concluding, if this is the acid test for the inclination toward ideological decline, that the problems created by the Industrial Revolution have been largely solved.

The effort to attune the party's ideology to present Italian realities is a complementary side of the vigorous campaign for polycentrism which the party has been conducting within the international Communist movement. Beginning in 1956, P.C.I. frankly asserted that the Soviet model could no longer be a specific guide to Communist parties in every country and that it would be necessary to find a "national path to socialism." Togliatti made this point forcefully in the last book he published before his death.[26] In November, 1961, the P.C.I. Secretariat formulated a resolution which said in part that "There do not exist and there cannot exist either a guiding party or state or one or more instances of centralized direction of the international Communist movement. Under existing conditions there must be and there must increasingly be a great articulation of the movement in a context of full independence of individual parties."[27]

These are brave words, and it is still much too early to conclude with any confidence what the result of the P.C.I.'s campaign will be.[28] What is important is the apparent P.C.I. conviction that it can come up with a new strategy—a new formula for achieving power—for Communist parties operating in Western European and other countries of advanced capitalism. It is important to bear in mind that, in doing this, the party purports to be able to provide an up-dated ideological rationale for action. Some of the "moldiness" of "Scientific Socialism" has certainly been scraped away. What remains, coupled with some of the newer ideas currently in ferment, amounts to much more ideology than one might detect from the simple notation that the language of the late forties and early fifties is no longer in vogue.

## Italian Christian Democracy

The genius of Alcide DeGasperi is that for a decade following the birth of the Italian Republic he was able to hold together within the Christian Democratic party (D.C.) strongly opposed ideological factions that managed to play down ideology in the interest of holding on to power. This was no mean achievement. Although the popular image of the D.C. is that of an opportunistic, anti-ideological "brokerage" party, the truth is that, from the outset, strong factions that would have emphasized ideology, even at the risk of splitting the party, had to be suppressed or defeated. DeGasperi's hegemonic control of the organization was secured only after he had managed to beat down early competition for leadership emanating from such ideologues as Giuseppe Dossetti, Amintore Fanfani, and Giovanni Gronchi. One might well conclude that, in an age of alleged ideological decline and after a decade of enjoying the many fruits of political power, ideology would have become a much less salient issue within the D.C.

Exactly the opposite tendency is apparent, however. Since the death of DeGasperi, and the advent of Fanfani as a major party leader in 1954, the ideological debate has not only intensified but has also broken into public view, revealing a party organization under deep internal stress. I believe that the facts will clearly demonstrate that since that date the role of ideology within the D.C. has actually increased rather than diminished, and a few central occurrences will serve to bear out this conclusion.

In September, 1961, the D.C. held at San Pellegrino the first of three annual "ideological" conventions. They represented a long and successful effort on the part of those in the party who had fought for making the party ideologically coherent, something more than the "brokerage" party the D.C. had been under DeGasperi's leadership. Looming over these proceedings were two of the party's perennial dilemmas: First, to what extent should the D.C., a party drawing much of its strength from the political right, articulate a left-wing ideology as a guide to policy? Second, how much ideological freedom could the party express *vis-à-vis* a Catholic Church to which it must necessarily remain fairly closely tied? Those who favored stronger articulation of a coherent left-wing ideology were strongly spurred by an undeniable gradual movement to the left by the Italian electorate, by the increasing willingness of the Italian Socialist party to consider active coalition with the D.C., and certainly not least by the kinds of ideological changes in the Vatican triggered by the innovating papacy of John XXIII.

Speakers at the conferences reviewed the party's ideological history, noting that at war's end it appeared that the party would lead the country left and that, in those years, DeGasperi himself stated that the old order based on the domination of rural landowners and urban industrialists would not remain intact. But it was lamented that whenever the D.C. confronted issues concerning which the party's ideology seemingly required socialist solutions, ideology was arrested in favor of not pushing to the breaking point the ideological centrifugal tendencies within the organization. As Franco Malfatti, one of the followers of Giuseppe Dossetti and Amintore Fanfani, points out, the revolutionary tone of early D.C. pronouncements was gradually transformed into the muted notes of a purely formalistic democracy and of a great concentration of governmental power at Rome.[29]

As the D.C. moved self-consciously toward the "Opening to the Left" which would bring the Socialists into the government, the party's ideologues would no longer accept the De Gasperi formula whereby all concern about or dedication to ideology was to be obscured in favor of the overriding value of party unity. At San Pellegrino, Malfatti put the new posture of the ideologues pointedly. "The problem of [party] unity," he said, "is a great one of fundamental importance but it is also a problem that runs the risk of losing all its value if used as a sedative, or as the Hymn of Garibaldi, every time there is conflict between clerical and anti-clerical elements."[30] If the party wished to be free of all internal ideological conflict, nothing would remain of it except an agreement "to hold power for power's sake."[31]

According to Achille Ardigò, a sociologist and long-time member of the party's national executive committee, the major milestones in the D.C.'s ideological evolution are the following:

First, the development of the concept of the political autonomy of Catholics, unconstrained by specific direction by clerical forces. Second, the growth of the idea of the autonomous function of intermediate groups (such as family, community, and social class) against the excesses of the centralizing, modern liberal state. Third, the defense and consolidation of liberty, in a government of laws, through an alliance of the democratic forces of the nation against political and ideological extremes. Fourth, the materialization of the ideology of the "new party" led by Amintore Fanfani. Finally, the emergence of a new concept of the state as an artifice of harmonious and planned development—the idea of the state as an instrument of dynamic intervention in the economic sphere and of the modification of the rights of property in favor of the well-being of the collectivity. It is the evolution of this last, self-consciously ideological stage that permitted the party's recent shift to the left and the acceptance of coalition with the Socialists.[32]

One can identify many reasons for this shift to the left, including Italian voting patterns that have clearly led the D.C. in this direction. To the many social and economic pressures leading to the emergence of a Catholic Socialism, one would have to add the liberating impact of John XXIII's revolutionary encyclical, *Mater et Magistra*. In the light of this radical departure from the conservative, often reactionary, political utterances of Pius XII, it is easy to understand why the D.C. left should be spurred to a more purposeful and ideological rationalized attack on Italian society's ills.

It is important to recognize that the San Pellegrino meetings mean not that the D.C. has moved left on a purely opportunistic basis, but, rather, on the basis of a "rediscovery" of the ideological formulations laid down by Dossetti and others in the late forties. To be sure the current ideology is not socialism and, indeed, leaders like Aldo Moro have been careful to distinguish D.C. ideology from socialism and communism. Nevertheless, the D.C. is today a dramatically less catch-all party than it was under De-Gasperi. It now has a somewhat official and publicly articulated ideology. If ideology is in fact in significant decline elsewhere in

Europe,[33] Italy will certainly have to be excepted from such easy generalizations. In the P.C.I., ideology has changed and appears to be vigorously reasserting itself; in the D.C. the era of suppressed ideology has passed, and ideological debate and commitment are clearly resurgent.

How, then, explain the imperfect, distorted, and erroneous perceptions of the decline-of-ideology writers?

## INTERPRETATIONS OF THE DECLINE-OF-IDEOLOGY LITERATURE

Several interpretations of the decline-of-ideology writings are possible, and I shall touch here on only two or three. First, one might simply dismiss this literature as reflecting a much too narrow focus on certain undeniable changes in the rhetoric, and even in the perceptions and prescriptions, of some contemporary Marxists. I say dismiss, rather then accord them serious intellectual attention, because: a) the narrow focus fails to include a broader conceptual framework that would permit comparative analytic attention to other aspects of Marxian and non-Marxian ideologies, and b) many of the observations limited to the crisis or travail experienced by Marxists since the Hungarian Rebellion and the XX Congress of the CPSU amount to nothing more than propaganda slogans.

Second, it is possible to sidestep the fascinating subject of broader comparative ideological analysis and concentrate instead on the central proposition that runs through much of this writing, namely, that ideology tends to wane as societies reach levels of social and economic modernization typified by several Western countries. It seems to me, however, that any attempt to assess these writings in such terms is fraught with a number of difficulties that can only be briefly mentioned here. For example, one will have to come to grips with Mannheim, who remains, after all, the first and most prominent scholar to touch on almost every aspect of the arguments mustered by contemporary writers, including the proposition that the birth and death of ideology depends on certain social, economic, and "ecological" factors.

But, Mannheim, as I have noted, intends a pejorative definition of ideology, thus greatly narrowing its application. For systems of ideas that are *not* incongruent with empirical realities, he uses the term "utopia." However, if I read him correctly, Mannheim's final test for deciding whether a system of ideas is ideological or utopian is almost invariably *post facto*—in the sense that what one identifies as yesterday's ideology becomes tomorrow's utopia when it can be shown that, somewhere in space and time, prescriptions or transcendent ideas turned out not to be incongruent with potential "social realities."[34] The pragmatic test is deceptively simple: If it works, it's utopian; if it doesn't, it's ideological. Outside of ascribing super-rational powers to the "omniscient observer," there is no readily apparent way of identifying the very thing one wishes to measure, except after the fact.

Beyond this conceptual problem, there are others implied by the "more modernization-less ideology" formulation. Such generalizations involve secular trends that span centuries. Thus, even if one can reach an acceptable working definition of ideology, the matter of measuring these trends—to say nothing of projecting them into the future—seems to me to involve a degree of precision in historical data gathering and measurement that is only a little better today (and in some ways much worse) than it was in Mannheim's time. My own impression about such long-range trends is that, despite some interesting changes in the symbology of ideology, we are far from seeing the end in Europe of ideology as I have defined it or, indeed, of ideology defined as dogmatic, inflexible, passionately articulated perceptions of reality and prescriptions for the future. Furthermore, since the long-term trend line is not unequivocally established, we cannot say whether short-term phenomena are part of a downward plunging graph line or merely a cyclical dip in a line which may be essentially flat or rising.

It also seems to me that the proposition we are discussing here suffers all of the limitations (which I have detailed elsewhere[35]) that one can identify with a good deal of the recent writing about political development. This formulation seems to rest on the assumption (or hope) that socio-economic-political development is moving in a deterministic, unilinear, culture-specific direction, whereby the future will consist of national histories that are monotonous repetitions of the "Anglo-American" story. In short, the decline-of-ideology writers seem to believe that "they" are becoming more and more like "us."

This leads to a possible third interpretation of the literature, namely, that most of this writing is not social science but, ironically, simply more ideology. The French scholar, Jean Meynaud, reacts in this summary way to the "decline" writers: "In reality, the deep intent of this theory is to establish that in wealthy societies socialism is definitely eclipsed. With many persons it [the theory of decline] is a rather banal aspect of anti-communism or, if one prefers, of a new version of conservative opportunism."[36] This view is strongly echoed by William Delany who says, "The end of ideology writers write not just as sociologists or social scientists but as journalists and an anti-totalitarian ideological cabal. Their work is ideology but, like almost all Western ideologies since the 18th Century, with a heavy 'scientific' component to give respectability and a sense of truth."[37]

These are admittedly harsh judgments. And yet, when one confronts the waning-ideology literature with actual developments in Western Europe, the gap between fact and "scientific" findings suggests exactly such evaluations. Indeed, it is entirely possible that, in the case of some of the decline writers, what they see may be little more than autobiographical projections, which may be fine for some novelists but is clearly quite sticky for social scientists. In any event, insofar as social science analysis of ideology is concerned, it is more than a little difficult to agree with an appraisal of the social sciences which begins by confiding that the American social scientist has been co-opted into something called the "establishment," and then goes on to say about "establishment" members:

Theirs is an alienation brought about by "superior wisdom," that is, by the ability to penetrate the ideologies of others and thereby to emancipate themselves. In this group is the social scientist, who is the objective observer. He penetrates all of the disguises created by the untrained mind or the ideological mind and attaches himself to the image of the wise. He represents the "establishment."[38]

I suppose that, if there is an American "establishment" and if the social scientist has come to play such a prominent role in it, one would expect that in the rationalization and defense of his well-ordered world the social scientist's words are likely to take on typically ideological overtones. In any event, it is difficult to imagine how the social scientist in the United States would now go about rebutting the reiterated Russian claim that Western social science is not much more than thinly veiled bourgeois ideology.[39]

This leads to a few concluding remarks about the extent to which phenomena associated with the alleged decline of ideology reflect in great measure certain kinds of adaptations to the crisis confronting Western intellectuals. The Italian case will serve as one concrete illustration of this, although similar patterns can also be explicated for other Western countries.

At the end of World War II, Italian intellectuals—like their counterparts elsewhere in Western Europe—felt deeply involved in a concerted and apparently promising effort to transform Italian society. This was a period in which "The sacred texts were dusted off and the people were enlightened in order to create the maximum degree of consensus and to realize the maximum degree of support and conversions."[40] But romantic notions of socialist revolution—widely fostered by intellectuals—were of very short duration. Failure of Italian society to move directly toward socialism caught many intellectuals flat-footed. They remained tied to a permanent anti-Fascism which led them to ritualistic rhetorical statements about Italian society's ills and the paths to salvation.[41] For almost fifteen years, these intellectuals repeated with startling monotony themes and prescriptions which were simply out of joint as far as the changing conditions of Italian society were concerned. In this sense, certainly, Aron and others are right in scoring the stultifying consequences of doctrinaire ideological formulations.

These were years of demoralization for intellectuals who expected revolutionary change and were treated instead to a great deal of temporizing under DeGasperi; but the intellectuals were also blinded to certain social and economic changes that made the traditional rhetoric of Marxism alien to growing numbers of Italians. The irony in all of this is that the intellectuals were the last to appreciate the need for new rhetoric and, indeed, for new ideological formulations. They had been preceded by political leaders not only in the Communist party, but in the ranks of Christian Democracy as well. The politicians evidently quickly understood that no large-scale intervention of the public sector in any kind of development was likely to proceed for long without some kind of *ideological* justification.

To some extent, the isolation of intellectuals from social realities was encouraged by the P.C.I. In keeping the party's intellectuals organizationally separated from mass members, the P.C.I. was able to capitalize on a tendency which is deeply rooted in Italian culture. As Guiducci points out, Italian intellectuals were strongly influenced by the Crocian idea that they were a caste apart, superior to and removed from the masses, and thus failed to maintain an open and realistic contact with the broader population. Even in a context of deep ideological commitment, they managed to adhere to "a position which is traditional with the Italian man of culture, estranged as he is from reality, tied as he is to a culture which is literary and humanistic in the narrowest sense of the words."[42]

The striking thing about Italy in recent years is that the country's intellectuals (largely of the left, but also of the right) seem to be emerging from the kind of isolation Guiducci mentions. Their confrontation of the realities of Italian society has not led, however, to a decline of ideology. Rather, I would suggest that what has happened involves in part ideological clarification and in part the framing of new ideologies to which striking numbers of Italian and European intellectuals now adhere. These new ideologies in a profound sense involve substituting new myths for old. The new myths, which form the core of the ideological structure of many intellectuals, are those of the welfare state and of economic planning. As Henri Jarme rightly puts it, "The myth of planning is only the socialist variant of the myth of progress."[43] But such myths, if Italy is any test, attract more than segments of former orthodox Marxists; they are woven as well into the kind of new ideology that Christian Democrats create.

To be sure, the emergence of new myths creates new symbols and vocabulary. This sort of change should not be construed, however, as an end of ideology. As Giovanni Sartori notes, "Granted that in an affluent society the intensity of ideology will decrease, a lessening of its intensity should not be confused with a withering away of ideology itself. . . . The temperature of ideology may cool down but this fact does not imply that a society will lose the habit of perceiving political problems in an unrealistic or doctrinaire fashion; and it implies even less that a party system will turn to a pragmatic approach."[44]

Two points are relevant here. First, it is obvious that many Italian intellectuals seem to have rediscovered a valid—or at least personally satisfying—function in society, namely, providing an ideological rationale, as well as rational alternatives, for economic planning activity. Second, in achieving this redefinition of role, the intellectual seems to have reaffirmed his responsibility for creating the ideological system within which contemporary activity is justified. Needless to say, some of these intellectuals will phrase ideology in the language of science and rationality, whether they are in favor of radical change or of the preservation of the status quo. There is certainly little evidence in Italy, in any event, that, say, a commitment to social science miraculously resolves the nagging problem of Mannheim's Paradox, nor, indeed, that it should.

When we turn to the decline-of-ideology writers, it is possible to detect that they, too, are in search of a definable role in contemporary American society. Whether that role involves the use of social science to criticize America's failing or to extol its consensual or managerial character is a fascinating empirical question. But surely the exploration of this problem would require of a mature social science a certain amount of caution and humility regarding the danger of translating highly selective data gathering or personal predilections or ambitions into sweeping historical projections and "scientific" generalizations. Clifford Geertz, I believe, has put this most succinctly: "We may wait as long for the 'end of ideology' as the positivists have waited for the end of religion."[45]

NOTES

1. This term is used by Clifford Geertz in "Ideology as a Cultural System," in D. E. Apter (ed.), *Ideology and Discontent* (London, 1964), pp. 48 ff. Although the present paper was prepared in draft before that volume appeared, I have benefited immensely in its revision from Geertz's perceptive essay. I have also profited from suggestions offered by my colleagues, Wendell Bell, James Mau, and Sidney Tarrow; and particularly from William Delany, whose analytical critique of papers on this subject delivered at the 1964 Annual Meeting of the American Political Science Association ("The Role of Ideology: A Summation") is itself a most insightful view of the problem.

2. I do not mean to suggest that American sociology speaks with one voice on this subject. There is, on the one hand, the claim of scientific objectivity and objection to the intrusion of values into research. But, on the other hand, there is also growing concern with the "global" questions, a retreat from the scientism implicit in some functionalist formulations, and increased demands for the need to engage in ethically relevant social research. See, for example, Peter Berger, *Invitation to Sociology* (Garden City, N. Y., 1963); Maurice Stein and Arthur Vidich (eds.), *Sociology on Trial* (Englewood Cliffs, N. J., 1963).

   It is also worth recalling that Max Weber, himself, to whom many claimants of the "scientific objectivity" of social science often turn for support, would never, in my view, have gone as far as some of our contemporaries in his brief for empirical science. As I read him, he considers a *science* of culture to be both "meaningless" and "senseless." See Max Weber, *On the Methodology of the Social Sciences*. Translated and edited by E. A. Shils and H. A. Finch (Glencoe, Illinois, 1949), pp. 49–112, and especially Part III. It is also possible to read Weber on the use of values in teaching as simply a strategy to be followed by scholars on the left who, in an authoritarian Bismarckian society, would be permitted to voice in the classroom only the values of the "Establishment." See, *ibid.,* pp. 1–47.

3. Talcott Parsons, "The Point of View of the Author," in Max Black, (ed.), *The Social Theories of Talcott Parsons* (Englewood Cliffs, N. J., 1962), pp. 313–315, 360–362.

4. Andrew Hacker, "Sociology and Ideology," in *ibid.*, pp. 289–310. In my view, Hacker raises most of the relevant questions about Parsons' seeming political "conservatism," and he underscores as well the essentially ideological reactions of Parsons to the work of someone like C. Wright Mills. Parsons' response to Hacker is to acknowledge that he (Parsons) is an "egghead," and a "liberal" whose views of American society and the functioning of the American political system are normatively unacceptable to Hacker and to " . . . a good many other American intellectuals, especially those who think more or less in Marxist terms. . . . " *Ibid.*, p. 350.

5. One exception would be Otto Kirchheimer, who was greatly concerned about the possible consequence of, say, the emergence of the "catch-all" political party in a country like the West German Republic. See his "The Transformation of the European Party System," in Joseph LaPalombara and Myron Weiner (eds.), *Political Parties and Political Development* (Princeton, 1966). Cf. his "The Waning of Opposition in Parliamentary Regimes," *Social Research* 24 (1957), pp. 127–156. I am uncertain as to whether what Kirchheimer describes is a decline of ideology, but it is noteworthy that he was one of those who didn't think that what he saw was "good" for Western societies.

6. Karl Mannheim, *Ideology and Utopia* (London, 1936), pp. 175–176. Mannheim's second chapter in this volume, pp. 49–96, from which the volume's title is derived, is of course the classic statement of the origins of the term "ideology," its particular and general formulations, its relationship to Marxism, and its catalytic impact on the sociology of knowledge.

7. The best recent short review of the literature that I have seen is Joseph J. Spengler, "Theory, Ideology, Non-Economic Values, and Politico-Economic Development," in Ralph Braibanti and J. J. Spengler (eds.), *Tradition, Values and Socio-Economic Development* (Durham, 1961), pp. 3–56, and especially Part V. Spengler himself opts for a somewhat pejorative definition which hinges on values that directly or indirectly impede a "rational" approach to the ends-means problem in economic development: see pp. 31–32.

8. L. H. Garstin, *Each Age Is a Dream: A Study in Ideologies* (New York, 1954), p. 3. I recognize that my usage here is quite broad and that it may be typical of what my friend Giovanni Sartori scores as the American tendency to assign to the concept, ideology, a very wide meaning, "without limits." Sartori argues that such definitions are "heuristically sterile and operationally fruitless" (personal communication to the author, November 16, 1965). Sartori may or may not be right; my point here is simply to break away from the extremely narrow definition implied in the "decline of ideology" literature.

9. Much of the burden of Geertz's essay, *op. cit.*, is to alert the social scientist to the great need for viewing ideology within a framework of "symbolic action." See pp. 57 ff.

10. I refer here primarily to the following: Raymond Aron, "Fin de l'age ideologique?" in T. W. Adorno and W. Dirks (eds.), *Sociologica* (Frankfurt, 1955), pp. 219–233; R. Aron, *The Opium of the Intellectuals* (New York, 1962); Talcott Parsons, "An Approach to the Sociology of Knowledge," *Transactions of the Fourth World Congress of Sociology* (Milan and Stresa, 1959), pp. 25–49; Edward Shils, "The End of Ideology?" *Encounter* 5 (November, 1955), 52–58; S. M. Lipset, *Political Man* (Garden City, 1960), pp. 403–417; Daniel Bell; *The End of Ideology* (Glencoe, Ill., 1960), especially pp. 369–375; and S. M. Lipset, "The Changing Class Structure and Contemporary European Politics," *Daedalus* 93 (Winter, 1964), 271–303.

11. Bell, *op. cit.,* pp. 370, 371.

12. Lipset, *Political Man, op. cit.,* p. 403.

13. Aron, *The Opium of the Intellectuals, op. cit.*

14. Lipset, *Political Man, op. cit.,* p. 407.

15. Lipset, "The Changing Class Structure . . . ," *op. cit.,* p. 272.

16. Lipset, *Political Man, op. cit.,* p. 406.

17. A number of colleagues who were good enough to read this manuscript urge that the empirical evidence challenging the "decline" thesis should not be limited to Italy. Roger Masters and Giovanni Sartori point out, for example, that the U.S. would provide additional supportive evidence. Nils Elvander notes that Tingsten himself, in his analyses of the Swedish Social Democratic Party, became "caught up in the intense struggle against the 'dead' ideology of the party, and when the battle was over he went on declaring ideology dead, not being able to see that it was revitalized again and again" (personal communication to the author, December 19, 1964). I am aware of this additional evidence and simply note that the Italian case is used here as an illustrative rather than exhaustive example.

18. Paolo Covilla, Giorgio Galli, Luigi Pedrazzi, Alfonso Prandi, and Franco Serra, "I Partiti Italiani tra il 1958 e il 1963." *Il Mulino,* 12 (April, 1963), 323.

19. G. Tamburrano, "Lo Sviluppo del capitalismo e la crisi teorica dei comunisti italiani," *Tempi Moderni,* 5 (July-September, 1962), 22.

20. See the editorial, "I Problemi del Mezzogiorno nei Congressi del PCI e del PSI," *Cronache Meridionali,* 4 (January-February, 1957), 57–58. The struggle of the P. C. I. to make the necessary ideological, strategic, and tactical changes in its approach to the Italian South is perceptively and exhaustively analyzed by Sidney Tarrow, *Peasant Communism in Southern Italy.* Ph.D. dissertation manuscript, Berkeley, University of California, 1965.

21. "I Problemi del Mezzogiorno . . . ," *op. cit.,* p. 59. Cf. Giorgio Amendola, "I Communisti per la rinascita del Mezzorgiorno," *Cronache Meridionali* 4 (May, 1957), 279. See, also, P.C.I., *Tesi e documenti del Congresso del PCI,* (Rome, 1963), 138.

22. Abdon Alinovi, "Problemi della politica communista nel Mezzogiorno," *Critica Marxista,* 1 (July-August, 1963), 4–8.

23. Palmiro Togliatti, *Il Partito Communista Italiano* (Rome, 1961), p. 55; Antonio Gramsci, "Alcuni temi della questione meridionale," in *Antologia degli scritti* (Rome, 1963), pp. 51, 69.

24. Tamburrano, *op. cit.*, p. 23.

25. *Ibid.*, p. 69. See the important statement by Bruno Tentin, one of the most important of the party's young leaders, intellectuals and ideological architects, "Tendenze attuali del capitalismo italiano," in *Tendenze del capitalismo italiano: Atti del convegno economico dell' Istituto Gramsci* (Rome, 1962) p. 43 ff.

26. Togliatti, *op. cit.*, p. 131.

27. See "Problemi del dibattito tra partiti comunisti," *ibid.*, p. 16.

28. The Italian Communists have pushed polycentrism very hard indeed, and do not react well to Soviet attempts to water it down. See, *L'Unità*, November 22, 1961, p. 11. On this general topic, see the excellent analysis by Donald L. M. Blackmer, "The P.C.I. and the International Communist Movement," Massachusetts Institute of Technology, mimeographed.

29. Franco M. Malfatti, "La Democrazia Cristiana nelle sue affermazioni programmatiche dalla sua ricostruzione ad oggi," in *Il Convegno di San Pellegrino: Atti del I Convegno di Studi della D. C.* (Rome, 1962), pp. 325–341. For examples of the early, postwar ideological statements of the party, see, for example, Alcide De-Gasperi, "Le Lineo programmatiche della D. C.," in *I Congressi Nazionali della Democrazia Cristiana* (Rome, 1959), p. 23; Gianni Baget Bozzo, "Il Dilemma della D.C. e del suo prossimo Congresso," *Cronache Sociali* Vol. 3 (April 30, 1949), 17; Achille Ardigó, "Classi sociali e sintesi politica," in *Il Convegno di San Pellegrino . . . ," op. cit.*, pp. 135 ff. It should be noted that the periodical *Cronache Sociali*, cited above, was the most important publication for those in the D.C. who, in the early postwar years, attempted to give the party a clear-cut left-wing ideological cast. Until recently, full collections of the magazine were extremely rare. The major articles from it, however, are now available in a two-volume work, *Cronache Sociali* (Rome, 1961).

10. Franco M. Malfatti, "L'Unità della D.C. e il problema delle tendenze," *Cronache Sociali*, 3 (February 15, 1949), 15.

31. Ardigò, *op. cit.*, p. 145.

32. *Ibid.*, pp. 155–165.

33. Exactly how much of the West is to be included in the generalizations about ideology's decline is never made too clear. Lipset, for example, is careful to hedge his European generalizations by frequently excepting Italy and France. My point would be that if these two countries are excepted, as they should be, one can scarcely pretend to speak with justification about *European* trends. See Lipset, "The Changing Class Structure . . . ," *op. cit., passim.* Moreover, there is also rather persuasive evidence that Lipset's generalizations are not currently valid, if they ever were, for a country like West Germany. See H. P. Secher, "Current Ideological Emphasis in the Federal Republic of Germany," a paper delivered at the 1964 Annual Meeting of the American Political Science Association, Chicago, September 9–12, 1964. Note particularly the extensive, German-language bibliography on this subject contained in the footnotes of this paper. In any event, the burden of Secher's argument is that German ideology is on the upswing, both in the SPD and in the Catholic sectors of the CDU/CSU.

34. See Mannheim, *op. cit.*, Ch. 4, "The Utopian Mentality." Mannheim notes that, "Ideologies are the situationally transcendent ideas which never succeed *de facto* in the realization of their projected content. . . . Utopias too transcend the social situation. . . . But they are not ideologies, i.e., they are not ideologies in the measure and in so far as they succeed through counteractivity in transforming the existing historical reality into one more in accord with their own conceptions" (pp. 176, 177). Mannheim later refines the definition of utopia, trying to tie it to the issue of incongruence from "the point of view of a given social order which is already in existence." Needless to add, it is ideology's decline that Mannheim applauds, and the decline of utopia that he greatly fears because the latter, he says, would make man nothing more than a "thing" unable to shape or understand history: *ibid.*, p. 236.

35. See my (ed.), *Bureaucracy and Political Development* (Princeton, 1963), Ch. 2; and my "Public Administration and Political Change: A Theoretical Overview," in Charles Press and Alan Arian (eds.), *Empathy and Ideology: Knowledges of Administrative Innovation* (forthcoming).

36. Jean Meynaud, "Apatia e responsibilità dei cittadini," *Tempi Moderni,* 5 (April-June, 1962), 33.

37. William Delany, "The End of Ideology: A Summation," *op. cit.,* p. 16.

38. Apter, *op. cit.,* pp. 37–38.

39. See A. A. Zvorykin, "The Social Sciences in the U.S.S.R.: Achievements and Trends," *International Social Science Journal,* 16 (No. 4, 1964), 588–602. J. S. Roucek, "The Soviet Brand of Sociology," *International Journal of Comparative Sociology,* 1 (1961), 211–219.

40. Antonio Carbonaro and Luciano Gallino, "Sociologia e ideologie ufficiali," *Tempi Moderni,* 4 (January-March, 1961), 31.

41. Nicola Matteucci, "Pensare in prospettiva," *Tempi Moderni,* 4 (April-June, 1961), 32. Cf. the important editorial, "Valori e miti della società italiana dell'ultimo ventennio, 1940–1960," *ibid.* (October-December, 1961), 22.

42. Roberto Guiducci, *Socialismo e verità* (Turin, 1956), pp. 23 ff. Cf. Gaetano Arfè, "La Responsibilità degli intellettuali," *Tempi Moderni,* 4 (January-March, 1961), 31–32; Paolo Prandstraller, *Intellettuali e democrazia* (Rome, 1963).

43. Henri Jarme, "La Mythe politique du socialisme democratique," *Cashiers Internationaux de Sociologie,* 33 (July-December, 1962), p. 29.

44. Giovanni Sartori, "European Political Parties: The Case of Polarized Pluralism," in J. LaPalombara and M. Weiner, *op. cit.*

45. Geertz, *op. cit.,* p. 51.

# 10 Empirical Relevance of the Hypothesis of Decline

## M. REJAI, W. L. MASON, AND D. C. BELLER

An important part of the analysis of political systems is an examination of ideologies or belief patterns that condition their operation. In addition to influencing the goals that will be pursued, ideologies have an important effect on the style of political life. Hence, a concern with diverse patterns of ideological belief has become a central aspect of contemporary political science.

Since the early 1950's, an increasing number of scholars have undertaken empirical studies of the role of ideology in political life. In particular, many have been concerned with the apparent waning of ideological politics in advanced, industrial societies—a

M. Rejai, W. L. Mason, and D. C. Beller, "Political Ideology: Empirical Relevance of the Hypothesis of Decline," *Ethics,* 78:4 (July 1968), 303–312. Reprinted by permission of The University of Chicago Press, copyright 1968 by The University of Chicago.

concern which has resulted in a significant body of literature on the "decline of ideology." Over the past few years, however, the decline hypothesis has been attacked by certain critics who have claimed constancy—or even "upswing"—in ideology in all parts of the world.

This article examines and evaluates the hypothesis of ideological decline and, in particular, the arguments of its critics.[1] The principal finding is that the criticisms launched against the decline thesis are based on dubious grounds and stem from serious misunderstandings. Perhaps the most alarming attribute of the antidecline writers is their apparent willingness to disregard the empirical significance of the hypothesis in question and to rely, instead, on semantic justification. To do so is to misunderstand some of the most important political changes over the past twenty years. In the pages that follow, we shall seek to show that the relevance of the hypothesis of decline is an empirical proposition as yet beyond the challenge of its critics.

# I

Raymond Aron should perhaps be assigned credit not only for having coined the phrase "end of ideology" but also for having elaborated upon it in some detail.[2] As early as 1953, he suggested that the strength of Communist ideology, for example, is directly proportionate to the degree of economic development in the country in which it may be found.[3] Two years later he formulated the hypothesis of decline and emphasized the passing of fanaticism in political belief and the erosion of ideas systems that were at one time sharp, distinct, and explicit.[4]

Perhaps the most significant impetus to the spread and acceptance of Aron's hypothesis was provided by a conference on "The Future of Freedom," sponsored by the Congress of Cultural Freedom in September, 1955.[5] Held in Milan, the conference was attended by some 150 intellectuals, scholars, politicians, and journalists from numerous countries. After five days of discussion and debate, there emerged among the Western representatives a clear consensus along the following lines: (1) total or extremist ideologies appeared to be in a state of decline: passionate adherence to universal ideological formulations were no longer relevant; (2) this decline was due largely to the increasing economic affluence in Western countries; and (3) this decline was crystallized in the fact that "over the past thirty years the extremes of 'right' and 'left' had disclosed identities which were more impressive than their differences."[6] By contrast, representatives from the non-Western countries insisted on the continued relevance of extremist ideologies.

Following the Milan conference, some of the American participants (who included Daniel Bell, John K. Galbraith, Sidney Hook, Seymour Martin Lipset, and Edward Shils) became centrally involved in further exploration and elaboration of the decline hypothesis. In a 1958 article, for example, Shils stated emphatically that the expectation that the age of ideology is passing is "not simply frivolously optimistic." While noting that in advanced Western societies "Marxism is decomposing," "nationalism . . . has lost its doctrinal grip," and "the asperities of the debate between socialism and capitalism seem to be fading," he reiterated the point that, "of course, ideological politics, Marxist, Islamic, Arabic, Hindu, Pan-African, and others, still exist in the new states outside the West in a vehement, irreconcilable form."[7]

Similarly, addressing himself to the problem of "exhaustion" of total ideologies in the 1950's, Bell wrote:

> Few serious minds believe any longer that one can set down "blueprints" and through "social engineering" bring about a new uptopia of social harmony. . . . Few "classic" liberals insist that the state should play no role in the economy, and few conservatives, at least in England and on the Continent, believe that the Welfare State is "the road to serfdom." In the Western world, therefore, there is today a rough consensus among intellectuals on political issues: the acceptance of a Welfare State; the desirability of decentralized power; a system of mixed economy and of political pluralism.[8]

Perhaps the most systematic comparative treatment of the decline thesis and its relationship to economic development (among other variables) has been undertaken by Lipset. Having noted the general phenomenon of decline in ideological polarization in Western societies, he wrote in 1960:

> This change in Western political life reflects the fact that the fundamental political problems of the industrial revolution have been solved: the workers have achieved industrial and political citizenship; the conservatives have accepted the welfare state; and the democratic left has recognized that an increase in overall state power carries with it more dangers to freedom than solutions for economic problems. This very triumph of the democratic social revolution in the West ends domestic politics for those intellectuals who must have ideologies or utopias to motivate them to political action.[9]

Elaborating on this theme a few years later, he noted that "the growth of bureaucracy and 'affluence' in western industrial democratic society has made possible a social system in which class conflict is minimized. Democratic politics has become the politics of collective bargaining." The causal relationships underscoring this proposition were stated in the following terms:

> Greater economic productivity is associated with a more equitable distribution of consumption goods and education—factors contributing to a reduction of intra-societal tension. As the wealth of a nation increases, the status gap inherent in poor countries . . . is reduced. As differences in style of life are reduced, so are the tensions of stratification. And increased education enhances the propensity of different groups to "tolerate" each other, to accept the complex idea that truth and error are not necessarily on one side.[10]

## II

During the past decade, a number of scholars have sought to verify the hypothesis of decline in specific modern societies. As early as 1955, Herbert Tingsten noted a direct relationship between economic development and the "leveling" of party and ideological conflicts in Swedish democracy. Having considered the major areas of traditional ideological cleavage in Swedish politics, he concluded: "The great [ideological] controversies have . . . been liquidated in all instances. . . . Liberalism in the old sense is dead, both among the Conservatives and in the Liberal Party; Social Democrat thinking has lost nearly all its traits of doctrinaire Marxism, and the label of socialism on a specific proposal or a specific reform has hardly any other meaning than the fact that the proposal or reform in question is regarded as attractive. The actual words 'socialism' or 'liberalism' are tending to become mere honorifics, useful in connection with elections and political festivities." Noting the emergence of "a community of values" between widely divergent parties and groups, he stated that the importance of ideology had been reduced to a point where "one can speak of a movement from politics to administration, from principles to technique."[11]

In his 1957 study of European parliamentary regimes, Otto Kirchheimer arrived at similar conclusions. He, too, identified the most significant changes in Europe as a temporizing of ideological formulations together with the emergence of a vast, homogenized, prosperous, and consumption-oriented middle class. He wrote: "The rise of the consumption-oriented individual of mass society . . . sets the stage for the shrinking of the ideologically oriented nineteenth-century party. . . . By and large, European parliamentary parties are reducing their special ideological . . . offering." The increasing consensus on the desired ends, Kirchheimer agreed with Tingsten, had led to "the transformation of political problems into administrative and technical routines."[12]

A 1965 study of Dutch politics yielded analogous findings. A. Hoogerwerf's comparative analysis of the election programs of the four major Dutch political parties for the years 1948 and 1963 revealed "a growing unanimity on a number of sociopolitical issues, viz. nationalization, a planned economy, and social [welfare] provisions." Ideological disputes, Hoogerwerf concluded, are becoming increasingly blurred. "Among the political leaders a shift is occurring from policy decisions to administrative decisions, i.e., from the choice of ends to the choice of means."[13]

Similarly, Robert E. Lane's secondary analysis of a wide range of public-opinion data from the United States and other Western countries over a number of years showed that the "Age of Affluence" has everywhere led to an increasing reduction of ideological tensions and a corresponding acceptance of the idea of the legitimacy of the opposition parties. The age of affluence, Lane found, is marked by the disappearance of "sense of crises," "sense of alarm," and "high stakes" in partisan politics. With particular reference to the United States, his data showed that only 5 percent of the population agree with the proposition that "Republicans probably endanger welfare," while only 3 percent believe that "Democrats probably endanger welfare." Lane thus concluded that in the age of affluence politics "becomes more a discussion of means than ends—its ideological component declines."[14]

An important study of postwar developments in European politics was undertaken recently by Lipset. Relying on massive empirical data from many parts of Europe, he reaffirmed the conclusion that ideological polarization was fast disappearing from the canvas of European politics. "Domestic politics in most of these societies," he noted, has become "reduced to the 'politics of collective bargaining,' that is, to the issue of which groups should secure a little more or less of the pie."[15]

Given the hypothesized link between economic development and ideological decline, one would expect the pattern to be repeated in all advanced, industrial societies—Western as well as non-Western. One would expect to find a relative decline in ideological politics, for example, in Japan. And this, indeed, appears to be the case. In a study of "Economic Growth and the 'End of Ideology' in Japan," Masaaki Takane concluded: "So far, no drastic results can be seen, but a trend toward the 'end of ideology' has been established. Presumably, if economic growth continues, and if there is no serious increase in tension in other parts of Asia, this trend will become stronger and more widespread."[16]

The most remarkable phenomenon in connection with the hypothesis of ideological decline, however, is not its empirical relevance for European or Japanese politics but its application even to such a country as the U.S.S.R. Writing on the "cumulative effect" of recent social, political, and economic developments in the Soviet Union, Zbigniew Brzezinski identified one of the most important consequences of these developments as "the reduced importance of both ideological issues and personalities." He went so far as to write: "Indeed, the effort to maintain a doctrinaire dictatorship over an increasingly modern and industrial society has already contributed to a reopening of the gap that existed in prerevolutionary Russia between the political system and the society, thereby posing the threat of the degeneration of the Soviet system."[17] Similarly, Frederick Barghoorn has written recently that the "existing Soviet political structures and the ideology which serves as a major source of their legitimacy are increasingly irrelevant to a more and more diversified society." He added: "The erosion of ideological dogma among the intellectuals is undoubtedly helping to undermine the psychological foundations of rule by a party which still makes a demigod of a man who died almost fifty years ago."[18]

The "erosion" of ideology in the Soviet Union is a theme identified also by Daniel Bell, who perceives the over-all direction of recent changes in that country as "the breakup, on all levels, of a monolithic society." Bell is explicit that although this does not suggest the disappearance of ideological politics, "in the abatement of the *dynamism* of a creed, and in the direction of the role of ideology as a 'weapon' against external and internal enemies, it may signify the 'end of ideology' in the sense that this polemical idea has been postulated."[19] A similar conclusion is reached by Robert C. Tucker in his study of the "deradicalization" of Soviet ideology.[20]

The end-of-ideology hypothesis, then, has occasioned a large body of scholarly output over the past decade. In general terms, this hypothesis seeks to establish a negative correlation between the degree of economic development and the intensity of ideological politics within a given country. The hypothesis has held up quite well in empirical investigations in a number of advanced, industrial societies.

## III

The hypothesis of ideological decline has generated an array of critics, of whom the most comprehensive and the most systematic appear to be Professors Henry David Aiken and Joseph La-Palombara.[21] The arguments of the antidecline school deserve serious consideration because they highlight some basic conceptual and methodological problems in contemporary social science. In the discussion that follows, we shall share the critics' concern with the meaning of "ideology" and its relative "decline" or "upswing," paying particular attention—as does La-Palombara—to the case of Italy.

Aiken and LaPalombara begin their substantive treatments of the decline thesis by adopting definitions of ideology that have serious deficiencies. As Bell points out, one of the chief defects of the Aiken essay is the multiplicity of senses in which the term "ideology" is used. In response to Bell's request for precision in defining ideology, Aiken states flatly: "It was not my purpose to define it, but to study and to characterize what other people . . . seem to think about it."[22] For Aiken, there are no useful distinctions between "political ideology," "political philosophy," "political discourse," and even "politics itself." Political ideology, he insists, "is nothing but political discourse." The end of ideology, he adds, "is, in a sense, almost tantamount to the end of politics itself."[23]

LaPalombara's definition of ideology suffers from similar imprecision. For him, ideology "involves a philosophy of history, a view of man's present place in it, some estimate of probable lines of future development, and a set of prescriptions regarding how to hasten, retard, and/or modify that developmental direction."[24] Beyond this, according to LaPalombara, ideology "tends to specify a set of values that are more or less coherent and . . . seeks to link given patterns of action to the achievement or maintenance of a future, or existing, state of affairs."[25]

What is apparent about these conceptions of ideology is that they are so broad as to be virtually useless for the purpose their authors have in mind. To his already broad definition, for example, LaPalombara adds still other broadening qualifications. Thus, ideology "may or may not be dogmatic," it "may or may not be utopian," it "may or may not emphasize rhetoric or flamboyant verbal formulations," it "may or may not be attuned to the claimed rationality of modern science," it "may or may not be believed by those who articulate it."[26] While this definition does touch upon such characteristics of ideology as its value content and programmatic orientation, it leaves out some critical elements generally included in conceptions of ideology.[27] It ignores, for example, the common observation that the basis of any ideology is a complex of beliefs held habitually and emotionally. This suggests what both LaPalombara and Aiken seek to deny: a degree of "distortion" or "unreality" in ideology. The proposition that ideology entails an element of "illusion" or "myth" has been stressed, at least since Karl Marx,[28] by most of the contributors to the literature. Thus Mannheim defines ideology as "more or less conscious disguises of the real nature of a situation."[29] Gustav Bergmann suggests that an ideological statement is "a value judgment disguised as, or mistaken for, a statement of fact."[30] Lasswell and Kaplan refer to ideology as "the political myth functioning to preserve the social structure."[31] Examples could be multiplied.[32]

Aiken and LaPalombara also neglect the point, commonly recognized, that ideology must necessarily be a part of the belief system of social groups. The tenets of ideology must find acceptance and manifestation in the behavior of a political society. Moreover, the significance of ideology will vary with the social group that holds it. Thus, for example, ideology as a systematic set of propositions articulated by the political elite may be quite different from ideology as an element of mass commitment.[33]

This important distinction is nowhere considered by Aiken or LaPalombara.

In short, while focusing their attention upon Western societies, Aiken and LaPalombara employ definitions of ideology so vague, so general, and so broad as to minimize their relevance for empirical investigation of those societies. In leaving out such critical attributes of ideology as its emotional belief component, its element of myth, and its social base, they rule out from the beginning the very aspects of ideology that seem to have been the concern of the writers against whom their work is directed. Instead, Aiken and LaPalombara insist on some curious assertions. They maintain, for example, that those definitions of ideology that identify an element of "deception" or "myth" are necessarily "pejorative" in character. They preclude from their consideration the point that the mere identification of "deception" or "myth" in ideology is an empirical propositon having nothing to do with "pejorative" activity. We are not suggesting that *some* definitions of ideology are not pejorative in character; we do say, however, that the categorical assertions of Aiken and LaPalombara cannot be substantiated.

An equally curious assertion is LaPalombara's accusation that the decline-of-ideology writers have equated "ideology" with "Communist ideology." Aiken is more careful here. He identifies "Marxism" as "the primary target" of the decline writers, asserting that "in prophesying the end of ideology, it is the end of Marxism of which they mainly dream."[34] LaPalombara, on the other hand, writes categorically:

> It seems . . . apparent that what these writers mean by ideology is not any given set of values, beliefs, preferences, expectations, and prescriptions regarding society but that *particular* set that we may variously associate with Orthodox Marxism, "Scientific Socialism," Bolshevism, Maoism, or in any case with strongly held and dogmatically articulated ideas regarding class conflict and revolution. Thus, "the exhaustion of political ideas in the West" refers to that particular case involving the disillusionment experienced by Marxist intellectuals when it became apparent that

many of Marx's predictions were simply not borne out, and when the outrages of the Stalinist regime were publicly revealed.[35]

Now, "the exhaustion of political ideas in the West" is apparently from Bell's *The End of Ideology*. However, it is manifestly unwarranted to suggest, as this passage seems to do, that the decline writers are not aware of the continued existence of a wide range of ideologies other than communism, that they have been blind to the ideologies of nationalism, the various democratic ideologies (including liberalism and conservatism), and the many politico-religious ideologies.[36] As far as we know, with the possible exception of LaPalombara, no writer on ideology has assumed the interchangeability of "ideology" and "Communist ideology."

# IV

LaPalombara's principal argument is that ideology, as *he* defines it, is not on the decline but, rather, is constant or on the "upswing" in Western countries. He "supports" this argument by drawing upon "empirical evidence" from one such country, Italy. Although he stops long enough to insist that similar empirical evidence can be found to justify the extension of the argument to the United States, Sweden, and other countries, nowhere does he actually give the matter serious consideration. He merely states that "Roger Masters and Giovanni Sartori point out, for example, that the U.S. would provide additional supportive evidence."[37] Despite his disclaimer to the contrary, it is clear that LaPalombara presents Italy as *the* illustrative case for an argument that is presumed to be of significance for the Western world as a whole.[38]

Given the hypothesized link between ideological decline and industrial development (a link which LaPalombara disputes), the choice of Italy as a test case raises serious problems. Of all the Western societies, Italy is most surely not one in which the problems of industrial revolution have been solved—a condition which Lipset and others suggest as a concomitant of decline of ideology. Nonetheless, LaPalombara proceeds to note, with apparent satisfaction, that the Communist Party of Italy (PCI) and its supporters "are far from concluding . . . that the problems created by the Industrial Revolution have been largely solved."[39] That, however, is precisely the point: no one suggests that the problems of industrialization have been overcome in Italy.

A fundamental difficulty associated with LaPalombara's treatment of the Italian case is that he never specifies the criteria that *would* satisfy him with respect to the proof or disproof of the hypothesis of decline. He does seem to imply, however, that one of two things may be involved: either ideologies must so converge within a society as to eliminate meaningful differences of outlook or ideological formulations must be abandoned altogether. He writes: "If by decline is meant that P.C.I. is becoming bourgeois or 'social-democratized,' or that it is abandoning any commitment to ideological formulations, I believe one should hesitate before leaping to such a conclusion."[40] Now, if convergence *is* the criterion of decline, LaPalombara's own data suggest that, even in Italy, recent modifications in the respective ideological postures of the Communist and Christian Democratic parties represent a movement toward greater ideological consensus than existed previously—that is, there has been a decline in ideological polarization. If, on the other hand, the abandonment of any commitment to ideological formulations is insisted upon, then his very broad definition of ideology drives the decline writers into the impossible position of having to demonstrate a lack of *any* consistent rationalization for policy goals before decline can be shown.

Once again, LaPalombara has pushed the issues out of focus. Using a definition of ideology so broad that almost any set of propositions held by anyone would qualify for inclusion, he attacks a thesis of decline based on a more restricted definition. Since he begins with a definition different from those typically used by decline writers, it is understandable, perhaps, that his finding should also be different—to wit, that ideology has not

declined in Italy. But this conclusion does not refute the decline-of-ideology thesis, for it is addressed to another question.

The ambiguity that haunts LaPalombara's analysis of the Italian case is largely a consequence of his failure to view ideology
as an operative variable in the political system. It may be interesting to learn that party intellectuals have not lost their ideological purity as the party has shifted position, but this does not tell
us much about the operation of the Italian political system. The
specific questions that make the phenomenon of decline a matter
of importance for the political scientist—but which La-
Palombara's definition of ideology does not permit him to consider—are those concerning the impact of ideology on specific
operational aspects of the political system. One of the most significant implications of the hypothesis of decline is that political
systems (and especially parliamentary systems) operate very differently when the partisan interests projected into them are of an
extremist, uncompromising nature than when those demands are
temperate and accommodationist. In the context of this proposition, the shift away from "extreme rhetoric" and "rigid and doctrinaire adherence to fixed schemes"—which LaPalombara himself associates with the PCI[41]—represents a reduction in the
ideological component of Italian political life. Consider La-
Palombara's own assessment of recent changes in PCI strategy:
"Nevertheless, the party's public posture has changed radically.
The most recent and important indication of this change is the
party's decision to seek alliances with elements of the middle
class—peasants, small land owners, artisans, small and medium
industrialists, and even with entrepreneurs who are not involved
with industrial monopolies. . . . The party's open strategy is to
attract to its ranks the mushrooming members of the middle and
tertiary strata that large-scale industrial development tends to
proliferate."[42] The willingness to make political alliances with
former foes and to accommodate ideological principles to electoral drifts *does* mean, we would submit, that in practical terms
ideological commitment has become subservient to pragmatic
considerations of political maneuver.

In short, what seems to be implied by LaPalombara's analysis
of the Italian situation is a decline in the intensity of ideological

commitment of both party leaders and party supporters, a decline in the exclusivistic quality of ideological formulations, and a decline in the mutual antagonisms among ideological groupings. This, we suggest, appears to involve an alteration in the style of Italian political life. The fact that party leaders (and/or followers) may continue to think in ideological terms—as ideology is defined by LaPalombara—does not seem nearly as important as the proposition that there has been a decline in the intensity and divisiveness of ideology in the Italian political system.

## V

The Aiken and LaPalombara attacks on the decline hypothesis, we have sought to demonstrate, are misdirected. The confusion that hinders their efforts is largely a consequence of two fundamental misunderstandings.

To begin with, Aiken and LaPalombara appear to misunderstand the substance of the decline thesis itself. The decline thesis, as we read it, does not refer to a total disappearance of ideological thinking; rather, it denotes a softening and blurring of ideological politics. It means, in simplified terms, a reduction in the amount of ideological conflict, polarization, rigidity, exclusiveness, etc., in a political system. It refers to the increasing irrelevance of "total" or "extremist" ideologies. Thus, Shils states, for example, that the decline thesis does not require the complete abandonment of ideological formulations. "Every society," he writes, "needs a certain amount of these ideals just as it would be ruined by too much of them."[43] Bell notes that the end of ideology "does not mean the end of 'belief systems' or the 'end of ideals.' " What it does signify is "an end to the 'war of beliefs.' "[44] The decline hypothesis, according to Bell, "has become a call for an end to apocalyptic beliefs that refuse to specify the costs and consequences of the changes they envision."[45] Lipset, who is equally explicit on this point, writes as follows:

As a final comment, I would note that not only do class conflicts over issues related to the division of the total economic pie . . .

continue in the absence of *weltanschauungen,* but that the decline of such total ideologies does *not* mean the end of ideology. . . . The "agreement on fundamentals," the political consensus of western society, now increasingly has come to include a position on matters which once sharply separated the left from the right. And this ideological agreement . . . has become *the* ideology of the major parties in the developed states of Europe and America.[46]

It seems clear, then, that the very meaning of the hypothesis of decline is misinterpreted and misconstrued by its critics.

The second difficulty underscoring the Aiken and La-Palombara attacks is that they appear to misunderstand the significance of the decline thesis. That thesis, we take it, is precisely a *thesis,* and its importance lies in its empirical relevance. It is meant to be a researchable question. Aiken is not seriously concerned with the empirical aspects of the problem. Although there are passing references to the American scene, nowhere does he attempt to examine and compare the intensity of ideological politics in different societies. LaPalombara, on the other hand, does employ the thesis-testing format in his analysis of the Italian case, but not really to test a thesis. He uses it to make an ideological argument (which he himself insists upon[47]) *against* a thesis which he takes as an ideological argument. By characterizing their respective endeavors as in part social-scientific and in part ideological (or philosophical), Aiken and LaPalombara present their own efforts as matters not amenable to analysis and testing.

## NOTES

1. We are grateful to Professor Seymour Martin Lipset of Harvard University for a critical reading of an earlier draft of this manuscript.
2. See Raymond Aron, "Fin de l'âge idéologique?" in T. W. Adorno and W. Dirks (eds.), *Sociologica* (Frankfurt: Europaische Verlaganstalt, 1955), pp. 219–233; and Aron, *The Opium of the Intellectuals* (New York: W. W. Norton & Co., 1962), pp. 305–324. The

M. REJAI, W. L. MASON, D. C. BELLER : 283

first American edition of *Opium* was published by Doubleday & Co. in 1957; the original French edition *(L'Opium des intellectuals)* appeared in 1955.

Seymour Martin Lipset has noted that two European writers, T. H. Marshall and Herbert Tingsten, "enunciated the basic thesis without using the term in the late 40's and early 50's." According to Lipset, Tingsten's earlier writings appeared in the Swedish newspaper *Dagens Nyheter,* while Marshall elaborated upon the theme in his 1949 essay "Citizenship and Social Class." See S. M. Lipset, "The Changing Class Structure and Contemporary European Politics," *Daedalus,* XCIII (Winter, 1964), 296, n. 1.

Lacking access to *Dagens Nyheter,* we are unable to evaluate Tingsten's early contribution; his later work (1955) will be considered presently. Marshall's basic argument is that, in their quest for political participation and citizenship, the new or rising classes tend to endorse violent and revolutionary action and that, once they are integrated into the existing order, extremism tends to be replaced by "collective bargaining." See T. H. Marshall, "Citizenship and Social Class," *Class, Citizenship, and Social Development* (New York: Doubleday & Co., 1964), pp. 65–122. Cf. Lipset, *op. cit.,* p. 272. However, the theme of decline of ideology remains essentially implicit in Marshall; nowhere is it spelled out.

3. See Raymond Aron, "The Diffusion of Ideologies," *Confluence,* II (March, 1953), 3–12.
4. Aron, *The Opium of the Intellectuals,* especially pp. 305–324.
5. A fairly detailed account of the conference appears in Edward Shils, "The End of Ideology?" *Encounter,* V (November, 1955), 52–58. See also S. M. Lipset, "The State of Democratic Politics," *Canadian Forum,* XXXV (November, 1955), 170–171.
6. Shils, *op. cit.,* p. 53.
7. Edward Shils, "Ideology and Civility: On the Politics of the Intellectuals," *Sewanee Review,* LXVI (July-September, 1958), 453–456.
8. Daniel Bell, *The End of Ideology* (New York: Collier Books, 1961), p. 397. The original edition was published by the Free Press in 1960.
9. S. M. Lipset, *Political Man: The Social Bases of Politics* (New York: Doubleday & Co., 1963), pp. 442–443. The original edition was published by Doubleday in 1960.
10. Lipset, "The Changing Class Structure . . . ," pp. 271–272.
11. Herbert Tingsten, "Stability and Vitality in Swedish Democracy," *Political Quarterly,* XXVI (1955), 145–147. Similar findings have been reported recently for Norway. See Ulf Torgersen, "The Trend towards Political Consensus: The Case of Norway," *Acta Sociologica,* VI (1962), 159–172.
12. Otto Kirchheimer, "The Waning of Opposition in Parliamentary Regimes," *Social Research,* XXIV (1957), 150–151, 153.
13. A. Hoogerwerf, "Latent Socio-political Issues in the Netherlands," *Sociologia Neerlandica,* II (1965), 174, 175.
14. Robert E. Lane, "The Politics of Consensus in an Age of Affluence," *American Political Science Review,* LIX (1965), especially 880–883, 893. Cf. Lane's "The Decline of Politics and Ideology in a Knowledgeable Society," *American Sociological Review,* XXXI (1966), 649–662, in which he seeks to establish a negative correlation be-

284 : *Empirical Relevance of the Hypothesis of Decline*

tween "knowledge" and "ideology." The argument is that in a "knowledgeable" society—which is also necessarily technologically, scientifically, and economically advanced—there is a marked decline in dogmatic and ideological thinking.

15. Lipset, "The Changing Class Structure . . .," p. 274.
16. Masaaki Takane, "Economic Growth and the 'End of Ideology' in Japan," *Asian Survey,* V (1965), 304.
17. Zbigniew Brzezinski, "The Soviet Political System: Transformation or Degeneration," *Problems of Communism,* XV (January-February, 1966), 8, 14.
18. Frederick Barghoorn, "Changes in Russia: The Need for Perspectives," *Problems of Communism,* XV (May-June, 1966), 41, 42.
19. Daniel Bell, "Ideology and Soviet Politics," *Slavic Review,* XXIV (December, 1965), 603 (italics in original). Cf. Daniel Bell, *Marxism-Leninism: A Doctrine on the Defensive; The 'End of Ideology' in the Soviet Union?* (New York: Columbia University Research Institute on Communist Affairs, 1965), p. 50. We are grateful to Professor Bell for calling our attention to these two studies.
20. Robert C. Tucker, "The Deradicalization of Marxist Movements," *American Political Science Review,* LXI (June, 1967), 343–358.
21. Henry David Aiken, "The Revolt against Ideology," *Commentary,* XXXVII (April, 1964), 29–39; Joseph LaPalombara, "Decline of Ideology: A Dissent and an Interpretation," *American Political Science Review,* LX (March, 1966), 5–16.
22. Aiken in Daniel Bell and Henry David Aiken, "Ideology—a Debate," *Commentary,* XXXVII (October, 1964), 75.
23. Aiken, "The Revolt against Ideology," p. 37; Aiken in Bell and Aiken, *op. cit.,* pp. 75–76.
24. LaPalombara, *op. cit.,* p. 7.
25. *Ibid.*
26. *Ibid.*
27. The conception of ideology presented in these pages draws on the following sources: Aron, *The Opium of the Intellectuals;* Apter (ed.), *op. cit.;* Bell, *The End of Ideology;* G. Bergmann, "Ideology," *Ethics,* LXI (April, 1951), 205–218; C. J. Friedrich and Z. Brzezinski, *Totalitarian Dictatorship and Autocracy* (New York: Frederick A. Praeger, Inc., 1961), especially Part III; A. Hacker, *Political Theory: Philosophy, Ideology, Science* (New York: Macmillan Co., 1961); T. P. Jenkins, *The Study of Political Theory* (New York: Random House, 1955), especially pp. 10–11, 62–64; R. E. Lane, *Political Ideology* (New York: Free Press, 1962); H. D. Lasswell and A. Kaplan, *Power and Society* (New Haven, Conn.: Yale University Press, 1950), especially pp. 116–133; Lipset, *Political Man;* K. Mannheim, *Ideology and Utopia* (New York: Harcourt, Brace, 1936); R. McDonald, "Ideology and Political Appeals" (unpublished Ph.D. dissertation, University of California, Los Angeles, 1963); Shils, "The End of Ideology?"; Shils, "Ideology and Civility"; F. M. Watkins, *The Age of Ideology* (Englewood Cliffs, N. J.: Prentice-Hall, Inc., 1964). We have also had an opportunity to examine Edward Shils's important article "Ideology," to appear in the forthcoming *International Encyclopedia of the Social Sciences*

(New York: Macmillan Co. and Free Press), for which we are grateful to Professor Shils and to Dr. Peter G. Bock of the *Encyclopedia.*

28. See especially Karl Marx and Friedrich Engels, *The German Ideology* (New York: International Publishers, 1947). They write on p. 14, for example: "In all ideology men and their circumstances appear upside down as in a *camera obscura.*"
29. Mannheim, *op. cit.,* p. 55.
30. Bergmann, *op. cit.,* p. 210.
31. *Op. cit.,* p. 123.
32. See, e.g., Apter (ed.), *op. cit.,* "Introduction," especially pp. 19–20; Aron, *The Opium of the Intellectuals,* Part I; Friedrich and Brzezinski, *op. cit.,* pp. 96–104; Hacker, *Political Theory,* especially p. 5; Jenkin, *op. cit.,* especially p. 10; Shils, "Ideology."
33. Cf. J. B. Christoph, "Consensus and Cleavage in British Political Ideology," *American Political Science Review,* LIX (1965), 629–642; and P. E. Converse, "The Nature of Belief Systems in Mass Politics," in Apter (ed.), *op. cit.,* pp. 206–261.
34. Aiken, "The Revolt against Ideology," p. 32.
35. LaPalombara, *op. cit.,* p. 8 (italics in original).
36. See, e.g., Aron, *The Opium of the Intellectuals,* chaps. viii and ix and Conclusion; Bell, *The End of Ideology,* especially pp. 397 ff.; Lipset, *Political Man,* chaps. iv, v, x, and xiii; and Shils, "Ideology and Civility," especially pp. 453 ff.
37. LaPalombara, *op. cit.,* p. 9, n. 17. LaPalombara makes no mention of the findings of the Lane study discussed above, even though Lane's article was published in an earlier issue of the same journal in which LaPalombara writes.
38. He insists that, since the decline thesis applies "to the West, and therefore to Europe as well as the North American continent, it may be instructive to look at one of these countries, Italy, to see *exactly how accurate* these generalizations are" (LaPalombara, *op. cit.,* p. 8; italics added).
39. *Ibid.,* p. 11.
40. *Ibid.,* p. 10.
41. *Ibid.,* pp. 9–10.
42. *Ibid.,* p. 10.
43. Shils, "The End of Ideology?" p. 57. Cf. Shils, "Ideology."
44. Bell, *Marxism-Leninism,* p. 50, n. 58.
45. Bell in Bell and Aiken, *op. cit.,* p. 70.
46. Lipset, "The Changing Class Structure . . . ," p. 296 (italics in original).
47. He writes: "I wish to acknowledge that my own effort in this paper may be in part—and quite properly—identified as ideological" (LaPalombara, *op. cit.,* p. 6).

# 11 Anti-Ideological Thought in France

## ROY PIERCE

## INTRODUCTION

A survey of the literature which deals with the theme of the decline of ideology reveals two main features: the word "ideology" is used in a variety of ways, and sometimes in more than one way in the same work; and some of the leading contributors to the literature have not simply been describing what they regard as an observable phenomenon or raising a question about whether such a phenomenon exists but rather arguing a case in favor of a decline of ideological politics.

Sometimes ideology is used to signify a millennial political theory, of which Marxism is held to be the purest current vari-

Prepared especially for this volume, this chapter is a revised version of a paper delivered at the annual meeting of the American Political Science Association, Chicago, September 1964. *Author's note:* In preparing this version, I have profited from William Delany's paper, "The Role of Ideology: A Summation," which was also delivered at that meeting, and from the comments of my colleague, Samuel H. Barnes.

ety; sometimes it is used to signify only a confidence in socialist institutions, which are not exactly accorded millennial virtues but which are held in such high symbolic esteem that they tend to be equated with the good consequences presumed to follow from them. Sometimes it is used to refer to those shorthand concepts (left, right, liberal, modern, etc.) which people employ to help them make up their minds about parties or policies; sometimes it is used to refer to any political doctrine which a group has constructed or adopted. Sometimes ideology is held to be a more or less coherent body of thought; sometimes it is held to be the very absence of thought. Sometimes the relation between ideas and reality is held to be the essential characteristic of ideology; sometimes the degree of congruence between idea and reality is held to be irrelevant to the definition of ideology. And so on.[1] It is clear that as long as people have various views of what an ideology is, it will be impossible to demonstrate to everyone's satisfaction that ideological politics has or has not declined (quite apart from the problem of how one would go about trying to measure it at time intervals).

At the same time as the word ideology is used in various ways, it is often not used neutrally. Groups which have what they regard as ideologies may regard them as desirable, but in the literature dealing with the decline of ideology, a prominent theme is that ideologies are harmful and that we would all be better off if ideological politics would disappear. This was the view of Albert Camus, the first person to use the expression "the end of ideologies." Camus was arguing a case, not describing a phenomenon, when he wrote in 1946 that if the socialists "renounced Marxism as an absolute philosophy, limiting themselves to retaining its critical aspect, often still valuable . . . they will demonstrate that this era marks the end of ideologies, that is of absolute utopias which destroy themselves in history by the price that they end up costing."[2] This statement, and others made by people whom I will refer to as anti-ideologists, is not neutral. The absence of neutrality has left the anti-ideologists open to the criticism that they themselves are ideologists, that whatever it is that is expressed by their anti-ideological position is itself an ideology, although the argument depends to some extent on whether the anti-ideologist and his critic understand the meaning of ideology in the same way.

I do not intend to try to cover here the still growing body of literature on ideology, as fascinating as I have found it to be to try to trace its main lines. Instead, I will limit myself mainly to some ideas contributed by French participants in the debates. French political thinkers have been prominent in developing the notion that ideological politics is harmful, and the cumulative analysis which they have produced expresses a multifaceted but perfectly intelligible political theory to which many of the current uses of the term ideology can be referred. Accordingly, the French contributors provide the closest thing that there is to a key to the solution of a triple problem. Why is there ambiguity and uncertainty over the meaning of ideology? Why do so many people hold a negative view of ideological politics? Is an anti-ideological position itself an ideology?

It has been suggested that there may be distinctive French and American views concerning ideological politics.[3] That may be so, but I will not try to discriminate between French and American views on the question. It appears more important to me to explain the fundamental approach to politics which underlies the French anti-ideologists' position. The significance of this approach extends far beyond the relatively narrow confines of a debate over whether or not ideology has declined. As I will try to show by comparing the approach to some views expressed by Karl Deutsch,[4] it really represents a political philosophy which is by no means limited to France.

## PROBLEMS OF DEFINITION

In its early post-World War II phase, the discussion of ideologies by French thinkers tended to have a fairly well-defined center of gravity within a field which contained the potentialities for many, varied, and diffuse applications. When Camus made the statement quoted above, he was defining an ideology as an absolute utopia which is not (or cannot be) reached because of the human damage which is (or would be) done in the effort to establish it. The statement surely refers primarily to the experience of Stalinist Russia. It may refer also to the experience of Nazi Germany, although in 1946, when the statement was made, nazism and fascism had been defeated and discredited. When Raymond Aron, who has been the principal French participant in the discussion of the decline of ideology, wrote *The Opium of the Intellectuals,*[5] he too was concerned primarily with criticizing Marxism-Leninism, in order to try to diminish its appeal for French intellectuals. But even as Marxism was the center of the discussion, it was clear that at least some of the things that both men were saying about it could be applied to other ideas about politics and that there was considerable ambiguity about just what these other ideas were and, therefore, about what an ideology is within their understanding of the term.

When read in conjunction with other things Camus had written earlier, and was to write not much later, his 1946 definition of ideologies as absolute utopias seems too limiting and the application he gave it seems too narrow. Camus had always been suspicious of abstract ideas. He was a critic of bourgeois democracy as well as of Stalinism; after reading *The Rebel,*[6] one wonders whether he was thinking, when he wrote the brief remark quoted, not only of the Russian Revolution of 1917 and the Nazi Revolution of 1933, but also of the French Revolution of 1789. The reference to absolute utopias parallels too closely other expressions—abstractions, general ideas, principles, systems—which Camus criticized, both before and after 1946, for one to assume that it stood sharply separated from some more fundamental set of considerations.

Aron too, while concentrating his attention in *The Opium of the Intellectuals* on Marxism, also spoke of liberalism, socialism, and conservatism as ideologies.[7] In *Espoir et Peur du Siècle,*[8] he subjected certain conservative values to the same kind of analysis that he had applied to Marxism in *The Opium of the Intellectuals;* he employed the concept of ideology to stand for the use of "abstract language" by pressure groups to support their particular interests and claims for prestige;[9] and he described the United States as more ideologically diverse than any country of Europe.[10]

More recently, Aron has tried to clarify his earlier formulations by writing that when he raised the question of whether the Western world was reaching the end of the ideological era, he defined ideology explicitly as "an overall system of interpretation of the historico-political world."[11] He refers to Hayek's liberalism and to Marxism as such overall systems, and then goes on to say that "it is difficult to trace the line of demarcation between ideologies that are formulations of an historical attitude or of a hierarchy of values, and that are inseparable from politics or, in any case, of all democratic politics, and the overall systems of interpretation to which I reserved the term ideology."[12]

I do not think that this statement resolves the definitional problem, but while I personally would prefer either a categorical and unambiguous definition of ideology or a moratorium on the use of the word, the definition of ideology seems to me to be less important in the context of French criticism of ideology, however the word is understood, than the kind of criticism brought to bear on the various concepts that are labeled ideological. This is because the criticism reflects a form of political reasoning and probably even a philosophy of politics that are important in their own right.

## ANTI-IDEOLOGICAL POLITICAL THOUGHT

What Camus and Aron have in common as political thinkers (as well as what both men have in common with the political ideas of Simone Weil) is that they each express, in different forms and with varying emphases, a particular form of political thought which (for reasons to be given shortly) I will call "open." Elsewhere I have showed the intellectual links among these three French political thinkers and analyzed their political ideas in detail;[13] here I will confine myself to a summary of the main characteristics of the current of thought which they represent as it applies to the debate over ideological thinking.

This current of thought perceives politics as men pursuing goals that reflect ideals, principles, or values.[14] But men pursue their goals through policies and institutions which may or may not actually express the values on behalf of which they are adopted. And men adopt policies and institutions within a field of circumstances or conditions which may or may not permit the policies or institutions to achieve the intended goals. This current of thought, therefore, is particularly sensitive to the difficulty of translating ideals, which are abstract, into policies or institutions, which are concrete. This sensitivity leads to a strict insistence on examining closely the relationships between goals, policies, and circumstances. Will the policy achieve the goal in the given circumstances? Will it conflict with other equally desirable goals? Will it set other forces into motion which can be expected to thwart the initial purpose? These are some of the questions which the anti-ideologist raises early in any discussion of political action.

In particular, the anti-ideologist tries to examine as closely as possible the link between abstract ideals and concrete practices. Men justify their political action in terms of ideals (liberty, equality); they idealize certain institutions (property, parliaments); they confer symbolic value (positive or negative) upon concepts whose concrete institutions are often indeterminate (socialism, capitalism, tradition). The anti-ideologist asks whether a particular action in particular circumstances will be likely to promote the ideal, and in what sense; whether and to what extent certain institutions in certain circumstances are likely to justify the claims made in their behalf; what precisely are the defining characteristics of a given social concept and how much and what kind of praise or blame their operations deserve.

It should be clear why there is confusion over the meaning of ideology as it is construed by the anti-ideologists. The latter want to relate abstract concepts, particularly emotive ones, to concrete referents. This is what is involved in ideological criticism (and in empirical social science). But there are various abstract concepts, of different types. Some, like Marxism, may represent what Aron calls "overall systems." Others may be less complex. But they all pose the same problem of the relationship between the ideal and the social reality. The anti-ideologist, of course, may not succeed in establishing the degree of the relationship; he does, however, believe that one must try to do so.

The anti-ideologist believes that it is necessary to do so because unexamined abstract concepts can in certain circumstances produce harmful results ranging from disappointed expectations to what Camus called "logical crime." For the extreme limit of ideological thinking is to identify ideals with the policies adopted or the institutions established to achieve the ideals. This is to confer on policies and institutions a value which, in the view of the anti-ideologist, no policy or institution merits automatically. Some policies or institutions are better than others, come closer than others to expressing the values they are designed to promote. But to equate the ideal with the prosaic risks dangers which range, depending on the situation, from reparable error to regimenting entire societies or committing violence on a global scale.

In a limited sense, the anti-ideologists' insistence on relating abstract concepts to concrete referents is related to the English philosophical school of linguistic analysis. But it goes beyond linguistic analysis in its encouragement, more often implicit than explicit, of social science. For it is clear that the purely logical ingredient of ideological criticism has its limits and that empirical testing of claims and counterclaims eventually becomes necessary. In this respect, the anti-ideologists are both practitioners and advocates of a social science designed to enable people to select the policies most likely to achieve their goals.

The anti-ideologists' manner of thinking about politics cannot easily be summed up in a single sentence. In 1964, I thought that insofar as it could be given a simple label, relativism would be the most appropriate. The main reason for selecting relativism as an appropriate descriptive term was its distance from absolutism, and it therefore seemed appropriate in the negative sense that the school rejects absolute political claims and, as illustrated by the quotation from Camus above, equated absolutes with the ideologies they condemned. The anti-ideologists assert repeatedly that politics never achieves more than the approximation of ideals, that it does not achieve salvation, that it always carries a risk of error.

The word absolutism is too pretentious, however, to apply properly to every situation in which a group might act in a fashion which would draw the criticism of the French anti-ideologists. Dogmatism might be the better word to apply to certain cases; in others, the word overvaluation would be more appropriate. From the perspective of this current of French political thought, ideological politics is characterized by the attribution of absolute value to any program, means of action, or institution; by a tendency to act dogmatically without regard to circumstances; by the persistent overvaluation of some principles or policies relative to alternatives.

If absolutism is not the only opponent, relativism loses its appropriateness as the proper descriptive label to give to the other side. Because of this, and because of other works which have a direct bearing on the subject, "openness" seems to me a better term.

## OPENNESS

There is obviously a close correspondence between such notions as absolutism, dogmatism and persistent overvaluation, and the interpretation of ideology suggested by Giovanni Sartori.[15] Following Rokeach's distinction between the open and the closed mind,[16] Sartori distinguishes between an open and a closed approach to politics. In his view, the closed approach is one of the dimensions of an ideological mentality. Openness and closedness here are defined in terms of permeability to evidence and argument; "ideologism can be legitimately understood to mean not only a rigid and dogmatic approach to politics, but also a principled and doctrinaire perception of politics."[17]

There is also a close correspondence between the outlook of the French anti-ideologists and the propositions, expressed partly in religious terminology and partly in communications terminology, which Karl Deutsch employs to describe the concept of autonomy of a political system.[18] The autonomy of a system, according to this analysis, depends on the capacity of the system to receive new information, relate it to its behavior and to its goals, and adjust its behavior and its goals in the light of that information. The inability of a system to perform those operations represents "self-closure,"[19] the insulation of the system from its environment and/or the failure to adjust to that environment.

In an attempt "to approach the ancient problem of morality and politics from the viewpoint of the study of communication and organization,"[20] Deutsch suggests that the avenue to social learning can be expressed as "humility," its obstacle as "pride." In language reminiscent of Camus, Deutsch writes: "The concepts of faith and humility exist to some extent as opposites in mutual tension. Faith implies commitment to some judgment of our own, even if it were only our judgment in choosing the right authority or the right book to obey; but humility might advise us to distrust our own judgments even in such cases. Taken together, the two concepts offer us no model of a perfect working arrangement, but rather indicate two boundary conditions between which a viable pattern must be sought."[21]

What emerges from the conception of openness, by which I have characterized the political outlook of the French anti-ideological school, is a way of thinking about politics rather than the specification of concrete forms of social or political organization. Specific policies or institutional recommendations depend on the nature of the problem and the circumstances in which it appears. Adherence to particular policies or institutions, as a matter of principle, is precisely what the anti-ideologists regard as ideological reasoning.

Does this mean that the anti-ideologists are without principles, without values? Of course not. Aron and Camus are not indifferent to the outcome of political struggles. But principles are not to be pursued at any cost, and no fixed hierarchy of values can be implemented in every situation. And underlying the whole anti-ideological philosophy is the primordial value of freedom of criticism and research. Under what other condition could learning, for the sake of which openness is urged, take place? Camus called freedom "the only imperishable value of history."[22] Aron wrote that "the authentic westerner is he who accepts totally from our civilization only the liberty that it leaves for criticizing it and the chance that it offers to improve it . . . . "[23] What Deutsch calls "spirit," in contrast to "eclecticism," expresses the inner configuration of purpose which underlies a policy.[24] What he calls "memory" and "tradition" function as the architects of the configurations of purpose which give meaning to a political decision, and which alone prevent a political system from being tossed like a cockleshell by the crosscurrents of its environment. But unless they also remain alert to the messages from the environment, "self-steering organizations are apt to cease to steer themselves and to behave rather like mere projectiles entirely ruled and driven by their past."[25]

But while these people all proclaim the need for values, they urge a skeptical attitude about all policies and institutions. Never assume that the institutions will reflect the values; never assume that the policies will achieve the goal. Instead, examine, weigh, hesitate, and after one has finally acted, do not become wedded to the decision made, the institution created, or the policy adopted. Circumstances may change, the results may not be what one expected.

## CRITICISMS

Is this open, anti-ideological philosophy of politics itself an ideology? I do not think so, at least if an ideology is defined in Sartori's terms as (in part) a closed cognitive structure.[26] The distinguishing property of the anti-ideologists' philosophy is precisely that it does not contain any fixed formulation of a right and proper organization of society, of a good policy, or even of a good set of institutions. The formal conditions of what is right and proper are delineated, but concrete decisions are to be worked out in a constant evaluation of goals, means, and circumstances. Aron calls this process the dialectic between man and his works;[27] Deutsch speaks of the tensions between humility and pride, lukewarmness and faith, reverence and idolatry, love and its opposites, and eclecticism and spirit;[28] Camus and Deutsch both underline the tension which is involved. The ideas that appear in this form of reasoning are not concrete images of political or social phenomena; they are conceptual categories within which concrete problems are to be analyzed.

It is possible, of course, that in the analysis of a concrete situation, someone who adheres to this open philosophy might make an ideological statement or even assume an ideological position of some central importance. He might, for example, confound a preference with a condition (say, in discussing the relationship between unequal rewards and economic growth) or describe as immutable something that is contingent (say, racial discrimination). To do so would be to bend the reality to fit the idea of it, a characteristic of ideological thinking. But even if this were done, the ideological ingredients would not be intrinsic to the method, but rather the result of inadequate application of the method. The test of ideology versus openness would lie in the thinker's response to the evidence presented by his critics.

It has been suggested that the arguments against ideological politics result in "approbation of the existing order," that they have contributed to the "consolidation of conformism," that they have a "place in the ideological arsenal of conservatism."[29]

There are aspects of the uses to which the anti-ideologist's philosophy has been put which lend support to this view. Aron's criticism of the Marxist ideology and of traditional conservatism was directed against people discontented with the prevailing political structure and social policies, and in this respect his own position was conservative, not, of course, in the traditionalist sense which he criticized, but in the sense of conserving the status quo against two very different kinds of critics. Aron wrote in 1966 that he had become more sensitive than he had been ten years earlier "to the risks of passivity and of indifference" that accompany the discrediting of overall ideological systems.[30]

I do not believe that the philosophy of the anti-ideologist necessarily supports the status quo. For one thing, the notion of a status quo is not entirely clear in a society where there is a constant pulling and hauling of social and political groups. Adapting policies to circumstances in a swiftly changing society would not necessarily be a conservative act. And to the extent that the anti-ideologist succeeds in establishing the concrete meaning of abstract notions, calculating probable consequences of alternate courses of action, and contributing to social science, he is helping to reduce the area of the unknown. This may be the least conservative feature of the openness of anti-ideological thought. For the advocates of change are probably always at a disadvantage simply because change means moving into the unknown. People may prefer a present that they know, despite its obvious imperfections, to a future that they do not know, despite its potentialities.[31] Reducing the extent of the unknown, therefore, may contribute to overcoming the natural defenses of conservatism.

It is probably the case that there are different emphases among people who hold an open political philosophy. Although I have suggested that there is a similarity in outlook between the French anti-ideologists and Karl Deutsch, there is an explicit thrust forward in Deutsch's position that has no counterpart in Aron's. Failures in what Deutsch calls the autonomy of the political system are "related to the overvaluation of the near over the far, the familiar over the new, the past over the present, and the present over the future."[32] Aron, perhaps, tends to place more emphasis on maintaining continuity between the present and the past, and between the future and the present. But the underlying significance of the open philosophy is that it accepts the necessity of arguing in specific cases over just these matters, and the outcome is not determined by definition in advance.

## IMPLICATIONS

It should be clear that if ideological political thinking has no single, discrete expression, if it is "not only a rigid and dogmatic approach to politics but also a principled and doctrinaire perception of politics," then it becomes extraordinarily difficult to produce some empirical measure of its increase or its decline.

It is simple enough, if some agreement can be established over which major parties profess "overall systems of interpretation and action," to chart their electoral record across some period. But the problem of measurement becomes much more difficult if one considers not only overall systems, but also any kind of overvaluation of policies or institutions because these are equated with the ends they are presumed to serve or the values they are assumed to express. All parties appeal to abstractions, become wedded to slogans, make exaggerated claims, oversimplify, and sometimes forget that they are not alone in the world and that the world changes.

Anthony Downs has tried to show that ideological appeals may be the inevitable consequences of the high cost of information for the great majority of political participants in a democracy.[33] Barnes and Converse have emphasized the organizational implications of maintaining consistent ideological expression among the poorly informed and the poorly educated.[34] The long-term trend, however, in societies which devote a large share of their resources to education, runs counter to ideological thinking (as it is understood here), as the number of people capable of securing and evaluating political information will increase.

At the same time, however, the web of relationships likely to be set off by the adoption or the rejection of almost any policy proposal becomes more complicated as our societies become more intricate in their economic and social activities, to say nothing of the interdependence of national societies. While people and governments may be more likely than ever before to make the kind of calculations advised by the anti-ideological school, the kind of decisions they are called upon to make and the extent and interconnectedness of the social grids over which the impulses of those decisions will spread may make it increasingly difficult for the probable consequences of those decisions to be accurately assessed in advance.

Lastly, it is apparent that since the debate over "the decline of ideologies" of the 1950s and early 1960s, large movements of discontent, populated mainly by university students, have appeared in the Western democracies. The inspiration of these movements is varied: some, particularly in France, are highly ideological in that they proclaim variants of anarchism, syndicalism, Trotskyism, Maoism, and so forth. Others are less ideological, and more concerned simply with specific social changes whose merits can be argued more easily within the framework of the anti-ideologist's conceptual categories (goals, means, circumstances).

Whether these movements will crystallize into a new wave of ideological politics, we do not yet know. Bertrand de Jouvenel thinks that the French student revolt of May-June 1968 may be the harbinger of a new social attitude, one which opposes the prevailing acceptance of the continual need for economic growth and the social changes which inevitably flow from assigning priority to it.[35]

Raymond Aron, on the other hand, without underestimating the significance of the student revolt, appears to believe that at least the anarchistic, syndicalistic, and other pre-Marxist underpinnings of the revolt are totally inadequate models for the organization of society because they are incompatible with the requirements of modern industrial society.[36]

And so the debate goes on. Whether new anti-industrial ideologies will take firm hold on the public mind, or whether the discussion of what the goals of society should be will take place within the assumption that science and technology are an immutable part of the environment, no one can say with certainty. The latter seems to me to be more probable. But in a debate over a subject of such magnitude, it would be surprising if the hallmarks of ideology did not repeatedly appear.

### NOTES

1. David Minar has prepared a useful classification of ways in which ideology can be defined: he shows that "by any definition, ideology is

thought," but that it can be and is "specifically distinguished by content, structure, function, or locus." "Ideology and Political Behavior," *Midwest Journal of Political Science,* (November, 1961), 326.

2. Albert Camus, "Ni Victimes Ni Bourreaux," in *Actuelles, Chroniques 1944–1948,* Paris, 1950, p. 154. The article originally appeared in *Combat* in November 1946.
3. William Delany, "The Role of Ideology: A Summation," *op. cit.,* p. 16; and Raymond Aron, *Trois Essais sur l'Age Industriel,* Paris, 1966, pp. 197–198.
4. To my knowledge, Karl Deutsch has never been involved in the discussion of whether or not ideology has declined.
5. The original French version was published in Paris in 1955; the English version was published in New York and London in 1957.
6. London, 1953; New York, 1954.
7. *L'Opium des Intellectuels,* Paris, 1955, p. 324.
8. Paris, 1957.
9. *Ibid.,* p. 48.
10. *Ibid.,* p. 51.
11. *Trois Essais sur l'Age Industriel, op. cit.,* p. 215.
12. *Ibid.*
13. *Contemporary French Political Thought,* New York and London, 1966.
14. They do not ignore the "who gets what, when, how" aspect of politics. Even in that framework, acts are justified in terms of ideals, principles or values.
15. "Politics, Ideology, and Belief Systems," *American Political Science Review,* LXIII (June, 1969), 398–411.
16. Milton Rokeach, *The Open and Closed Mind,* New York, 1960.
17. "Politics, Ideology, and Belief Systems," *op. cit.,* p. 403.
18. *The Nerves of Government,* The Free Press of Glencoe, 1963.
19. *Ibid.,* Chapter 13.
20. *Ibid.,* p. 214.
21. *Ibid.,* p. 232.
22. *The Rebel, op. cit.,* p. 291.
23. *L'Opium des Intellectuels, op. cit.,* p. 69.
24. *The Nerves of Government, op. cit.,* pp. 240–242.
25. *Ibid.,* p. 207.
26. The other element of ideology, according to Sartori, is its emotive dimension. *Op. cit.,* p. 403.
27. *Trois Essais sur l'Age Industriel, op. cit.,* p. 234.
28. *The Nerves of Government, op. cit.,* pp. 229–242.
29. Jean Meynaud, *Destin des Idéologies,* Etudes de Science Politique 4, Lausanne, 1961, pp. 123, 124, and 133–134.
30. *Trois Essais sur l'Age Industriel, op. cit.,* p. 216.
31. For a related view of why "more people are capable of reaction than reform," see Richard M. Merelam, "The Development of Political Ideology: A Framework for the Analysis of Political Socialization," *American Political Science Review,* LXIII (September, 1969), 750–767; the quotation is from p. 766.
32. *The Nerves of Government, op. cit.,* p. 229.

33. *An Economic Theory of Democracy,* New York, 1957.
34. Samuel H. Barnes, "Ideology and the Organization of Conflict: On the Relationship between Political Thought and Behavior," *Journal of Politics,* 28 (August, 1966), 513–530; Philip E. Converse, "The Nature of Belief Systems in Mass Publics," in David Apter, ed., *Ideology and Discontent,* New York, 1964, pp. 206–261, especially pp. 246–249.
35. "L'Explosion Estudiantine" in *Analyse et Prévision,* VI (September, 1968), 561–582.
36. *La Révolution Introuvable,* Paris, 1968, pp. 32, 113, and 137.

# 12 *The Student Movement and the End of the "End of Ideology"*

## MICHAEL NOVAK

One would have thought, a few years ago, that the age of ideology was at an end. But now young people have discovered that pragmatism, too, has the characteristics and effects of an ideology. They have observed, in particular, its low resistance to a new, toughened strain of tyranny. Technological progress, they recognize, demands stability and unity over periods of time long enough to bring plans and projections to fulfillment; it thus depends upon control over natural resources, industrial facilities, future human desires, and world conditions. Any government dedicated to the uses of advanced technology finds it in the national interest to produce and to enforce stability ("controlled dynamic growth") on a worldwide scale.

Michael Novak, "An End of Ideology?" *Commonweal,* March 8, 1968, pp. 679–682. Reprinted by permission of Commonweal Publishing Co., Inc.

Thus university students have been among the first to discern and to condemn the dangers of the philosophy heretofore dominant in the intellectual life of this country. Many among the brightest and most emotionally mature students, as studies like that of Joseph B. Katz have shown, are won over by the experiences, emotions, and arguments that have given birth to "the New Left." These are the students who rebel most strongly against liberal professors, liberal journals, and the general civility and temperateness of liberalism. Moreover, so sharp is this rebellion that communication between "Old Left" and "New Left" is scarcely possible. Fundamental presuppositions have been changed. Basic value judgments are made differently. If we had an accurate map of what is at stake, perhaps it would become possible to disagree with clarity and precision, instead of with rudeness, contempt, and theological odium.

The argument of the students, naturally enough, is grounded in what they see and hear daily at the universities. The war in Vietnam has taught them that their professors share the basic values and interests of the American government and of the leaders of the new technological industries, whatever the highly publicized public differences between academy and town on questions of procedure. Thus the recent statement by fourteen "moderates"—some of them giants in academic life—justifying present United States policy in Asia reaches the students as no surprise. They have long known what William Pfaff recently wrote in *Commonweal:* that the war in Vietnam is essentially a pragmatist's war, essentially a liberal war. Protest against the war was slow in coming, precisely because it fitted the American intellectual temper so well. Richard Rovere's recent account of his own dilemma in *The New Yorker* illustrates the point.

What, then, is the American intellectual temper as students perceive it? First, let us be clear that we are talking about a minority of students, although probably the most significant minority in terms of perception and talent; and a growing minority. Second, we need a context in which the argument is not unduly loaded against either the older intellectual community or the radical students.

Historically, "the movement" is at best five or six years old. The young do not have a full-blown theory by which to situate their own position over against alternatives. They arrive upon the scene when there seems to be a vast consensus, a tradition that has been appropriated with growing extension and solidity since at least the first days of the New Deal. That tradition is antimetaphysical; it values compromise and adjustment; it prides itself upon its diagnosis of "real" interests and its estimate of immediate "realizable" possibilities; it thinks itself, in a word, unusually "realistic." As the young see it, however, this tradition has been operative with a social and political vision that has been reduced to automatic and trivial sequence. It is tired, repetitive in tactics and strategy, and increasingly out of contact with the dynamic energies of our time. The pragmatic tradition misread the conditions that resulted in the war in Vietnam and the conditions of despair and pride in the black community. Moreover, pragmatists seem blind to the fact that they, too, are ideologues. They neither defend nor criticize their own presuppositions, value judgments, predilected standards (like quantification), and political biases. They have tried so hard to be "objective" that they have failed to examine their own subjectivity—including economic status and professional commitments—for sources of distortion. Because mathematics is "objective," they think they are.

The students spot plenty of distortion. An occasional paper of the Center for the Study of Democratic Institutions, *Students and Society,* for example, offers unusually clear student testimony on this point. The word for professors is "technocrat." The American intellectual community seems to prefer "how to" questions, questions of prediction and control. Such questions demand as much quantification as the material will bear ("and then some"). Effectively, this preference removes the intellectual community from facing value questions and questions of ends—these are "soft" questions, and those who deal with them are considered unprofessional. Rewards go to hard-nosed analysts who provide the power of prediction and control.

Many professors do not seem sensitive to what their students are thinking or feeling; many would be surprised to think that, precisely as professors, they ought to be. Concentration is upon "objective" materials. Much worse, the limits of reality, for academic purposes, are established by professional circles in each discipline; what is important to such a circle is important, what is irrelevant to it does not, professionally, exist. The gap between the professional disciplines and the real world—where "real" means of concern to living human beings—could grow to great lengths before professionals would notice. But students have noticed. And to them specialization seems to be an escape from responsibilities as a human being. Professors perform their professional tasks, and then retreat to their comfortable upper middle class homes and private lives, like kept women of the American way of life. Their dignified phrases about truth and academic freedom could be claimed just as well by auto repairmen.

The close ties between major universities and the new technological industries, moreover, and the new dependence of state and national governments upon academic research and advice, have changed the role and character of the universities in society. In a rough way, the university is to our society what the church used to be: its spiritual center, its source of guidance and legitimation. Its duly ordained experts are the clergymen of the new era: Walter Rostow as *éminence grise*. We have not yet devised ways of guaranteeing the separation of university and state.

Radical students turn upon their professors as protestant reformers upon complacent and powerful medieval churchmen. The note of disappointed innocence is poignant: how *could* you, *you* above all? The one hope of cutting through the American myths of cherry pie, virginity, self-reliance, anticommunism, crusades for freedom, and hard work lies in the university. Yet university professors appear to prefer the comfort of their sinecures to preaching the original revolutionary message of our land, the message transmitted through our bill of rights, our constitution, the Statue of Liberty's call to the oppressed and poor of the world.

It is important to make clear that the protest of the reformers is not merely a protest of activists against theoreticians. The student protestants are saying that the old *doctrines* are wrong, the *theories* are inadequate, the professors are blind to too many realities of life. The reformation is theoretical as well as practical. We have to revise our *conception* of knowledge and of the role of science, our *view* of ourselves and of our world. The issues involved, in fact, sound like metaphysical or theological issues.

## GUT REACTIONS

The students, however, have been well taught by pragmatic teachers; they do not know how to raise metaphysical questions; they retreat, instead, to gut reactions. They look at the war, the ghettos, the increasing reaction of right-wing and liberal forces of "law and order," and they *feel* indignation. The corruption riven through American life by the interests of the comfortable is so palpable they can taste it and smell it. "All you have to do is open your eyes, man. If it don't make you feel sick, ain't nothin' no one can do for you." When one young man I know loses his bitterness—the center upon which he now pivots his personality —he pulls out a wrinkled photograph of babies disfigured by napalm: his Spanish Jesus mutilated on the cross. Among the students there is an unmentioned litmus test: they study you to see if you feel what they feel. Liberals who talk "realistically" and "pragmatically," radicals believe, cannot possibly feel what their words imply; they know not what they do.

Yet the young are trapped. They reject the technocrats but have pitifully few intellectual alternatives. When John Dewey and other great architects of the current pragmatic realism were teaching, they at least carried with them, implicitly but powerfully, the humanistic tradition of their own earlier schooling; they advised their students, however, not to bother with the old masters of the prescientific era. Some among the second generation of behavioral scientists, political scientists, social scientists, and analytical humanists, consequently, speak only one intellectual language. In rejecting that language, the present generation of students finds itself mute about its most urgent feelings. They do not *wish* to be anti-intellectual, but the one available intellectual language is abhorrent to them. Moreover, it is impossible for them to return to the classics, the great books, or the humanists—the recovery of a tradition that has now lapsed would turn them into historians, whereas it is the present and the future they most want to absorb and to comprehend. Had they the language, one feels, many of them would like to articulate clearly what is happening now, and thus produce new classics expressing our own new cultural era. Mute instead, they can only say that those over thirty don't understand.

And surely they are right in feeling in their bones a new culture coming to birth. They need a vision of man adequate to the new time, and a political and social theory adequate to that vision. It ill becomes the older generation, which (overburdened by vast wars) has since 1932 provided so little by way of long-range vision or creative political and social theory, to demand that the students produce the longed-for vision and program in one stroke: instant ideology. The radical students need help. Specifically, they need fresh theories, new intellectual tools, openness to breakthroughs and readiness for originality. In many cases, all they need is someone to help them to articulate what they have already experienced and cannot quite say.

Thus, for example, the radicals speak in indignant tones of corruption, sickness, and selling out; but they do not really mean to say that they think of themselves as pure, or that total purity of motive and conscience is possible for a human being. The vision of man which they seek must be utopian in the sense that it is an alternative to the present series of pragmatic adjustments and gives promise of a new cultural epoch. It need not be utopian in the sense that it represents a naïve innocence about man. Reflecting on the first five or six years of the movement, the radicals have learned that you can't trust anyone *under* thirty, either; not even yourself.

The radicals recognize that the rugged individualism of Ayn Rand, the inner-directed personality of David Riesman, and the natural, atomic individual imagined by John Stuart Mill and the

English empirical tradition are not now (if they ever were) viable models of human behavior. The social sciences—and political events—have taught them too well that the supposedly private, autonomous world of the self is in fact conditioned and shaped by the institutions in which human beings live, move, and have their being. The sense of reality is, itself, a social product. Consequently, the radicals aspire to political consciousness in the proper sense: to become conscious of one's own identity is to become aware of institutional power already at work in oneself. The road to personal liberation is not private or through meditation, but political. Awareness grows through conscious, reflective, accurate action. The separation between thought and action, which present university life enforces, seems to the students illegitimate; and they argue the case on theoretical grounds.

The students seek fresh theories at many crucial places in the analysis of social reality. For example, when older liberals speak of "academic freedom and academic decorum" in connection with recent demonstrations on campuses, they are thinking of McCarthyism, loyalty oaths, and the disruptive techniques of the Nazis in the 1920's. But the students are thinking of the enormous power of television and newspapers to establish the mainstream of public discourse. They see clearly how the honeyed discourse of public officials—which is ordinarily reported straight—instantly smothers the imaginations and emotions of all within their reach, and how a sweet coating is put upon all intentions and actions of the United States. The inherent respectability of official sources gains a multiplied, overwhelming power, and the entire burden of counterargument, unmasking, and reporting of contradictory interpretations passes over onto the few who are equipped for it. Commonly, the mass media cannot follow the subtleties of the argument; moreover, officials merely announce; dissenters must document. Thus, a time-lag of days, weeks, or months may be required before a rebuttal can be published. Worse, the very structure of the mass media makes dissenters seem querulous, nitpicking, obsessed; officials are encouraged to pose as noble and long-suffering.

The balance of power in the formation of public opinion has

been altered by the advent of television. The society of independent, rational individuals envisaged by John Stuart Mill does not exist. The fate of all is bound up with the interpretation of events given by the mass media, by the image projected, and by the political power which results. The few with access to further information cannot compete with the many. Moreover, it is not so much "further information" that is at stake; it is the "image," the symbolic presentation of values, presuppositions, angle of vision, frame of reference, that is established by the media. In a society with respect for its political institutions, officials have only to act with decorum and energy in order to benefit by such respect and to have their views established as true until proven false.

Thus people are at the mercy of their government in a new and frightening way. The forces of "law and order"—army and police—are so powerful in the United States that no conceivable challenge could be raised against them. The technological society demands unity and thus the whole apparatus is concentrated in an awesome way in the hands of the federal government. "Freedom of speech," therefore, can no longer be governed merely by standards of decorum. The assumption that officials are speaking the truth can no longer be safely entertained by those who value their liberty. The credibility gap is not due to the personality of President Johnson; it now inheres in the office and in all public offices.

What, then, does freedom of speech mean in a technological society? How can one defend onself against McCarthyism on the one hand, and official newspeak on the other? The solution of the students has been to violate the taboos of decorum and thus embrace Vice President Humphrey, the CIA, Dow Chemical, and other enemies in an ugly scene, hoping that the unpopularity of the radicals will rub off on those embraced. They want to make the heretofore bland and respectable wear that tag which most alarms American sensibilities: "controversial."

This tactic suggests that it would be an advance in academic freedom never to allow a public official to share the privileges of academic discourse, unless followed immediately by a devil's ad-

vocate in open debate. We desparately need protection against
our government, its agencies, and its industrial allies. We desparately need a theory of free speech and tolerance which takes account of advances in technology, in expanded population, and in
industrial wealth and power. We need defense against the owners, advertisers, and official users of the mass media, and against
those who rely upon traditional decorum and the need for law
and order to make effective public challenge impossible. Given
television and affluence, a government no longer needs a brazen
Gestapo; it can win acquiescence by granting bread and circuses
and announcing noble sentiments.

Thus many seeds of immense theoretical importance are ger-
minating in the consciousness of the young. Never was it so clear
that the role of the teacher—and today of the publicist—is as
Plato described it: that of a midwife. Professors are not the fathers of the new consciousness, they are only the midwives, looking on with alert and critical wonder at what the young, seeded
who knows how or where, bring forth.*

* For a critique of the closure of moral purpose and intelligent inquiry
on the part of the radical movement, see also my "The Volatible Coun-
terculture," *Christianity and Crisis,* May 25, 1970, 107–113.

# 13 *Toward a Radical Alternative*

## KENNETH KENISTON

During the 1960's, it was the lot of Americans to live in mounting historical crisis, but not to understand it. The symptoms of the crisis were everywhere: deepening involvement in a war most Americans believe we should never have entered; poverty and urban deterioration in the world's richest nation; persistent racism in a society committed for two centuries to human equality; the growing disaffection of the best educated generation in history. But when it came to defining what was the matter, most have not even tried. As a result, the symptoms of the crisis have constantly been confused with its causes, while

Kenneth Keniston, "Three Books That Suggest a Radical Critique of Modern America," *New York Times Book Review,* September 6, 1970, pp. 3, 20. © 1970 by The New York Times Company. Reprinted by permission. *Editor's note:* The books under review are Philip E. Slater, *The Pursuit of Loneliness: American Culture at a Breaking Point* (Boston: Beacon Press, 1970); Richard Sennett, *The Uses of Disorder: Personal Identity and City Life* (New York: Alfred A. Knopf, 1970); Paul Goodman, *New Reformation: Notes of a Neolithic Conservative* (New York: Random House, 1970).

311

the best efforts of both young and old have been wasted in episodic attacks on these symptoms.

American liberalism was of course caught unprepared by the events of the last decade; indeed, it systematically denied the possibility of a crisis. "Ideology" was said to be dead and the most pressing cultural problem was "mass culture." Keynesianism had solved the problem of business cycles. Respectable trade unions and collective bargaining had brought the class conflict to the conference table. The American consensus, incremental change and the interplay of interest groups had transformed revolutionary impulses into party politics. By overstressing the "mechanisms of social control" that guaranteed "equilibrium," liberals had deprived themselves of concepts with which they could perceive, much less understand, what was happening.

Paradoxically the same was largely true of the "New Left." Emotionally, the new radicalism was indeed exquisitely attuned to the crisis. But intellectually, the new radicals made a virtue of not having an "ideology." Rejecting the rigidities of Marxism, they proposed a politics that was down-to-earth, participatory, and humane—and very American. Their critique of American society was from the start shallow and eclectic, uncritically mixing American populism, liberal reformism, and ever-larger doses of C. Wright Mills and [Herbert] Marcuse.

As the crisis deepened in the late sixties, the "old New Left" began to splinter, in good part because it lacked a solid intellectual basis. Some radicals turned back to Marxism, now leavened with Mao Tse-tung, Che Guevara, and Frantz Fanon. This move, though it connected American radicalism to the Third World, did so by identifying the world's most economically developed nation with the most underdeveloped. And for some, it even generated the fantasy that the modern American working class would become the vanguard of an impending revolution. What it overlooked was how basically modern American technology differs both from the nineteenth-century capitalism and from the underdeveloped nations.

Another faction of the New Left swung toward the cultural revolution—toward light shows, macrobiotics, Timothy Leary, acid, Zen, Norman O. Brown, astrology, encounter groups, and meditation. For many cultural revolutionists, the most important "struggle" was to develop "unalienated consciousness," spontaneous human relationships, and a rediscovery of the subjective world. Yet the cultural revolution has shown itself extraordinarily vulnerable to co-optation by *Time, Life,* and Madison Avenue; at worst, it risks becoming a harmless caricature of American culture rather than a viable alternative to it.

Even when, as in 1970, the symptoms of the national crisis—Mylai, Cambodia, Kent State, Jackson State—became evident even to the most complacent liberal, no one knew what was really the matter, much less what was to be done. Indignation prevailed over insight, polemics over profundity, and anger over analysis. Indeed, the concept of a "radical critique" of a contemporary American society still remains more of a slogan than an achievement.

The three books reviewed here, however, together suggest that such a radical critique may yet be born. The works of Philip Slater and Richard Sennett, in particular, show a refreshing willingness to deal with contemporary American society on its own terms rather than in strained analogies to nineteenth-century capitalism or to twentieth-century colonialism. All three books rest on a recognition that the current American crisis is the product of all that has happened since Marx's work. All three books are friendly to yet often sharply critical of the militancy of the young. All three books incorporate the insights of psychoanalysis into an understanding of the psychological substrata of social change. All three reject the "liberal" assumption of equilibrium, stressing instead change, challenge, and conflict. And all three are "radical" in the best sense, in that they go to the root.

*The Pursuit of Loneliness* by Mr. Slater, chairman of the sociology department at Brandeis, is a brilliant, sweeping, and "relevant" critique of modern America. It deserves a more intensive discussion than can be provided in a brief review. Slater's main thesis is simple: the untrammeled individualism of American society lies at the root of most of our present perplexities. Individualism engenders the awful loneliness of Americans, while it makes us unwilling to direct the technologically motored process of social change. The merit of Slater's work, however, lies not so much in his main thesis as in the brilliance with which its many subthemes are developed. Central to Slater's analysis is his constant awareness that modern affluence has rendered obsolete the traditional assumption that there was not enough to go around, generating a pervasive conflict between the "old [scarcity] culture" and the "new [post-scarcity] culture." Today, the ambivalent individualism of the old culture is contested by the ambiguous collectivism of the new, the hoarding of the old by the consumption and tribalism of the new, and so on.

Despite his sympathies with the new culture, however, Slater refuses to join it either in its apocalyptic radicalism or its apotheosis of the world of pure consciousness. Instead, he remains "political," arguing that any solution must involve an alliance between liberals and radicals to reassert control over the social process. Whether one agrees or not, Slater's is an insightful, well-written, and thought-provoking book that illumines each of the many aspects of American culture it touches.

*The Uses of Disorder* by Mr. Sennett, who teaches sociology at Brandeis and is director of the Urban Family Study Center and codirector of the Cambridge Institute, has modest goals, but is a notable achievement. Sennett sets out merely to write another book about cities. But in fact, he has ended up writing the best available contemporary defense of anarchism. Sennett believes that the homogenization of modern American life arose out of the "adolescent" conformisms perpetuated by preaffluent society. But in an affluent world, he argues, more "adult" levels of psychological functioning become possible, and with them a new kind of fruitful urban anarchy and diversity. Sennett's ideal city would be much like the "mixed neighborhoods" that surround university communities today. Such anarchic communities should be small and without police or rules. They would require men and women to deal with each other as face-to-face equals, to generate from their own self-interests the minimal rules necessary to make life livable, and to abandon their "adolescent" insistence on homogeneity.

Sennett's diagnosis of homogeneity differs profoundly from Slater's of individualism: Sennett's goal is the anarchy of "adult" self-interested men, whereas Slater's is greater acceptance of the needs of the collectivity. Like all anarchists, Sennett is an optimist about human nature, and is convinced that post-affluent "adulthood" will permit ideally anarchic cities where immediate self-interest alone will suffice to create livable communities. However questionable this faith, the issues Sennett raises are fundamental and profound. His book is utopian in the best sense —it tries to define a radically different future and to show that it could be constructed from the materials at hand. With this book, the process of redefining nineteenth-century anarchism for the twentieth century is begun.

Paul Goodman's *New Reformation* is essentially what Sennett would term an "old culture" book. For all of Goodman's traditional anarchism and Reichian psychology, he constantly appeals to an Aristotelian sense of balance, of rational order, and of measuredness. In *New Reformation* Goodman repeats many of the themes of his ten previous books of social criticism. But in this work he turns to examine the revolt of the young as an essentially religious reformation.

Goodman admits that his tone is at times petulant and querulous, and his intent, as always, didactic. Like both Sennett and Slater, he is post-Marxist and post-Freudian, critical yet admiring of the radicalism of the young. And like any anarchist, he is critical of the Leninist cast of some modern radicals, and remains optimistic that the dissolution of old authority relations would lead to a more spontaneous and better society. Yet Goodman, unlike most modern anarchists, insists again and again on the relevance of history, of learning, of the humanities, of reason and of science—and herein lies his loving quarrel with the young. His pleading, sane, frank, troubled, and by now tired voice is one of the truest and wisest in American life.

It is unlikely today that history will again allow us men like Marx and Freud. Events now move too fast for an individual genius to found a movement based upon the slow unfolding of his own ideas. The speedup of modern history makes most men's ideas obsolete during their lifetimes, while the instant consumption of both men and ideas by the media effectively prevents that lengthy period of gestation that characterized the great intellectual innovators and movements of the past. At best, what we can hope for today is the development of a new mood of social analysis and criticism that will be the work of many, not one genius.

Slater and Sennett, despite their important differences, suggest the directions in which a new social criticism might move. Post-Marxist and post-Freudian, aware of the interplay of human development and historical change, committed to radical change but unaligned with any radical faction, they assume that we will fail to fathom the modern crisis with the formulae of the past. Products of the technological society, they are aware of its voracious destructiveness, its dehumanizing assumptions, its conformism countered by defensive individualism, and its persistent devaluation of the subjective, the chaotic, the passionate, the cooperative, the anarchic and the immeasurable.

Yet they also acknowledge that technological society has produced unprecedented freedom from want, from insecurity, from poverty, hunger, and disease, and propose that these real gains make possible the most radical visions of a possible future. The problem today is thus not to destroy the technological world that is generating the contemporary crisis, but—for the first time in history—to put technology to work to place man in control of the social process he has created.

# For Further Reading

Abrams, Mark. "Party Politics after the End of Ideology." In Erik
Allardt and Y. Littunen, eds., *Cleavages, Ideologies, and Party
Systems.* Helsinki: The Academic Bookstore, 1964.

Adorno, T. W., Else Frenkel-Brunswik, Daniel J. Levinson, and R.
Nevitt Sanford. *The Authoritarian Personality.* New York:
Harper and Bros., 1950.

Aiken, Henry D. *The Age of Ideology.* New York: Mentor Books,
1956.

Aiken, Henry D. "The Revolt against Ideology," *Commentary,* 37
April 1964), 29–39.

Allardt, Erik. "Patterns of Class Conflict and Working Class Consciousness in Finnish Politics." In E. Allardt and Y. Littunen, eds.,
*Cleavages, Ideologies, and Party Systems.* Helsinki: The Academic Bookstore, 1964.

Apter, David E. "Introduction: Ideology and Discontent." In D. E.
Apter, ed., *Ideology and Discontent.* New York: Free Press,
1964.

Aron, Raymond. *The Industrial Society: Three Essays on Ideology
and Development.* New York: Frederick A. Praeger, 1967.

Aron, Raymond. "Nations and Ideologies," *Encounter,* IV:1 (January 1955), 23–33.

Aron, Raymond. *The Opium of the Intellectuals.* New York: W. W.
Norton & Co., 1962.

Barnes, Samuel H. "Ideology and the Organization of Conflict: On
the Relationship between Political Thought and Behavior,"
*Journal of Politics,* 28:3 (August 1966), 513–530.

Bell, Daniel. *Marxism-Leninism: A Doctrine on the Defensive; The
"End of Ideology" in the Soviet Union?* New York: Columbia
University Research Institute on Communist Affairs, 1955.

Bell, Daniel, and Henry D. Aiken. "Ideology—A Debate," *Commentary,* 37 (October 1964), 69–76.

Benda, Julien. *The Betrayal of the Intellectuals.* Boston: Beacon Press, 1955.

Bendix, Reinhard. "The Age of Ideology: Persistent and Changing." In D. E. Apter, ed., *Ideology and Discontent.* New York: Free Press, 1964.

Bergmann, Gustav. "Ideology," *Ethics,* LXI (April 1951), 205–218.

Birnbaum, Norman. "The Sociological Study of Ideology (1940–60)." *Current Sociology,* IX:2 (1960), 91–172.

Bourn, J. B. "Philosophy and Action in Politics," *Political Studies,* 13 (October 1965), 377–385.

Brown, Bernard E. "Elite Attitudes and Political Legitimacy in France," *Journal of Politics,* 31:2 (May 1969), 420–442.

Brown, Steven R. "Consistency and the Persistence of Ideology: Some Experimental Results," *Public Opinion Quarterly,* 34:1 (Spring 1970), 60–68.

Brzezinski, Zbigniew. *Ideology and Power in Soviet Politics.* New York: Frederick A. Praeger, 1962.

Burns, James MacGregor. "Political Ideology." In Norman MacKenzie, ed., *A Guide to the Social Sciences.* New York: Mentor Books, 1966.

Christoph, James B. "Consensus and Cleavage in British Political Ideology," *American Political Science Review,* 59 (September 1965), 629–642.

Connolly, William E. *Political Science and Ideology.* New York: Atherton Press, 1967.

Converse, Philip E. "The Nature of Belief Systems in Mass Publics." In D. E. Apter, ed., *Ideology and Discontent.* New York: Free Press, 1964.

Corbett, Patrick. *Ideologies.* New York: Harcourt, Brace & World, 1965.

Cox, Richard H., ed. *Ideology, Politics, and Political Theory.* Belmont, Calif.: Wadsworth Publishing Co., 1969.

Crosland, C. A. R. *The Conservative Enemy,* London: Jonathan Cape, 1962.

Crosland, C. A. R. "The Future of the Left," *Encounter,* 14:3 (March 1960), 3–12.

Crossman, R. H. S. "The Spectre of Revisionism: A Reply to Crosland," *Encounter,* 14:4 (April 1960), 24–28.

Dahrendorf, Ralf. *Class and Class Conflict in Industrial Society.* Stanford, Calif.: Stanford University Press, 1959.

Dahl, Robert A. "Epilogue." In R. A. Dahl, ed., *Poltical Oppositions in Western Democracies.* New Haven: Yale University Press, 1966.

"The Diffusion of Ideologies," *Confluence,* II (March, June, and September 1953). A series of articles on this topic by Hannah Arendt, Raymond Aron, John K. Galbraith, Bertrand de Jouvenel, and others.

Dion, Léon. "Political Ideology as a Tool of Functional Analysis in Socio-Political Dynamics: An Hypothesis," *Canadian Journal of Economics and Political Science,* 25:1 (February 1959), 47–59.

Edinger, Lewis J. "Political Change in Germany: The Federal Republic After the 1969 Elections," *Comparative Politics,* 2:4 (July 1970), 549–578.

Friedrich, Carl J. "Ideology in Politics: A Theoretical Comment," *Slavic Review,* 24:4 (December 1965), 612–616.

Friedrich, Carl J. *Man and His Government: An Empirical Theory of Politics.* New York: McGraw-Hill Book Co., 1963.

Geertz, Clifford. "Ideology as a Cultural System." In D. E. Apter, ed., *Ideology and Discontent.* New York: Free Press, 1964.

Germino, Dante. *Beyond Ideology: The Revival of Political Theory.* New York: Harper & Row, 1967.

Hacker, Andrew. *Political Theory: Philosophy, Ideology, Science.* New York: Macmillan, 1961.

Harris, Nigel. *Beliefs in Society: The Problem of Ideology.* London: C. A. Watts & Co., 1968.

Hoffer, Eric. *The True Believer.* New York: Mentor Books, 1958.

Hughes, H. Stuart. "The End of Political Ideology," *Measure,* II:2 (Spring 1951), 146–158.

Janowitz, Morris, and David R. Segal. "Social Cleavage and Party Affiliation: Germany, Great Britain, and the United States," *American Journal of Sociology,* 72:6 (May 1967), 601–618.

Jenkin, Thomas P. *The Study of Political Theory.* New York: Random House, 1955.

Johnson, Harry M. "Ideology and the Social System," *International Encyclopedia of the Social Sciences.* New York: Macmillan and Free Press, 1968. Vol. 7, pp. 76–85.

Kirchheimer, Otto. "Germany: The Vanishing Opposition." In Robert A. Dahl, ed., *Political Oppositions in Western Democracies.* New Haven: Yale University Press, 1966.

Kirchheimer, Otto. "The Transformation of the Western European Party Systems." In Joseph LaPalombara and Myron Weiner, eds., *Political Parties and Political Development.* Princeton, N. J.: Princeton University Press, 1966.

Kirchheimer, Otto. "The Waning of Opposition in Parliamentary Regimes," *Social Research,* 24 (Summer 1957), 127–156.

Lane, Robert E. "The Decline of Politics and Ideology in a Knowledgeable Society," *American Sociological Review,* 31 (1966), 649–662.

Lane, Robert E. *Political Ideology.* New York: Free Press, 1962.

Lasswell, Harold D., and Abraham Kaplan. *Power and Society.* New Haven, Conn.: Yale University Press, 1950.

Lerner, Daniel, Ithiel de Sola Pool, and Harold D. Lasswell, "Comparative Analysis of Political Ideology: A Preliminary Statement," *Public Opinion Quarterly,* XV (Winter 1951–52), 715–733.

Lichtheim, George. *The Concept of Ideology and Other Essays.* New York: Vintage Books, 1967.

Loewenstein, Karl. "Political Systems, Ideologies, and Institutions: The Problem of Their Circulation," *Western Political Quarterly,* 6:4 (December 1953), 689–706.

Lowenstein, Karl. "The Role of Ideologies in Political Change," *International Social Science Bulletin,* V:1 (1953), 51–74.

MacRae, Duncan G. *Ideology and Society.* London: Heineman, 1961.

MacIver, Robert M. *The Web of Government,* rev. ed. New York: Free Press, 1965.

Mannheim, Karl. *Ideology and Utopia.* New York: Harcourt, Brace & Co., 1936.

Merelman, Richard M. "The Development of Political Ideology: A Framework for the Analysis of Political Socialization," *American Political Science Review,* 63:3 (September 1969), 750–767.

Meyer, Alfred G. "The Function of Ideology in the Soviet Political System," *Soviet Studies,* 17:3 (January 1966), 273–285.

Minar, David W. "Ideology and Political Behavior," *Midwest Journal of Political Science,* V:4 (November 1961), 317–331.

Mukerji, Krishna P. *Implications of the Ideology Concept.* Bombay: Popular Books, 1955.

Parsons, Talcott. "An Approach to the Sociology of Knowledge," *Transactions of the Fourth World Congress of Sociology.* Louvain: International Sociological Association, 1959, 25–49.

Partridge, P. H. "Politics, Philosophy, Ideology," *Political Studies,* 9 (October 1961), 217–235.

Rejai, Mostafa. "Ideology." In Philip P. Wiener, ed., *Dictionary of the History of Ideas,* 6 vols. New York: John Scribner's Sons, 1972.

Rogow, Arnold A., and Harold D. Lasswell. *Power, Corruption, and Rectitude.* Englewood Cliffs, N. J.: Prentice-Hall, Inc., 1963.

Rokeach, Milton. *The Open and Closed Mind*. New York: Basic Books, 1960.

Roucek, J. S. "A History of the Concept of Ideology," *Journal of the History of Ideas*, V:4 (October 1944), 479–488.

Sartori, Giovanni. "Politics, Ideology, and Belief Systems," *American Political Science Review*, 63:2 (June 1969), 398–411.

Schweitzer, Arthur. "Ideological Strategy," *Western Political Quarterly*, 15:1 (March 1962), 46–66.

Shils, Edward. "The Concept and Function of Ideology," *International Encyclopedia of the Social Sciences*. New York: Macmillan and Free Press, 1968. Vol. 7, pp. 66–76.

Shils, Edward. "The End of Ideology?" *Encounter*, V (November 1955), 52–58.

Shils, Edward. "Ideology and Civility: On the Politics of the Intellectuals," *Sewanee Review*, LXCI (July-September 1958), 450–480.

Shklar, Judith N. *Political Theory and Ideology*. New York: Macmillan, 1966.

Steck, Henry J. "The Re-Emergence of Ideological Politics in Great Britain: The Campaign for Nuclear Disarmament," *Western Political Quarterly*, 18 (March 1965), 87–103.

Stjernquist, Nils. "Sweden: Stability or Deadlock?" In Robert A. Dahl, ed., *Political Oppositions in Western Democracies*. New Haven, Conn.: Yale University Press, 1966.

Sutton, Francis X., Seymour E. Harris, Carl Kaysen, and James Tobin. *The American Business Creed*. Cambridge, Mass.: Harvard University Press, 1956.

Tarrow, Sidney. "Economic Development and the Transformation of the Italian Party System," *Comparative Politics*, 1:2 (January 1969), pp. 161–183.

Tingsten, Herbert. "Stability and Vitality in Swedish Democracy," *Political Quarterly*, 26:2 (1955), 140–151.

Torgersen, Ulf. "The Trend towards Political Consensus: The Case of Norway," *Acta Sociologica*, VI (1962), 159–172.

Tucker, Robert C. "The Deradicalization of Marxist Movements," *American Political Science Review*, 61 (June 1967), 343–358.

Van Duzer, Charles H. *Contribution of the Ideologues to French Revolutionary Thought*. Baltimore: Johns Hopkins University Press, 1935.

Wahlke, John C., and Avery Leiserson. "Doctrines, Ideologies, and Theories of Politics." In J. C. Wahlke and Alex N. Dragnich, eds., *Government and Politics: An Introduction to Political Science*. New York: Random House, 1966.

Waltzer, Herbert. "Political Ideology: Belief and Action in the Arenas of Politics." In Reo M. Christenson et al., *Ideologies and Modern Politics*. New York: Dodd, Mead, 1971.

Walzer, Michael. "On the Role of Symbolism in Political Thought," *Political Science Quarterly,* 82:2 (June 1967), 191–204.

Waterman, Harvey. *Political Change in Contemporary France*. Columbus, Ohio: Charles E. Merrill, 1969.

Waxman, Chaim I., ed. *The End of Ideology Debate*. New York: Funk and Wagnalls, 1968.

Young, James P. *The Politics of Affluence: Ideology in the United States Since World War II*. San Francisco: Chandler Publishing Co., 1968.

Zeitlin, Irving M. *Ideology and the Development of Sociological Theory*. Englewood Cliffs, N. J.: Prentice-Hall, Inc., 1968.

# Index